Washington Revealed

WASHINGTON REVEALED

The Only Guide to Washington, D.C. That Allows You to Focus on Your Individual Interest

Maxine H. Atwater

JOHN WILEY & SONS, INC.

New York • Chichester • Brisbane • Toronto • Singapore

Library of Congress Cataloging-in-Publication Data

Atwater, Maxine H.
Washington revealed : the only guide to Washington, D.C. that allows you to focus on your individual interest / by Maxine H. Atwater.
p. cm.
Includes bibliographical references and index.
ISBN 0-471-54673-9 : $12.95
1. Washington (D.C.)—Description—1981—Guide-books.
2. Walking—Washington (D.C.)—Guide-books. I. Title.
F192.3.A85 1992
917.5304'4—dc20 91-28555

Printed in the United States of America
10 9 8 7 6 5 4 3 2 1

Printed and bound by Courier Companies, Inc.

To Lloyd, Esther, and Maxine V. Atwater, my father, mother, and aunt, whose support and love have empowered me to fulfill yet another dream.

PREFACE

What motivates a writer to work alone indoors for hundreds of hours through sunlit days that invite her to come outside and play? If not madness, it has to be a dream even more enticing than the beautiful world of flowers, trees, and people that beckons.

For me that motivating dream has been quite simply to change the way people experience Washington, D.C.

The possibility that Washington offered more than the obvious came to mind about five years ago, when I began a second career as a tour guide. Working for some of the major companies in Washington, I soon learned the facts and details that make up the commentary of most tour guides. But I felt dissatisfied. Wasn't there something more to say or do to give people a richer experience of the capital city?

Special-interest tours seemed like the answer. By focusing on specific subjects such as art, gardens, or literature, people could appreciate Washington in new ways. With details on the sites that related to their special interests, they would see the city that natives know.

Visitors needed to have the city's sightseeing attractions broken down into categories. They needed a guide to relay background information and to suggest how best to see the sites. This is that guide.

Assisting me in its creation were these people, to whom I proffer bouquets and accolades: Friends and advisors—Libby Dudley, Riki Jones, Barbara Peters, Gary Arlen, Barbara Chabrowe, Tom Ballentine, Judy Mackeness, Bill Blackwell, Jean Manchester, Jim Moriarty, Diane Rose, Henry Kent, and Joan Searby.

Catalysts—Liz Steingrabber of John Wiley & Sons and Robin Diener of Chapters Book Store, whose enthusiasm for my literary tours helped to create Special Interest Tours, Inc., and this book.

Public affairs people and other experts—Pam Baker, National Museum of Natural History; Kathleen Betts, Anderson House; Larry Betzler, Reservations Inc; Susan Bliss, Freer & Sackler Galleries; Susan Butler, National Museum of American History; Tom Caldwell, U.S. Navy Memorial; Henry Cathey, National Arboretum; Colleen Crowly, Dyke Marsh; Wanda Dowell, Fort Ward; Demetrios Dukas, artist; Susan Foster, National Museum of American History; Ann Hartzel, Pennsylvania Avenue Redevelopment Corp.; Jan Herman, U.S. Bureau of Medicine and Surgery (Old Naval Observatory); Tom Hurney, National Museum of Natural History; Ruth Kaplan, National Gallery of Art; Isabel Kayser, INTELSAT; Laura Lester, The Phillips

Collection; John Listman, Museum of the National Guard; Philip McClain, landscape architect; Rick McWalter, National Geographic Society; Julia Malone, Northern Virginia Regional Park Authority; Virginia Mecklenburg, National Museum of American Art; Barbara Moffitt, National Geographic Society; Mike Monroe, Renwick Gallery; Donald Murphy, National Theater; Ann Odem, Hillwood Museum; Joyce Peterson, National Air and Space Museum; Eleanor Preston, Tudor Place; Phyllis Rosenzweig, Hirshhorn Museum; Mark Sayer, Pentagon; Robert Sheldon, Library of Congress; Candace Shireman, Heurich Mansion; Susan Silverstein, Navy Museum; Nancy Tuckhorn, DAR. Museum; Fredrica Wechsler, National Academy of Sciences; Bill Wyss, Arts and Industries Museum.

Thanks to Greg Orfalea for permission to reprint a portion of his poem "Kite Day at the Washington Monument" published in *Washington and the,* edited by Francis Coleman Rosengberger, published by University Press of Virginia, 1977.

Contents

WASHINGTON REVEALED

Introduction

Today, when it comes to seeing the sights of a city, many crave the personal touch. If you're one of these people, you resist being herded along the standard tourist tracks. Instead, you want the sights you see and the information you hear to relate to your interests. Rather than following the trails worn deep by the masses, you chart your own course.

Organizing your sightseeing around a special-interest automatically breaks you away from the herd. You not only see new sites but also discover new aspects of familiar ones. Additionally, as you pursue a special interest you tend to find yourself getting special treatment as well. You share the excitement and delight of experts who show you their collections: the horticulturist who points out a hybrid, the antiquarian who turns the pages of a rare book, or the Civil War professor who brings a memorial to life with a poignant story.

This book opens the door to special-interest sightseeing. With its pages as your guide, you can now discover many of the special sights in Washington, D.C. To see others, you may need to join a group of people with similar interests. Some of the best that the capital offers can be seen only on specially arranged group tours. For these sights, you'll need a tour company that can make those arrangements.

The best tours combine relevant sites with background commentary. Words and visual impressions work together to increase your understanding and pleasure and to etch memories to last a lifetime. Sometimes the words you hear will determine how you perceive what you're viewing. A landmark like the U.S. Capitol building, for instance, can be seen from various viewpoints. In addition to its political symbolism, the Capitol can be seen as a tour de force of engineering, as the subject of a poem, as a social stage, as an art gallery, and—with its surrounding greenery—as a rare arboretum.

Also, while tracking your favorite subjects and things, you often discover little-known sites. Without the focus of a special-interest pursuit, you might never step inside a certain site or an outstanding item.

Finally, by pursuing your special interests, you gain an insider's knowledge of Washington. It's up to you whether you give in to temptation and flaunt what you've learned or simply relish your wisdom in silence.

Here are examples of the sights you'll see as you venture into Washington's world of special-interest sightseeing:

- Miniature soldiers fighting the Battle of Long Island (page 120).

- The country's most outstanding eighteenth-century waxwork, a gift to Martha Washington (page 17).
- Three eight-foot Tiffany windows, the largest remnants of the artist's work in Washington (page 36).
- Clanking nineteenth-century machinery illustrating the peak of America's early technology (page 195)
- A 1909 Studebaker coach once used to carry senators and representatives from their offices to the U.S. Capitol (page 191).
- A microscope from Louis Pasteur's lab (page 106).
- One of the country's largest collections of Ansel Adams photographs (page 31).
- A chandelier from the bedroom of Catherine the Great (page 28).
- A statue of poet Kahlil Gibran, inscribed with his poetry (page 71).
- 230 quilts and 190 coverlets that make up one of the most important textile collections in the United States (page 11).
- A garden of the flowers mentioned by Shakespeare in his works (page 71).

You'll discover these sights and more as you unravel the tangled skeins of this complex city. And as you follow your chosen threads, you'll uncover the glorious, the rare, and the unexpected.

How to Use This Book

Over a hundred sites are featured in this book, grouped by special-interest category. Often a site is listed under more than one category. When it is, a reference at the end of the entry notes the other chapters where you can find information about the site.

Sometimes categories overlap. For instance, the military highlights at the National Air and Space Museum also might be considered technological highlights. Choosing the appropriate category was a judgment call that is open, of course, to argument.

Since some sites are featured in numerous special-interest categories, addresses, hours, and other details are given only once: At the end of book, in the **Where and When** section. Thus, for information on all sites mentioned in the text, refer to that section (page 206).

The book is designed to be helpful to sightseers traveling by foot, by Metro subway, or by bus or car. Each **Highlight Walk** organizes a specific special-interest category into a single geographic area. Sites along a specific route are described in the order in which you'll come upon them on the suggested route. The map accompanying each **Highlight Walk** traces the route and pinpoints the featured sites.

Other destinations, in the **More Sites** sections, are divided by additional geographic areas, including Capitol Hill, Dupont Circle, Embassy Row–Georgetown, Foggy Bottom, the Mall, Midtown, and 17th Street. You can use this section to design your own tour. The final category, **Beyond** lists sites found in other parts of Washington, and in Maryland and Virginia. Occasionally, **Notes** give information about minor sites to be seen in a specific neighborhood or offer ideas for lunch or refreshment stops along the way.

Some chapters also include additional information related to the special-interest subject. For instance, in the Music and Theater chapter, you'll find a listing of top concert stages.

For more information on Washington sightseeing, refer to the **Tourist Resources** section at the back of the book.

CHAPTER 1

ANTIQUES

Drawing Room, Hillwood Museum (*Courtesy of Hillwood Museum*)

Although you may see greater arrays of fine antiques in other cities, you most often see them as museum exhibits. In Washington, D.C., however, antiques come to life. Instead of merely being displayed, antique furnishings become backdrops for historic events.

This is particularly true of the Diplomatic Reception Rooms of the White House and the State Department. In these two famous sites you see rooms where monarchs, world leaders, and diplomats are entertained. The antique furnishings that you might appreciate elsewhere only for their artistic merit take on new importance here. Chairs, tables, desks, and settees become statements about America and its people. With only a little imagination, you can glimpse the American personality captured by craftsmen in these period pieces.

More information about American life-style and taste comes through as you tour Washington's wealth of antique exhibits and houses furnished with period pieces. Some exhibits feature American-crafted furniture. Others reveal the preferences of America's twentieth-century scions for European, Russian, and Oriental antiques.

You'll see the best of Washington's antique furnishings and decorative arts at the sites described here. In addition to museum houses and exhibits, you'll also find a fascinating array of antiques in Washington area shops.

Because the city is located halfway between New England and the South, antiques from both areas find their way here. Also, since Washington is close to the Blue Ridge Mountains and the Shenandoah Valley, you'll find country pine and other unpainted pieces.

Because the city is a center for antiques, you may in a single day of browsing find eighteenth- and nineteenth-century pieces from Boston, Philadelphia, Richmond, and Charleston. Using the shops as classrooms, you can educate yourself about regional characteristics, perhaps noting the differences between inlay work done in Baltimore and that fashioned in New England.

If you want to learn about antiques, plan to be in town during one of the major antique shows, which bring together local dealers with those from across the country and throughout the world. Most agree that the best showing of fine quality antiques is the Washington Antique Show, which is held each year in early January. This show, begun in 1954, is a fund-raiser that involves celebrities, including the spouses of top officials. Because of its social allure, the show draws some of America's top dealers. About 50 dealers exhibit American and European furnishings, paintings, maps, fine silver, porcelains, Oriental rugs, tapestries, and rare books. The show frequently features exhibit tours, lectures, concerts, and dealer appraisal opportunities.

To find out about antique-related events, refer to *Where Magazine* and to the *Washington Post*'s "Weekend" section, which comes out on Fridays. You'll also find information about Washington antique shops (including those in Georgetown and the District), and about shops in nearby Kensington, Maryland, and Alexandria, Virginia.

In the pages that follow, you'll find information on the capital's finest antique collections. By following the **Highlight Walk** and visiting the other sites featured in **More Antiques**, you'll see the rich variety the city offers. You'll also step inside some of Washington's most magnificent rooms. Many will transport you across the years and give you a glimpse of the people who have called Washington home.

HIGHLIGHT WALK
17TH STREET AND FOGGY BOTTOM

Within a single block of 17th Street, you'll discover three fascinating antique exhibits. By adding a visit to the State Department Diplomatic Reception Rooms, you'll assure yourself an incomparable day. You'll see a superb combination of American and European antiques: the French glove table possibly commissioned by Napoleon; the transplanted drawing room from a Parisian duke's townhouse; and 33 period rooms filled with fabulous antiques.

To make this the ultimate tour for antique lovers, you'll need to reserve a space on the State Department tour. If you make your State Department reservation for 2:45 P.M., you'll have time to reach and visit all the sites suggested in one afternoon. Plan on beginning this tour by 12:30; allow at least twenty minutes to walk between the Daughters of the American Revolution (DAR) Museum and the State Department.

1. RENWICK GALLERY

In addition to paintings and modern decorative arts, you'll see some interesting antiques at the Renwick Gallery. In the Grand Salon, whaling cases hold antique decorative pieces primarily from the nineteenth century. Highlights include Russian glass, Staffordshire enamel, Venetian blown glass, and a large collection of Sevres porcelain.

In the adjacent Octagon Room you'll see a small but rich collection of Renaissance Revival furnishings. The focal point is a mahogany French glove table with Sevres porcelain embellishments. Possibly one of three works commissioned by Napoleon, the table features a porcelain centerpiece painting of Napoleon's coronation. Circling the painting are 16 oval porcelain plaques depicting Napoleon's marshals and insignia. Carved and inlaid

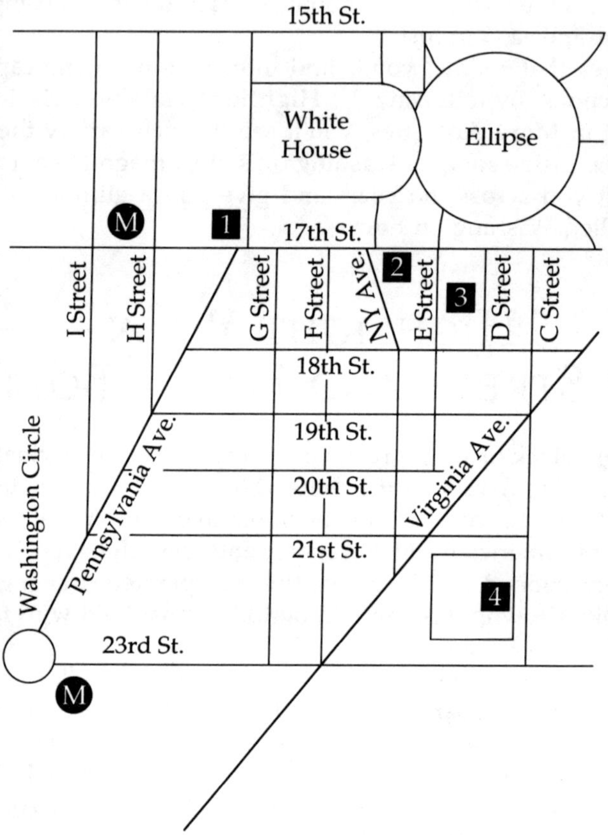

M Metro

1. Renwick Gallery, 17th Street and Pennsylvania Avenue NW
2. Corcoran Gallery of Art, 17th Street and New York Avenue NW
3. DAR Museum, 1776 D Street NW
4. State Department, C Street and 22nd Street NW

Route

From the Farragut West Metro subway station, walk south on 17th Street to Pennsylvania Avenue and the Renwick Gallery of Art. Continue along 17th Street to first to the Corcoran and then the DAR Museum. From the DAR, follow D Street to 18th Street, crossing Virginia Avenue to C Street. Continue on C Street to 22nd Street, and turn right to the State Department. From the State Department, it's a six-block walk to the Foggy Bottom Metro station.

wood chairs from the same period, made in New York in 1870, complement the table. The armchairs feature gilt brass lion heads on the ends of their arms.

For more information on the Renwick, see **Art**.

2. Corcoran Gallery of Art

For those visiting the Corcoran Gallery of Art to see nineteenth- and twentieth-century American art, coming upon a room straight out of a French king's palace can be something of a surprise.

Even those who knowingly seek out the ornate grand salon risk being awestruck. There is no single more ornate room in Washington. Ivory silk curtains embroidered in varicolored threads decorate windows. Above, clouds float on a gray-blue ceiling painted with classical figures and cupids bearing garlands. Antique furnishings of the Louis XVI and Louis XVIII periods reign.

The room was moved from Paris and reconstructed in its entirety in the New York townhouse of Senator William Andrews Clark. In 1925, Clark bequeathed his art collection, including this room, to the museum. A special wing was built in 1928 to display Clark's collection, which, together with the Corcoran collection, makes up the nucleus of the museum.

Of the original 50 pieces in the Clark collection, about 30 re-create the drawing room from the Hôtel de la Tremoille in Paris, built during the reign of Louis XVI. Some of the pieces are thought to have come from the collections of a French nobleman. Highlights for the antique lover include:

- *Nineteenth-century Empire-style ormolu and marble clock, and two candelabra.* The clock depicts the goddess Diana in her chariot, driving a pair of hunting hounds. The clock's white enamel dial is set in the wheel of the chariot. The candelabra of bronze are female figures holding torches in their outstretched hands.

• *Pair of eighteenth-century gilded wood torchères.* The in-curving shaft, set on a tripod base decorated with garlands of flowers, supports a basket with 16 scrolled branches. Lily-shaped cups, festooned with crystal stars, hold candles.

• *Eighteenth-century inlaid tulipwood commode.* Designs of branches and flower vases are inlaid in various natural woods and framed by acanthus wreaths of ormolu. Medallions and panels depicting pastoral subjects add to the beauty of the piece.

• *Suite of carved and gilded love seats and armchairs.* The seats and backs of the pieces are covered with a fine Beauvais tapestry.

For more information about the Corcoran Gallery, see **Art**.

3. DAR Museum

Flames don't flicker in the parlor and kitchen fireplaces of the period rooms here, but you'd almost think they do. That's because the 33 rooms so vividly re-create early American life-styles. A kitchen, a children's playroom, parlors, and dining rooms bring the past to life. The state rooms, furnished primarily by Daughters of the American Revolution (DAR) members, provide a unique assemblage of eighteenth- and nineteenth-century American antiques. As you tour the period rooms that cover three floors in the marble palace that serves as headquarters for the DAR, you'll see hundreds of treasures. Among the most noteworthy, as selected by the collection curator:

Maine Room

• *Circa 1810 card table.* This unique piece combines features characteristic of both Philadelphia and the South. The construction technique marks it as the work of a Philadelphia cabinetmaker, while the running inlay of pointed ovals and diamonds gives it definite Southern overtones.

District of Columbia Room

• *Washstand.* A delicate example of the style that became popular in the early 1800s. This piece, decorated with twisted brass wire stringing, was most likely purchased in Wakefield, Virginia.

Pennsylvania Foyer

• *Walnut armchair that combines Queen Anne and Chippendale features.* The serpentine arms with scroll knuckle terminals, incurvate arm supports, and serpentine stretchers are all Queen Anne elements; the bowed and eared crest rail, square seat, and claw-and-ball feet echo Chippendale characteristics.

Massachusetts Room

- *Mahogany side chair.* Given by John Hancock to the Fessenden family after their property was damaged during the Battle of Lexington. The chair illustrates the way cabinetmakers added distinct local design elements to the basic English style. The features that show that the piece is American include the diamond figure-eight carvings, the shaped rear legs, and the raked talons of the claw-and-ball feet.

Virginia Room

- *Armchair.* This piece may have been part of the furnishings at the Governor's Palace in Williamsburg. The impressed "Virginia" on the seat rail probably marked the chair as property of the Colony, simply on loan to the governor for use in his palace residence.

Tennessee Room

- *Pair of Empire-style armchairs.* These were part of the set of 24 ordered by President James Monroe for the White House in 1817.

Wisconsin Room

- *Wedding chest.* Mary Burt, the original owner, married a Farmington, Connecticut, marshal in 1695. Note the peculiar iconographic notations: swastikas, commalike tendrils, and stylized fish-shaped tulips.

Over 5,000 antiques are displayed in the period rooms and in the newly remodeled DAR Museum Gallery. The hall, according to the *Washington Post*, once a "mishmash of members' mementos," is now "a matchless museum."

The gallery features an impressive collection of decorative arts, including fine examples of furniture, ceramics, glass, paintings, silver, costumes, and textiles. This collection encompasses the breadth of American historical craftsmanship. Among the antiques not to be missed:

- Circa 1820 Spode supper set.
- New England whaler's handcarved wooden domino set.
- Silver tankard, circa 1740.
- Silver beaker made by Paul Revere.
- Pincushion with the stitched greeting "Welcome Little Stranger," given at the christening of Elizabeth Rea Rhodes on September 10, 1786.

The highlight of the collection, however, may be the museum's early American textile collection, which is one of the most important in the United States. In order to display larger quantities of its collection of 230 quilts and 190 coverlets, the museum features unique sliding racks on which eight pieces can be displayed. Two additional cases exhibit whitework quilts, with backlighting to show off the embroidery. On any one day you're likely to see examples of the finest pieces from the collection: quilts made before 1860, those with detailed family histories worked into the design, and whitework pieces, including the Marseilles style, which is embroidered, stuffed, and candlewicked.

4. State Department

When world leaders come to Washington, they often don't have time to step inside a museum. Until recently, that meant they left without discovering our country's cultural heritage. To solve the problem, the State Department has in effect brought the mountain to Mohammed. The suite of Diplomatic Reception Rooms, where foreign dignitaries are entertained, has been turned into a museum equivalent.

Fifteen connecting rooms showcase our country's fourth- or fifth-greatest collection of eighteenth- and early nineteenth-century American antiques. Unlike a museum exhibit, however, this $50 million collection of furnishings and decorative arts gleams and shines in period rooms designed to complement them.

The architectural detail and ornamentation of the rooms echo the best aspects of America's built history. Architect Edward Mason Jones understood early American architects so well that he could think from their viewpoint. He used as his inspiration the most beautiful rooms in early America: Monticello, Mount Vernon, Stratford Hall, Powell House in Philadelphia, and Marmion, the Virginia manor house now in the Metropolitan Museum of Art in New York. Elements of all of these went into his masterpiece, the Thomas Jefferson State Reception Room. In creating this room of perfect proportion and simple elegance, Jones referred to the design books Jefferson had collected for his own library.

Some of the other rooms designed by Jones are more ornamented. For the John Quincy Adams State Drawing Room, for instance, Jones used hand-carved architectural detail inspired by the great mid-Georgian Philadelphia houses. In the entrance hall, the intricately worked plaster ceiling and elaborate frieze incorporate a rich array of design elements. Variety adds richness. The simplicity of the maple mantelpiece, the fluted Corinthian columns, and the expanse of King of Prussia marble flooring contrasts with elaborate rococo ceilings, ornamental cartouches, plaster medallions, and a treasury of carved grapes, leaves, garlands, masks, musical instruments, and gilded eagles.

Amidst the splendor, crystal chandeliers shine. Oriental carpets lie on beautiful mahogany and Georgia pine floors, one laid in mahogany squares in the pattern used at Monticello. Oil paintings, prints, and etchings of the American landscape and famous leaders, and others illustrating historic moments, enhance the rooms. Among the most outstanding are a Gilbert Stuart portrait of John Jay, Thomas Sully's likeness of Thomas Jefferson, and a portrait of Benjamin Franklin painted by Jean-Baptiste Greuze in Paris.

But if you're an antique fancier it's the furniture, made during America's golden age of cabinetmaking, that will haunt your dreams. The collection, valued at $30 million, boasts the finest American Queen Anne, Chippendale, Hepplewhite, and Sheraton pieces. On regularly scheduled tours, docents take you through eight of the most impressive rooms. Although your guide will point out many of the most outstanding antiques, be on the lookout for these rare eighteenth-century show-stoppers:

- *Boston Chippendale bombe chest with drawers that curve outward.* This is one of the greatest masterpieces in the collection.

- *Five-legged gaming table, marble-topped console table, and large desk-bookcase from New York.* These splendid examples by Duncan Phyfe and Charles Honoré Lannuier are considered the best examples of New York furniture prior to the Revolution. *Antiques* magazine called the 1770 mahogany desk-bookcase with paneled doors and ball feet "one of only a few so masterfully executed."

- *Philadelphia Chippendale desk-bookcase with a bust of John Locke centered between carved scrolls.* Note the carved peanuts on many of the Philadelphia pieces, which the city's craftsmen favored as an embellishment.

- *Philadelphia Chippendale tallcase clock made for a Revolutionary War patriot.* The most ambitious American clock ever attempted, it shows not only the zodiac and the phases of the moon, but also the meeting dates of various Pennsylvania courts. (Tallcase clocks were not known as grandfather clocks until the nineteenth century.)

- *Philadelphia mahogany and satinwood sideboard.* Critics, noting the lavish inlay and serpentine design, have called it one of the best examples of the period anywhere. The piece was once on loan to the Metropolitan Museum of Art.

Some antique furnishings boast not only artistic merit but also historic importance. Among these pieces:

- *English Sheridan desk.* Representatives signed the Treaty of Paris on this table in 1783.

- *John Hay's desk chair.* A secret compartment is hidden beneath the seat.

• *Thomas Jefferson's table desk.* Jefferson used it when he wrote the Declaration of Independence.

The story of the transformation of the eighth-floor Diplomatic Reception Rooms (plus offices and a ceremonial room on the seventh floor) begins in 1961. In that year Clement E. Conger, deputy chief of protocol for the State Department, took on the job of furnishing the recently completed entertainment rooms. Starting from scratch, Conger determined to furnish the rooms with the finest examples of early American design. With no government funding, he had to rely solely on the gifts of individuals and corporations. Congers proved to be skillful at fund-raising, however, and today the Diplomatic Reception Rooms are enriched with over 4,500 to 5,000 objects valued at $60 million.

With the ultimate in diplomatic charm, Conger persuaded individuals, corporations, and foundations to donate $30 million in money or in antiques. So successful were his efforts that in 1970, President Nixon asked him to serve as curator for the White House. By the time he left that post, Conger had raised $15 million in objects and money for White House refurbishment. He also brought outstanding antiques out of storage and got rid of the department store reproductions. As a result, the White House today looks much as it did in 1817, following its restoration after the War of 1812. (See White House entry.)

More Antiques

Georgetown–Embassy Row

Anderson House

One critic calls the Anderson House a piece of social archaeology. This great town residence remains as a unique example of the opulent life-style of wealthy Americans in early twentieth-century Washington. Built by diplomat Larz Anderson in 1905, the mansion brims over with rich antiques. Among the pieces collected by Anderson on his travels through the world are eighteenth-century paintings, sixteenth-century Flemish tapestries, and Oriental art objects including a forest of jade trees and an eighteenth-century Ukiyoe Japanese screen.

On guided one-hour tours or on your own, you can feast your eyes not only on the antiques themselves, but also on the lavishly designed rooms. The high point for antique lovers is the dining room decorated with eight tapestries commissioned by King Louis XIII. The tapestries, woven in Brussels in the sixteenth century, were created by the most skillful master weavers of their time: DuBreuil and the ateliers of Jacques Geubels and Jean Raes.

For more information on Anderson House, see **Gardens, Literature,** and **Military.**

DUMBARTON HOUSE

When the British burned Washington's buildings during the War of 1812, they destroyed most public examples of the unique Washington Federal style. But thanks to the survival of some period residences, you can get an idea of how the capital city looked in the eighteenth century.

One of the best examples is Dumbarton House. This house, built in 1799, breaks with the earlier Georgia plantations of the Chesapeake Tidewater (including Stratford Hall). Its style, which expands on Adamesque elements, features embellishments executed by craftsmen and artisans. You can see original examples of plaster work in this style in two rooms on the first floor of Dumbarton House. Elements such as these were used as models in recreating the eighteenth-century appearance of the White House and U.S. Capitol interiors.

Dumbarton House, purchased in 1928 by the National Society of Colonial Dames, was restored in 1932. Beginning then, and continuing to recent years, members have donated some furnishings and the society has purchased others. From the beginning, the society decided that only furniture corresponding to the house's 1799 date of construction should be displayed. As a result, Dumbarton House provides a rare picture of early Washington. It also houses a collection of early nineteenth-century English and American decorative arts. The eight rooms open to the public are filled with outstanding examples of furniture, silver, textiles, ceramics, and paintings. Also of interest are the historic pieces. These include documents signed by Thomas Jefferson and George Washington; Martha Washington's coach coat; and Chinese export porcelain owned by Eliza Custis Law.

Among the furniture highlights from the shops of American cabinetmakers:

Entrance Way

- *Philadelphia Chippendale corner-cabinet.* Made in 1780. Note the Chinese fretwork above the glass doors. Also, don't miss the pair of Massachusetts Sheraton card tables, circa 1810, of mahogany and satinwood. The checkered line inlay adds interest.

Blue Parlor

- *Pair of George III Adam card tables.* Circa 1790. The tops are painted with a panoply of birds, flowers, and musical instruments. The frieze combines painted bellflower swags with satinwood line inlay borders.

Off the Blue Parlor

• *Baltimore Hepplewhite walnut slant-front desk.* Note that the 15 inlaid stars indicate the desk was made after Kentucky and Tennessee were admitted into the Union—between 1792 and 1796.

Federal Dining Room

• *Hepplewhite dining table.* Made in Deerfield, Massachusetts, in 1790, the piece is in three sections: The two ends are hinged, and the central section has two tapering legs.

• *Sheraton dining chairs.* These 11 chairs were made in Boston or Salem about 1790, altogether their square backs and black leather seats make them seem almost modern.

• *Portrait.* Considered one of the property's most noteworthy holdings, it is signed by Charles Wilson Peale and dated 1789. It portrays the children of one of the house's early owners, Benjamin Stoddert.

Off the Dining Room

• *Philadelphia Sheraton secretary-bookcase.* Circa 1795. The mahogany piece features contrasting satinwood doors and drawers.

Music Room

• *Russian cobalt glass chandelier.*

• *Baltimore Hepplewhite inlaid mahogany Pembroke table.*

• *George III mahogany sofa with serpentine crest rail.*

• *Three piece tea service.* Circa 1780, by William Garrett Forbes of New York.

Dumbarton House reopened in 1992, following a renovation that included the addition of a new office and meeting complex, and a courtyard patio and landscaped garden.

For more information on Dumbarton House, see **Gardens**.

Tudor Place

If antiques could talk, what stories they'd tell. At Tudor Place the babble would be deafening. That's because many of the antique furnishings in this residence-turned-museum have been treasured for six generations by one family.

Thomas and Martha Custis Peter purchased Tudor Place in 1805 with the $8,000 Martha inherited from her step-grandfather, George Washington. They wished to add a house to the preexisting buildings on the property, so they consulted with their friend William Thornton, architect of the U.S. Capitol. His neoclassical design for the residence is superb, especially the two-story portico on the south front. The portico, which features a semicircle of columns, joins a concave wall of glass panes to complete a circle.

Upon entering the reception hall at the center of the house, you see the curve of the portico windows unite the indoors with the outside landscape. Your eye sweeps unobstructed from room to garden. A grassy carpet becomes an extension of the Persian rugs underfoot. The light pouring in through the windows spotlights the fabulous antiques that seem to fill each room.

In addition to telling the story of the Peter family, antiques speak of the nation's history too. For here, preserved with reverence, are mementos and artifacts from George Washington's life. Perhaps only a loving family member would think to save the bar of soap used by Washington. It is here, together with more than 130 objects and manuscripts from the Mount Vernon collection.

Numerous pieces, including some that once belonged to George Washington, vie for attention. Among those chosen by the curator for their historic or aesthetic importance:

- *Miniature painting of George Washington.* Presented to Martha Custis Peter on the occasion of her marriage.

- *Waxwork scene presented to Martha Washington.* It symbolizes the parting of George and Martha at the onset of the Revolutionary War and originally stood on a chest in the Washingtons' Mount Vernon bedroom.

- *Six dining chairs.* Made in Philadelphia in 1755–75, they were used there by George Washington while he was president.

- *1855 silver tray crafted by Ball, Black & Company.* The piece features a fine engraving of Neptune bordered with a ship's chain. The richly chased handles are fashioned to resemble ship's rope entwined with anchor-attached cables.

- *French marble, gilt bronze, and enamel clock.* This piece, circa 1795, has a three-part dial painted by Jean Côteau, one of the foremost dial painters of the neoclassical period.

- *English ebonized wood bracket clock in the form of a Corinthian temple.* Circa 1680. The clock, one of the first pendulum clocks made in England, is by Eduardus East, clockmaker to Charles I and Charles II.

- *Qianlong porcelain punchbowl.* Chinese, circa 1765. This rare bowl, decorated with an English hunt scene, is believed to be one that Thomas Peter bought at the public sale following the death of Martha Washington.

- *Desk-bookcase-linen press.* Made in the Washington-Alexandria area in 1800.

On one-hour tours of the house, you'll see these and other important antiques. Since antiques can't talk, a docent will tell you stories about the important pieces you see, the Peter family, and early Washington life.

For more information on Tudor Place, see **Gardens**.

Dumbarton Oaks

Dumbarton Oaks is a treasure trove of antiques, especially the Garden Library, which is occasionally open to the public. In it, flower-decorated pieces complement flower-filled paintings by the great masters. See **Art**, **Gardens**, and **Music**.

Midtown

The White House

In addition to being beautiful, antiques bring history to life. Seeing the furnishings and decorative objects that Thomas Jefferson, Abraham Lincoln, and other presidents have known provides a connection with them through the centuries. Furnishings in the White House have changed radically over the 200-year history of the mansion. Each president, in an attempt to keep up with the fashions of the day, has added his own touch. As a result, furnishing styles have followed the course of America's early decorative taste. The first major furnishings in the White House were the gilded Empire-style pieces, fashionable in France in the early nineteenth century. President James Monroe, who had purchased the pieces in Paris during his diplomatic service, brought them with him when he came to the president's house in 1817. Empty for three years, the president's house was renovated following the War of 1812, during which it had been burned by the British. Monroe completed the refurnishing of the residence by adding pieces purchased by James Madison and ordering an array of goods from France.

Although it has passed through Victorian and Art Nouveau furnishing styles, the White House we see today looks much as it did in Monroe's day. As the oldest period furnishings in the White House, Monroe's choices form the core of the historic collection. Although only one of Monroe's original pieces remains—the pier table in the entrance hall—antiques similar to the originals stand in their places.

Gone are the haircloth chairs and sheepskin rugs of the Lincoln administration. Torn down is the Tiffany screen commissioned by Chester Arthur, which once ornamented the cross hall. No more do the blue glass panels decorated with gold scrollwork top Blue Room windows. Benjamin Harrison's figured carpets, upholstery, and wallpaper have vanished. We now see the White House not just as a residence but as a symbol. Since the beginning of the twentieth century, awareness of the role of the White House as a site of historic preservation has grown.

This awareness most notably began in 1902, when Teddy Roosevelt oversaw reconstruction of the mansion's interior. Roosevelt called on an architectural firm famed for its historic style, McKim, Mead and White. When it came time to redecorate the state rooms, Teddy and his architects swept away all Victorian fancies. In place of carpets, parquet floors gleamed. Other rooms took on "the plain composure of stone. Spare, austere, consciously historic, the White House entered its second century," according to the White House Historical Association.

Movements to preserve White House history continued. In 1949, to make sure the historic authenticity of the mansion would be preserved, President Harry Truman got Congress to create the Committee for the Renovation of the Executive Mansion. In the 1960s, the Kennedys pressured Congress to set up a Fine Arts Committee for the White House and to appropriate funds so that historic pieces could be acquired. President Johnson in 1964 formed a commission to recommend furnishings in public rooms. During the renovation in 1969, the Nixons worked to preserve the historic character of the White House and added to the collection of valuable pieces.

To take in the wealth of American eighteenth- and nineteenth-century antiques enhancing the White House, you probably need more than one visit. When you join public tours of the White House—even the VIP tours—you see a great deal in a short time. On your first visit an architectural detail, a story, or a vision of Dolley Madison pouring tea may take precedence. Antiques may come into focus only on a second visit.

It also helps if you know what to look for—the furnishings of greatest historic and/or artistic merit that shouldn't be missed. With this in mind, here's a listing of the most important pieces in the five rooms you'll see on the general tour and in the three more rooms most often shown on the VIP tour.

HIGHLIGHTS:

Blue Room

- *Gilded chairs.* Six of the originals, ordered by President Monroe from French cabinetmaker Pierre-Antoine Bellange in 1817. The pieces, sold at auction in 1860 by President Buchanan, were returned to the White House almost 100 years later. The French Empire chairs are decorated with carved sprigs of olive trees. Monroe's original upholstery design—an American eagle woven into the center of a laurel wreath—has been copied, but in blue instead of his original choice of crimson and gold.
- *Pair of English console tables.* Made in England by a French craftsman between 1785 and 1790.

• *Pair of Sevres porcelain vases.* Made around 1800, decorated with scenes of the Parisian suburb where Benjamin Franklin lived while he was minister to France.

• *Hannibal clock on the mantel.* The work of Denière and Matelin, noted French bronze casters. Purchased by Monroe.

Red Room

• *Mahogany secretary-bookcase.* Circa 1815, attributed to Charles-Honoré Lannuier. Note the Gothic lancet arch motif on the glass of the doors, the gilded female heads topping the pilasters and on drawer fronts, and the hinged writing board.

• *Marble-topped round table.* Lannuier's labeled masterpiece and the most important piece of American Empire furniture in the White House.

• *Rosewood fire screen.* Circa 1817, attributed to Lannuier. Note the side columns with gilded bronze capitals and bases, the green-painted animal legs, and gilded leaf knees.

• *Sofa table of mahogany and fruitwoods.* From the workshop of French-born cabinetmaker Charles-Honoré Lannuier. This, the most important piece of American Empire–period furnishing, features a trompe l'oeil marble top inlaid in a geometric pattern. On top of the carved legs, note the bronze female heads.

• *Card table.* Features the carved lyre design of the New York Empire style.

• *Eighteenth-century bronze doré clock.* Made by Pierre Joseph Gouthière, a Parisian bronze caster. The clock plays pastoral music on a miniature organ inside the gilded case.

Green Room

• *Pair of porcelain vases.* Made between 1832 and 1837, in Philadelphia, by Tucker & Hemphill. Note that one is painted with a portrait of President Andrew Jackson, the other with a protrait of the Marquis de Lafayette.

• *French bronze doré clock.* Made by eighteenth-century artisan Robert Robin, clockmaker to Louis XV and Louis XVI.

• *Mahogany worktables.* Two extremely rare pieces attributed to Duncan Phyfe, made in about 1810. These worktables, designed for fine sewing or miniature painting, feature an ingeniously designed hinged lid that slides open to reveal trays and compartments. Note the rich details of Phyfe's work: the mahogany veneers that contrast with the satinwood-faced drawers and pigeonholes.

• *Duncan Phyfe settee.* Dated about 1810, with tied reeds and clustered wheat ears carved on the crest rail.

• *Two matching French candlesticks.* Bought by James Madison from James Monroe in 1803.

• *Sheffield coffee urn.* Circa 1785. John Adams considered it among his "most prized possessions." The ellipse above the spigot bears the initials JAA (John and Abigail Adams).

• *Mahogany drum table.* Circa 1800. Attributed to the workshop of Duncan Phyfe. Note the green leather top, the cross-banded apron with three drawers, the ring-turned pedestal, and the knee legs decorated with square-ended acanthus leaves.

China Room

• *Porcelain dessert plate.* From the state service of President James Monroe, made in France in 1817 by Philip Louis Dagoty and Edoward d' Honoré.

• *Cut glass decanter.* 1816, Pittsburgh. Attributed to Backwell, Page & Backwell, and presented to President James Madison by the maker. Note the engraved American eagle emblem with an M breast shield.

For more information on the White House, see **Gardens**.

Elsewhere In Midtown

In many of Washington's museum houses, you'll find lovely antiques that help re-create a period. One is the Octagon House, which has been restored to reflect the period when Dolley and James Madison lived there following the burning of the White House in 1814. Here you'll see some lovely Chippendale, Hepplewhite, and Sheraton pieces. The dining room table settings are changed each month to show various pieces from the collection, including a Staffordshire tea service. The Decatur House also displays American antiques in its Federal and Victorian-period rooms.

For a close-up look at some wonderful European and American antiques, stop by the lobby of the Madison Hotel. Hotel owner Marshall Coyne displays his personal collection, which includes an elegant Louis XV piano, three Louis XVI desks, and nine antique clocks from Europe and America. The collection continues on the second landing with Chinese furnishings, prints, and bronzes.

Beyond

Mexican Cultural Institute

On the second floor of the Mexican Cultural Institute, now open as a showcase for that country's artists, you can also see some interesting antiques. The house, built in 1912 for President Taft's Secretary of the Treasury, retains some of the original Louis XV furniture. Most interesting is the Louis XIII–style music room. Supposedly inspired by Château Fontainebleu, the huge room boasts a handpainted pipe organ and an unusual semicircular medieval fireplace. See **Art**.

National Museum of American History

Finally, antiques are often part of the displays at the National Museum of American History. Look for the fine American pieces included in the "First Ladies' Gowns" and "Life in 18th Century America" exhibits. The displays of American silver, porcelain, and glass are outstanding. For more information on the museum, see **Literature**, **Music**, and **Science**.

Mount Vernon
Mount Vernon, Virginia

Much like his gardens, the furnishings at Mount Vernon tell us a great deal about George Washington's tastes and values. The pieces that Washington collected over a 40-year period reflect his love of beauty, order, and dignity. Rather than ostentation, Washington chose to reflect in his selection of furnishings his own preference for simplicity—with style.

Although not a slave to fashion trends, Washington did often choose the new and unusual for his plantation home. One example is the unique fan chair he bought after seeing it demonstrated in Philadelphia in 1787. Although the original chair has disappeared, you can see a similar eighteenth-century contraption in his study. Attached to the chair is an overhead fan and foot pedals. To create a breeze and to shoo flies away, Washington would sit in the chair and pump the pedals.

In addition to the American-made fan chair, Washington purchased pieces from France, England, and China. He also mixed periods. In the large dining room, you'll see how he incorporated Federal furniture from Philadelphia with a pair of mahogany candlestands he purchased 40 years earlier in Williamsburg. You can also see his effective mix of American, French, English, and even Chinese pieces. These include such eighteenth-century pieces as a sideboard made by a Philadelphia cabinetmaker, a writing desk from France, and a mahogany spirit box made by Philip Bell of London. Despite this mixture, the overall effect is harmonious.

Getting a sense of the harmony that Washington created through his selections is one thing. Focusing on the details of the best pieces is quite another. That's because in the spring and summer, the press of people passing through the mansion at any one time doesn't allow much time for lingering. But you may have time to ask a question, perhaps about the location of a particular piece. It helps if you know what you're looking for. Highlights here are some of the not-to-be-missed antiques, significant for both their quality and their historic importance. The antiques are listed in the order in which you'll see them as you walk through the mansion.

George and Martha Washington's bedroom at Mount Vernon (*Courtesy of Mount Vernon Ladies' Association*)

HIGHLIGHTS:

Large Dining Room

• *Twin Hepplewhite sideboards.* Placed on either side of the Palladian window, they were made by John Aitken in Philadelphia in 1797.

• *Chairs.* Beneath the windows are 9 of the original 24 Washington had made for this room.

• *Mahogany candlestands.* Washington probably purchased these from the shop of Anthony Hay in Willliamsburg.

Little Parlor

• *Harpsichord.* Purchased by Washington for his step-granddaughter, Nelly Custis, from Longman & Bordering in London. The woods are mahogany, spruce, white pine, and inlaid satinwood.

Small Dining Room

• *Mahogany liquor chest (spirit box).* Ordered by Washington in 1760 from Philip Bell of London. The square case holds 16 bottles and features brass lifting handles and casters.

Blue Room

• *Martha Washington's Chinese dressing glass.* Oriental cypress, made between 1790 and 1795.

Yellow Room

• *English chest of drawers with writing slide and compartmentalized top drawer.* This piece served as a dressing table.

General and Mrs. Washington's Bedchamber

• *Washington's bedstead.* Mahogany, sycamore, white pine, and yellow poplar. The dimity hangings are reproduced from an eighteenth-century fragment.

• *Mrs. Washington's writing desk.* Made in France, of mahogany and white oak.

Study

• *Fan chair.* Invented by John Cram of Philadelphia in 1786.

• *Swivel desk chair.* By New York City cabinetmaker Thomas Burling, used by Washington early in his presidency.

• *Tambour secretary.* Made in Philadelphia by John Aitken for Mount Vernon.

• *Terrestrial globe.* Made by London mapmaker George Adams in 1790.

• *Dressing table.* Mahogany and white fir with a marble top, made in France between 1775 and 1785.

Rivaling the importance of these antiques is the story of how they came to be assembled at Mount Vernon almost 200 years after Washington's death. After Martha Washington died in 1802, her possessions were removed from Mount Vernon. Those that were willed to her heirs were scattered among the homes of her grandchildren at Arlington House, Woodland, and Tudor Place; the furnishings that George Washington had willed to a number of friends ended up in the homes of private citizens; the remainder were put on the auction block.

In 1853, a group of women headed by Ann Pamela Cunningham of South Carolina formed an association to purchase and preserve Mount Vernon. The Mount Vernon Ladies' Association purchased the estate in 1858 and set about bringing it back to the way it looked in 1799, when George Washington died. As part of that effort, they asked that original furnishings be returned.

In response, possessions that had been in safekeeping for over 50 years began coming home. From Arlington House, the home of Martha's grandson, came the Hepplewhite sideboard, the Washington bedstead, the Pembroke table, and Nelly's harpsichord. Heirs of Martha Washington's granddaughter at Tudor Place returned her writing desk, in which two letters from George to Martha had been discovered (see **Tudor Place** listing).

The families of the friends to whom Washington had willed his dressing table, tambour secretary-bookcase, and swivel chair also returned these possessions. The swivel chair, which Washington left to his friend Dr. James Craik, came back to Mount Vernon via the Hermitage. Andrew Jackson's heirs had held onto the chair that their presidential relative received as a gift from Dr. Craik.

Objects sold at the 1802 auction also came home. Dr. William Thornton's heirs sent back the Williamsburg candlesticks that Thornton had purchased. George Washington's great-grandnephew, the last of the family to own Mount Vernon, presented the terrestrial globe that he had acquired after Martha's death.

For more information on Mount Vernon, see **Gardens**.

Hillwood Museum
Northwest Washington

A Russian czar would be at home at Hillwood. He might even weep with nostalgia upon seeing jewel-encrusted gold chalices, Fabergé's imperial Easter eggs, and the chandelier from Catherine the Great's bedroom.

In addition to boasting the most representative collection of Russian decorative arts outside the Soviet Union, this museum-mansion oozes with opulence. Priceless objects, including some incomparable antiques, fill 40 richly decorated rooms.

Wedding veil, 1881. Hillwood Museum, on loan from the Smithsonian Institution. (*Courtesy of Hillwood Museum*).

The fact that so much wealth is concentrated in one site isn't an accident. In 1937 and 1938, the creator of Hillwood, heiress Marjorie Merriweather Post, was living in Moscow with her ambassador husband when the Soviet government, seeking to finance itself, sold artworks confiscated from the palaces of the imperial family. Mrs. Post was on hand. She had the opportunity to buy seventeenth- and eighteenth-century silver chalices made for the Orthodox Church at a mere five cents per gram weight.

The objects acquired in the 1930s formed the nucleus of Mrs. Post's collection, which was later expanded to include a broad spectrum of Russian decorative arts. Today, one sees hundreds of these treasures, ranging from porcelain, glass, and jeweled objects to textiles and furniture.

Mrs. Post, who purchased the 25-acre Hillwood estate in 1955, had the house redesigned to suit her life-style and to exhibit her art collection. Her will—she died in 1973 at Hillwood—bequeathed the estate to the Smithsonian Institution. Operational problems prompted the Smithsonian to return Hillwood to the Marjorie Merriweather Post Foundation. In 1977, Hillwood opened to the public as a private museum.

On regularly scheduled tours you will visit a dozen rooms, including the Russian porcelain room, French drawing room, icon room, library, dining room, and breakfast room.

HIGHLIGHTS:

Front Hallway

- *Pair of glass umbrella stands.* From the Russian Imperial Glass Factory.
- *French nineteenth-century commode.* With marquetry and gilt bronze, similar to one in Windsor Castle.

Russian Porcelain Room

- *Services.* Commissioned in 1777 and 1783 by Catherine the Great for use at the dinners she gave for knights of four imperial orders.
- *Plates.* Made for the coronation of Alexander II in 1856.
- *Glass goblets with white medallions.* The inscriptions commemorate the triumphal march of Alexander I into Paris in 1814, after the defeat of Napoleon.

Pavilion

- *Nest of tables from the Anichkov Palace.* Legs are carved in the Old Russian style similar to the ornamental carvings found on peasant houses.
- *Two ivory chests.* Made in north Russia in the eighteenth century of carved walrus ivory.

French Drawing Room

• *Three tapestries woven at Beauvais factory.* Based on sketches by François Boucher.

• *Suite of two large sofas and eight armchairs.* The tapestries on the chairs are said to have been ordered by Louis XVI as a gift to Prince Henry of Russia.

• *Ornate circular table of semiprecious stones.* Tigereye and lapis lazuli adorn the top, and amethyst drops adorn the skirt and stretcher.

Icon Room

• *Crown in diamonds.* Made around 1840 for the bride of the future Alexander II and worn by the brides of Alexander II and Nicholas II.

• *Two imperial Easter eggs.* Among 90 pieces by Carl Fabergé, jeweler to the imperial court.

• *Practical and amusing objects by Fabergé.* Including a gold music box, a stamp box, a menu holder, a lorgnette, and a crochet hook.

• *"Mother and Child" icon.* With a gold cover encrusted with emeralds and diamonds.

• *Renaissance-style cabinet.* Made of wood painted to look like ebony, with gilt bronze and lapis lazuli.

• *Three tables.* Tops are made of malachite cut into small pieces and assembled like a mosaic.

Dining Room

• *French Regency–style oak paneling.* From an old house in Paris.

• *Nineteenth-century rose-red Aubusson carpet.* Said to have been made as a gift from the French court to Emperor Maximilian of Mexico.

• *Empire-style candelabra.* Of dark lapis lazuli with gilt bronze, from a Russian imperial palace.

Breakfast Room

• *Chandelier.* Of glass and gilt bronze, possibly once installed in the bedroom of Catherine the Great.

Surrounding the Hillwood estate are extensive gardens including a French parterre, a greenhouse of prized orchid plants, and a Japanese landscape garden; the dacha (Russian summer house) displaying decorative arts; the Adirondack-style lodge, which houses a collection of American Indian artifacts; and the C. W. Post Wing, which houses pieces from the Arts and Crafts and Art Nouveau movements.

For more information on Hillwood, see **Gardens**.

Chapter 2

Art

Romaine Brooks, *Self-Portrait*, 1923 (*Courtesy of National Museum of American Art, Smithsonian Institution, Washington, D.C.*)

Although New York and Chicago boast more art museums and galleries, Washington offers a combination of quantity, quality, and accessibility that can't be beat. In addition, many of the capital's art spaces don't charge admission fees because they're government run. If you're an art-lover pursuing a special period or style, you can see more art more quickly and less expensively in Washington than anywhere else.

Because some of the embassy staffs recognize the importance of culture in international relations, many additional doors are opening. Now art lovers can almost travel the world as they visit the new embassy art galleries and exhibit spaces. Some nations have already built new cultural centers, while others are adding galleries and auditoriums to their embassies. Among them:

- Canada included in its new embassy, completed in 1989, a gallery and a 150-seat theater.
- Mexico opened a cultural institute in its former embassy building on 16th Street.
- Austria built a 450-seat auditorium and gallery at its new embassy and a cultural center on International Court off Connecticut Avenue.
- Japan moved its Information and Culture Center to larger quarters on Lafayette Square's Galleria; the center includes a gallery and 150-seat auditorium.
- Venezuela bought a new embassy building in Georgetown and added an art gallery and a 150-seat auditorium.

One observer notes that if the trend continues, visitors will come to Washington in the future not only to see the exhibit at the National Gallery of Art but also to see the art along Embassy Row. With 150 embassies, the possibilities are mind-boggling.

But even without that exotic element, the abundance of choices overwhelms the art lover in Washington. Concentrated within downtown Washington and Georgetown are 12 major art museums. When you add the 6 or more smaller museums and over 80 private galleries, you come close to 100 possible destinations.

Narrowing those options down to a realistic day or two of sightseeing takes planning. One way to plan is by choosing to visit the museums and galleries that feature the art period or style you most enjoy. It also helps to know what the highlights are in each collection. That way, if time or your concentration is limited, you'll be sure to see the most important pieces.

Being aware of the highlights of a museum collection also serves the generalist who simply wants to see the best that each institution offers. By concentrating on the choices of the curators, you can enhance your appreciation of art. In this fast-paced world, seeing the best of each category could also be the most efficient way to define your special interests in art. And with a particular focus, enjoyment expands.

This chapter presents information on Washington's major art museums and galleries and on the highlights of their collections. You'll also find details about nonmuseum sites that display works of art.

Highlight Walk 17th Street

On this walk of about two miles, you'll see some of Washington's finest collections and discover a little-known site or two. Among the surprises in store are the only museum collection of Ansel Adams photographs on the East Coast; American decorative arts exhibited in a Victorian palace; America's first private art collection; what may be the finest Tiffany windows in Washington; a showcase of Latin art; and a gem of a gallery tucked away in a federal institution.

1. Wilderness Society

You expect to see works of art when you enter an art gallery—but an office building? The fact that one of the world's only collections of Ansel Adams museum prints awaits discovery in such a space surprises most people. And what a collection it is. Because Adams was one of the Wilderness Society's staunchest allies in the fight to save the wilderness, he gave the society a set of 75 of his most famous prints. (Only in the Ansel Adams gallery at Yosemite National Park can you see another such permanent collection.) By visiting the Wilderness Society, you see the best of his work: prints that focus on both the intimate details of nature and on grand vistas, including those in Yosemite and in New Mexico. When viewed in their totality, the works offer a rare view of America's wealth of parks, mountains, shores, and forests.

2. Renwick Gallery

When millionaire William Corcoran decided to build a gallery to hold his art collection, he looked to Paris for inspiration. At the Paris Exposition of 1855, held in a new wing of the Louvre, Corcoran saw a new architecture that today is called Second French Empire. Impressed with its opulence, he envisioned an American version set in the nation's capital. Corcoran commissioned architect James Renwick to design a splendid Victorian salon as

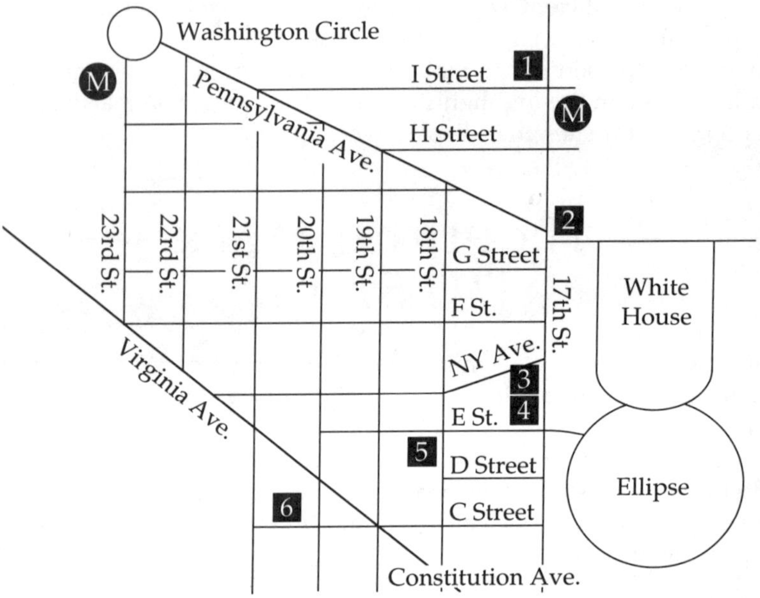

M Metro

1. Wilderness Society, 900 17th Street NW
2. Renwick Gallery, Pennsylvania Avenue and 17th Street NW
3. Corcoran Gallery of Art, 17th Street and New York Avenue NW
4. American Red Cross National Headquarters, 17th Street and D Street NW
5. Art Museum of the Americas, 201 18th Street
6. Federal Reserve Board Gallery, C Street between 20th and 21st Streets NW

Route

From Farragut West Metro station, walk south on 17th Street, stopping at a trio of art galleries as you go: the Wilderness Society, the Renwick Gallery, and the Corcoran Gallery of Art. At the American Red Cross National Headquarters, step inside to see the Tiffany windows. Then continue along D Street to 18th Street and the Art Museum of the Americas. Continue along C Street to the Federal Reserve Board. From the Federal Reserve Board, it's about eight blocks to either the Foggy Bottom or Farragut West Metro subway stations.

backdrop for his art. Sandstone ornaments, ironwork cresting, and niches for statues echoed the elegance of the Louvre. But instead of the granite of the Parisian building, Renwick chose red brick. In place of acanthus leaves, capitals were embellished with an American symbol—ears of Indian corn (as used in the U.S. Capitol). At the top of a palatial stairway, Renwick unfurled a sumptuous 90-foot-long room—the Grand Salon. As on the day it opened to the public, this room today remains a Victorian fantasy. Walls painted a raspberry hue are dramatic backdrop for a collection of 34 oil paintings. Pink velvet settees circling a torch-bearing sculpture, Viennese café tables, and potted palms complete the parlor setting.

In 1965, the building was transferred to the Smithsonian Institution for restoration. In 1972, it opened as an extension of the National Museum of American Art, focusing for the first time on America's rich heritage of design, crafts, and decorative arts.

The gallery's permanent collection includes a wealth of distinctively American works in a wide range of styles and disciplines. Works are classified by medium: ceramic, fiber, glass, wood, and metal. In 1992, the exhibit space for the permanent collection will be doubled, which means that you'll see up to 250 pieces at any one time.

HIGHLIGHTS:

- William Daley, *Oval Chamber*. Ceramic. This exceptionally large (three-foot-high) handsome sculptural form is by an artist known for his distinctive way of handling geometric design elements. It beautifully illustrates Daley's skill at combining architecturally inspired motifs.
- Peter Voulkos, *Rocking Pot*. Ceramic. The most important artist in the development of post–World War II American ceramics. In this piece, Voulkos used clay as a medium for contemporary sculpture, moving the medium into a new realm.
- Wendell Castle, *Ghost Clock*. Wood. A renowned art–furniture maker, Castle uses exotic materials and imaginative designs. This work, which appears to be a cloth-covered clock, is not made of fabric but of a single piece of mahogany. The curator calls it "an astonishing sculptural deception."
- Rudy Autio, *Listening to the East Wind*. Ceramic. The artist's work helped break down the boundaries between sculpture and ceramics. Created in 1986, this major piece reflects the artist's mature style, his draftsmanship, and his use of figurative image.
- Richard Mawdsley, *Feast Bracelet*. Metal. Intricate workmanship and meticulous attention to detail make this the artist's best-known work.
- Albert Paley, *Portal Gates*. Metal. One of the country's leading metalsmiths, Paley was commissioned by the gallery to create this work. The

Albert Raymond Paley, "Portal Gates," Renwick Gallery (*Courtesy of National Museum of American Art, Smithsonian Institution, Washington, D.C.*)

gate complements the building's rich architecture. Using a malleable steel, the artist created detailing seldom seen in ironwork.

• Mary Lee Hu, *Choker #38*. Metal. This prime example of the artist's work embodies her unique vocabulary of form based on direct manipulation. The combination of fine and sterling silver and, of 18- and 24-karat gold wires contrasts brilliantly with the colored lacquered copper wires.

• Cynthia Schira, *Reflectioni*. Fiber. The artist fuses her creative response to the flatness of the Kansas plains with inspiration from her study of textile history and techniques. The piece epitomizes her technique of creating subtle images on her large-scale panels by bringing to the surface a brocade weft of dyed rayon and bound-resist dyed cotton braid tapes.

• Tom Patti, *Bi-Axial Tubated Green Riser*. Glass. This superb example of the artist's innovative use of glass is exquisitely conceived. Using twentieth-century industrial technology, Patti pioneered new techniques of fusing and laminating common green-tinged plate glass to produce a series of works unique in the contemporary American studio glass movement.

• Harvey K. Littleton, *Opalescent Red Crown*. Glass. A unique example of the possibilities in molten hot glass. In this tight cluster of ten individual elements, there is a visual tension between the elegant vertical pieces and the internal shafts of terra-cotta color.

3. Corcoran Gallery of Art

The Corcoran Gallery of Art, Washington's oldest art museum, boasts one of the country's greatest collections of American art. Washington banker and philanthropist William Wilson Corcoran opened the gallery in 1869 to show the works he had collected. First housed in the Renwick Gallery, the collection was moved to its present site in 1897.

In the years since its endowment, the museum has expanded with the addition to two European collections: One is the William A. Clark Collection, which is noted for its Dutch, Flemish, and French Romantic paintings. This collection also includes works by Daumier and Degas, and an impressive selection of landscapes by Barbizon school painters. The second is the Walker Collection, which concentrates on French painting from the late nineteenth and early twentieth centuries.

Selected highlights from the permanent collection of 11,000 works are rotated frequently. In addition, the gallery exhibits temporary shows, including international collections and artist retrospectives.

Highlights:

American, Eighteenth and Nineteenth Century

• John S. Copley, *Portrait of Thomas Amory II*. 1770–72.

• Samuel F. B. Morse, *The Old House of Representatives*. 1822. Painted during a session of Congress in 1822, the picture shows 86 identifiable people, including congressmen, Supreme Court justices, and even a visiting American Indian chief.

• Frederic Church, *Niagara*. 1857. This work, the most famous of the Hudson River School paintings, put American art on the international map. When it was exhibited in London and Paris, art critic John Ruskin declared that American painting had come of age.

• Mary Cassatt, *Susan on a Balcony Holding a Dog*. 1883.

Twentieth Century

- Ad Reinhardt, *Number 5 (Red Wall, 1952)*. 1952.
- Cy Twombly, *Battaglia di 1550*. 1963.
- David Bates, *Cottonmouth*. 1988.
- Donald Lipsky, *Waterlilies #32*. 1990.

For more information on the Corcoran Gallery of Art, see **Antiques**.

4. American Red Cross Headquarters

The largest suite of Tiffany windows on public view glimmers and glows at the American Red Cross Headquarters. Fashioned in the Tiffany Studios in New York City, the ten-foot-tall windows remain as they were installed for the dedication of the building in 1917.

In few other places in the capital will you see such an example of Tiffany's glorious art. At one time, many of the city's buildings and homes were lit by the multicolor light cast by Tiffany windows. President Chester Arthur even commissioned a screen of colored glass for the White House. But that piece and the others have gone. Other than the windows that remain in a few churches (St. Mary's, for one), most Tiffany glass was removed with the decline of Art Nouveau.

What remains are the three theme windows that enhance the Board of Governors Hall here. The windows show Tiffany's innovation, the use of stained glass to tell a story. The three windows tell the story of ministry to the sick and wounded. Tiffany portrays figures in flowing robes and knights in armor, set against a backround of luminous, cloud-filled skies.

In the central panel, a fallen warrior receives food and aid from a faithful comrade; in the left (north) panel, female warriors carry banners as Charity offers a healing draught; in the right (south) panel, noblewomen do good deeds. Of particular note in the central panel is the white steed bedecked with jeweled trappings; the jewels are embedded colored glass stones, an example of one of Tiffany's innovations. Also of interest for its extraordinary beauty is the right panel, which features Una from Spenser's *Faerie Queene*. With a crown atop her long ribbon-entwined hair, and wearing a flowing robe, she carries a basket of flowers.

5. Art Museum of the Americas

The most comprehensive collection of twentieth-century Latin American art in the United States awaits discovery in Washington's newest and least-known museum. The 700 works that make up the permanent collection represent every important art trend in the past 40 years.

Here in the only museum in the United States devoted solely to Latin American art, you can survey the finest works of the major artists of the southern hemisphere under one red-tiled roof.

Appropriately, the collection fills a Spanish Colonial–style villa, once the home of a Latin diplomat. Now the white walls of the second and third floors of the mansion are brightened with artworks. In addition to temporary exhibits, about a third of the permanent collection is displayed at a time. Sculpture, which makes up about 15 percent of the collection, is shown in staircase niches and in the loggia and gardens.

The museum, established in 1976 by the Organization of American States to mark the bicentennial of the United States, stands behind the OAS building. In addition to displaying the works of such masters as Orozco, Tamayo, Matta, Cuevas, and Soto, the museum also shows the works of new artists. The museum presents a dozen temporary exhibits each year. Many of these shows examine various aspects of the art and cultural traditions of Latin American countries.

HIGHLIGHTS:

Twentieth Century

- Cándido Portinari, *Retorno da Feira (Return from the Fair).* This artist's murals were chosen to decorate the United Nations headquarters.
- Carlos Merida, *Purpura de Tormenta: Seires de los Cielos de Tejas (Stormy Purple: Texas Skies Series).* This muralist, painter, and printmaker draws from Mayan decorative motifs and from rhythms of pre-Columbian dance.
- Amelia Peláez, *Mar Pacificio (The Hibiscus).* The artist reinvents reality as she masterfully contrasts native and foreign elements, such as the native hibiscus flower, architectural moldings, and cane weavings.
- Roberto Matta, *Hermala II.* A member of the Surrealist group in Paris in 1937, he may be unsurpassed in his ability to convey images of the subconscious.
- Jesús Rafael Soto, *Hurtado Scripture.* The artist's kinetic compositions in Plexiglas won him a place in the forefront of the avant-garde.
- Fernando de Szyszlo, *Cajamarca.* He uses as inspiration decorative elements found in the textiles and imagery of pre-Columbian Peru.
- Kazuo Wakabayashi, *Azule Preto (Blue and Black).* Since his work was seen in the 1965 Rockefeller Center exhibition, the artist has been acclaimed as a leader in the nonfigurative trend.

6. FEDERAL RESERVE BOARD

In the atrium of this financial institution, in a grand setting of travertine marble floors and fluted columns, reigns one of Washington's least-known galleries. Created in 1975 by a presidential directive, the gallery mounts a number of shows each year. Borrowing from both private and public collections, shows range from the classical to the modern, from Biedermeier furniture to "fine art graffiti." If you relish Art Deco details, note the light fixtures on the ground floor, which are etched with astrological signs. Tours of the building can be arranged for groups.

Note: For a fascinating detour one block off 17th Street, arrange a VIP tour of the White House and focus specifically on the art. In the Vermeil Room, you'll see Claude Monet's *Morning on the Seine*, a painting given to the White House by the Kennedy family in memory of John F. Kennedy. On the regular tours you'll pass several important paintings, including George Caleb Bingham's *Lighter Relieving a Steamboat Aground* in the Green Room; Albert Bierstadt's *View of the Rocky Mountains* hangs in the Red Room.

More Art

Georgetown–Embassy Row

Dumbarton Oaks

When Robert Bliss retired from the foreign service in 1933, he and his wife Mildred came back to their country house in the Washington area. They had purchased the Rock of Dumbarton estate with its nineteenth-century house in 1920, and during their absence it had been remodeled and a great garden planted.

The house became a showcase for the books and art that they had collected in pursuit of their three loves: Byzantine art, pre-Columbian art and archaeology, and landscape gardening. In 1940, the Blisses turned over their precious collection and home to Harvard University. Using the estate and funds from the Bliss endowment, Harvard supports continuing research in their three areas of interest, maintains separate libraries for each, and sponsors fellowship programs.

When Robert Bliss began to collect pre-Columbian art in Paris around 1910, he was the first to buy pre-Columbian pieces for their aesthetic value. Prior to this time, pre-Columbian materials were collected principally as archaeological evidence of the great culture of ancient America, with little thought to their artistic merit.

The Bliss collection of pre-Columbian art shows some of the finest artistic achievements of the native peoples of the New World. The 250 objects on display show peaks of creativity, expression, and skill. The works are exhibited in a special pavilion that the Blisses asked architect Phillip Johnson to design in 1962. With the aim of enhancing the collection, Johnson designed a building made up of eight circular glass pavilions. The extensive use of glass gives the impression that the objects are enveloped by the woods outside.

HIGHLIGHTS:

• *Palenque.* Panel, depicting a Mayan ruler rising from the underworld. This is one of the finest pieces in the collection because of the great subtlety and delicacy of the carving.

• *Incan tunic, once worn by an emperor.* The designs woven into the cloth are a pattern of squares and rectangles that convey a message whose meaning is lost. This may be the greatest piece of all because of its fine quality.

• *Were-jaguar mask.* This Olmec period jade sculpture combines human (were) and feline forms into a unique and haunting abstraction.

• *Aztec gold pieces.* Necklaces, earrings, and lip-plugs formed by the lost-wax process. A highlight among the pieces is a necklace fashioned into delicate shields with tiny bells attached.

• *Peruvian funerary gold hoard from the grave of a ruler.* Among the dozen pure gold objects are 1,200 sequins once attached to a piece of clothing, pectoral and ear ornaments, a ceremonial spear thrower, a headband, two large rings worn on arms or legs, and a mask that adorned the ruler when he was buried.

One of the world's finest Byzantine collections also glistens and gleams at the Dumbarton Oaks Museum. The Blisses' interest in the period was stimulated when they attended the *Exposition Internationale d'Art Byzantine* in Paris. The collection now boasts more than 1,400 objects. Among them are icons, sixth-century ecclesiastical silver vessels and enamel crosses, and one of the world's largest collections of period coins.

Objects exhibited in the "treasure room" span the 1,127-year period when Constantinople served as the center of the Christian empire. During this period—from A.D. 326 to 1453—Byzantium sheltered an artistic culture of unrivaled opulence and refinement. Artistry flourished, particularly metalwork, enameling, ivory carving, and manuscript illumination.

The collection is organized into the three periods of Byzantine art: Early Byzantine, from 326, when Roman Emperor Constantine established his capital in Constantinople, to the rise of the Iconoclasts in 726; Middle Byzantine, from the restoration of images in 843 to the sack of Constantinople by the Crusaders in 1204; and Late Byzantine, from the recovery of the capital by the Romans in 1261 to its defeat by the Ottomans in 1453.

HIGHLIGHTS:

• *Mosaic Icon of the Forty Martyrs.* A miniature artwork in which hundreds of tiny enamel and precious metal cubes are pressed into wax. It is one of the first pieces to signal the birth of emotional art that came into favor during the Renaissance.

• *Tenth-century carved ivories.* These pieces are of unrivaled quality and refinement. Particularly noteworthy is *Virgin with Two Saints.*

• *Gilt-silver paten Communion of the Apostles.* The representation of figures on silver patens is so rare that this is one of only a handful in the world, and the only one in the Western hemisphere.

• *Sapphire cameo with bust of Christ.* Made in Constantinople in the tenth century, this piece shows the carver's supreme skill. The purity of the stone's color wins the praise of most visiting scholars.

• *Gold openwork pendants and bracelet.* Fashioned in Constantinople in the late fourth century, these are noted for the fine crafsmanship with which the artist cut through gold to create silhouette patterns.

• *Marble sarcophagus.* One of the world's largest, made in Rome in the early fourth century. Executed at a time when Christianity was recognized, it shows pagan influences.

• *Sion Treasure.* A hoard of 60 ecclesiastical silver pieces discovered in Turkey in 1963. The pieces are important because they were found together and thus give scholars their first physical evidence of the lavishness of early church furnishings.

At Dumbarton Oaks, fine European masterworks enrich the walls of the garden library, which is open on occasion. Flowers are the themes of oils by Odilon Redon, Seurat, Vuillard, and Renoir. Especially notable are two works by Degas, a watercolor sketch and *The Rehearsal.*

For more information on Dumbarton Oaks, see **Antiques, Gardens,** and **Music**.

The Phillips Collection

The bowls of fresh flowers, comfortable furniture, and windows overlooking the street make you feel as if you're a guest in a private home. The artworks on the walls, however—masterpieces of American and European modernism—leave little doubt that you've found your way to one of the world's great museums.

The Phillips collection, housed in the one-time residence of founder Duncan Phillips, is the oldest museum of modern art in the country. Phillips bought many of his most important artworks during the golden age of collecting between 1910 and 1920. He chose what he liked and hung it on his walls. In 1920, Phillips opened two rooms of his home to the public; eventually the entire building was opened. Now the former residence includes an annex, needed to make room for exhibits of at least some of the 2,500 works the museum owns.

Following the dictates of his own taste instead of fashion, Phillips collected modern pictures that he felt communicated joy. When he found an artist he admired, Phillips would often buy a number of his or her works. Among the multiwork holdings are those of Degas, van Gogh, Ryder, Vuillard, Rouault, Dufy, Braque, and Picasso. Nineteenth-century European works include Impressionist masterpieces. The best known is the golden moment captured by Renoir in his famed *The Luncheon of the Boating Party.*

As one of the early collectors of American modern art, Phillips got some of the country's best works. As a result, the collection today is strong in such pioneers of early twentieth-century American art as John Marin, Arthur Dove, Karl Knaaths, and Augustus Tack. The museum also holds outstanding works from such European artists as Paul Klee, Pierre Bonnard, Oscar Kokoschka, and Nicholas de Stael.

HIGHLIGHTS:

Modern European

- Paul Cézanne, *Self Portrait.* 1878–80. Nowhere does the artist better resolve the dualism between objective reality and subjective thought.
- Vincent van Gogh, *The Road Menders.* 1889. A highly complex composition, a work that van Gogh himself liked very much.
- Pierre Bonnard, *The Palm.* 1926. The unique qualities of the artist's long career come together here.
- Edouard Vuillard, *Woman Sweeping.* 1892. Conflicting patterns become one harmonious whole.

American, Eighteenth and Nineteenth Century

- Albert Pinkham Ryder, *Moonlit Cove.* 1880–90. Golden luminosity comes through in this, one of the artist's better-preserved canvases.
- Thomas Eakins, *Miss Van Buren.* 1886–90. Instead of a flattering portrayal, we see to the soul of the subject, her essence and personality.
- John Henry Twachtman, *Emerald Pool.* 1895. The artist's sensitivity to subtly graded color relationships caused Pierre Bonnard, who visited the Phillips Collection in 1926, to name this his favorite American painting.

Twentieth Century

- Georges Braque, *The Philodendron.* 1952. Simplicity here makes way for spontaneity, the breaking through of emotional expression.
- Pablo Picasso, *The Blue Room.* 1901. Here you see the harbingers of Cubism.
- Piet Mondrian, *Painting No. 9.* 1939–42. A step toward the pure color the artist uses toward the end of his life.
- Maurice Prendergast, *Ponte della Paglia.* 1898–99 and 1922. Before the oil painting entered the Phillips Collection in 1922, the artist overpainted carefree accents of brilliant color on his previously exhibited work.

• John Marin, *Fifth Avenue and Forty-Second Street.* 1933. Experimenting with oils, the artist incorporates disparate techniques; the work becomes a sampler for methods of paint application.

• Arthur Dove, *Flour Mill Abstraction.* 1938. The seemingly arbitrary geometric forms here cause some historians to see Dove as a harbinger of Abstract Expressionism.

• Milton Avery, *Girl Writing.* 1941. "He translated his sense of people, places, and the things he knew best into planes of characteristic color and light without the intrusion of distracting detail," writes Eleanor Green in *Master Paintings from the Phillips Collection.*

• Georgia O'Keeffe, *Ranchos Church.* 1929. The artist found she could say things with color and shapes that she couldn't say in another way. The painting followed her seeing Arthur Dove's work in a 1916 exhibition.

Saint Sofia Greek Orthodox Cathedral

A thousand years ago, when the mosaics of Istanbul's Sofia Cathedral were at their best, they looked pretty much like the ones you see today representing heaven on earth at Washington's sister cathedral.

Beyond the unadorned exterior of the Greek Orthodox Cathedral of Saint Sofia on Embassy Row lies the world's only complete re-creation of the now-crumbling Byzantine originals. The mosaics, which embellish the walls and the dome of the cathedral, were executed over a 20-year period by artist Dimetrios A. Dukas. Paul Underwood, who before his death was the Byzantine authority at Dumbarton Oaks, worked with Dukas to make sure his re-creation was as faithful to the original as possible.

Dukas's drawings, selected in a competition of American and European artists, were at first to be executed as paintings. Dukas, however, suggested that instead they be done as mosaics. When the committee saw his first effort, the mosaic that decorates the dome, they agreed to use the medium for the walls of the sanctuary, nave, and apse. Dukas was able to find the same materials for his works that ancient artists knew: Italian marble, glass, gold leaf, and terra cotta.

Completed in 1984, the mosaics form a heavenly pageant of saints, angels, Mary, and Christ on his jeweled throne. The figures, done in the style of the Macedonian dynasty, are simple, bold, and abstract in form—in contrast with the later realistic style. A booklet available at the site, titled "An Encounter with the Sublime," explains the subject matter of the mosaics and includes a fascinating explanation of the distinction between the classical Greek concept of beauty and the sublimity of Byzantine art.

Textile Museum

The pre-eminent museum in the Western hemisphere focusing exclusively on handmade textiles and carpets, the Textile Museum offers art of another kind. In the exhibit galleries of twin townhouses you'll see treasures drawn from the museum's holdings of over 12,000 textiles and 1,400 carpets. The shows, which change periodically, can feature Egyptian and Peruvian textiles, including an important collection of Peruvian tapestries; weavings from the East and American southwest; and rugs from a around the world, representing many periods. For more information on the Textile Museum, see **Gardens**.

Washington National Cathedral

Artists, using all the disciplines of their craft and the creativity of their genius, still work here. But instead of painting with oils on canvas, they paint with light.

On 214 stained glass windows created over an 80-year period, glass artists have articulated light. Like other artists, they demonstrate their mastery of color harmony, composition, and scale; they also express their passionate vision. As a result, the fiercely radiant colors of the windows make jewels look subdued by comparison. Only fireworks come close to the intensities of light made real here in stained glass. You see the full spectrum of the glass designer's art in the aisles, chapels, transepts, and clerestories of the cathedral. Rows of windows beneath its high, vaulted roof become a textbook of styles, color combinations, and subject matter.

The first windows, in the Bethlehem chapel, were created and fabricated in England in 1912. With their white flesh tones, large amounts of green, and minimal use of reds and blues, the windows typify the English traditions in stained glass coloring. In contrast, the French process of staining glass used in subsequent windows displays a rich variety of primary colors.

Like color, style has changed over the years. Until 1953, the windows created by artists followed the neo-Gothic tradition. But after that date, convention gave way to more urbane and adventurous styles. Since that time, a lively progression of artists from eight countries has expressed individual vision in unique ways. Much as in the world outside, tastes changed within the cathedral during its construction.

By comparing the early windows with the later ones, you'll see differences in window clarity. In the earlier days, some artists became fascinated with the mellow look of glass in old cathedrals. To imitate this dusky look, they applied film over the inside of the windows and spattered black specks on the outside to resemble the pitting found on old glass. But other people believed the windows were muddied and their liveliness reduced, and the entirely transparent window returned in later works. Free of film, the windows in the Mellon and Wilson bays are cleaner and brighter.

Differing characteristics like these, plus other fascinating details, are pointed out on the the stained glass tours that cathedral docents offer by special arrangement.

For more information on Washington National Cathedral, see **Gardens, Literature,** and **Music**.

Anderson House

For art lovers, one painting at the Anderson House makes a visit worthwhile—*Triumph of the Dogaressa,* painted by José Villegas in 1882 and exhibited as the artist's best work in the great galleries of Europe. Villegas was appointed curator of the Prado, an office that recognized him as Spain's leading artist.

For more information about Anderson House, see **Antiques, Gardens, Literature, Music,** and **Military**.

Foggy Bottom

Kennedy Center for the Performing Arts

Washington's grandest showcase of the arts reigns on the banks of the Potomac River in Foggy Bottom. When this memorial to John F. Kennedy was built, nations from around the world who wanted to play a part sent their gifts. Italy sent 3,000 tons of marble for exterior sheathing. Another 40 countries presented decorative objects and furnishings: rugs, chandeliers, mirrors, planters, silk fabric, sculpture, tapestries, paintings, an alabaster vase, shadow puppets, brass oil lamps, porcelain vases, and an ancient amphora. You can see some of the items on a stroll through the center, but for the choicest viewing, you'll need a ticket. That's because some of the best artworks are exhibited in the foyers inside the Opera House, the Concert Hall, and the Eisenhower Theater.

Even without a theater ticket, however, you'll see some fine works. Highlights include Australian tapestries in the South Gallery, representing the Creation; the fiberwork sculpture from Brazil in the Hall of States; paintings from Peru in the Hall of Nations; a reproduction of a third-century mosaic on the roof terraces, and impressive bronze panels from Germany along the entrance plaza.

A good way to see all the theaters with their private spaces is by joining the center's free tour. For more information on that tour and the center, see **Music**.

State Department

Outstanding historical American artworks are part of the period furnishings at the State Department Diplomatic Reception Rooms. Paintings illustrate early American life and depict famous leaders and events. Among the outstanding paintings you'll pass on the standard tour is Benjamin West's recreation of the signing of the treaty that ended the American Revolution.

Other high points: Thomas Sully's full-length oil portrait of Thomas Jefferson, Fitz Hugh Lane's *View of Boston Harbor*, Charles Wilson Peale's portrait of George Washington, Childe Hassam's *Streets of Provincetown*, and Thomas Moran's *The Cliffs of Green River, Wyoming*.

The Mall

National Museum of African Art

You may not hear the chants or drums or catch the flash of metal spear by firelight, but the sense that you are in Africa pervades. Earth-colored walls and floor coverings, subdued lighting, and fringes of potted greenery create the mood. The objects on display seem to be inhabited still by the spirits that once wore and held them. Masks, headdresses, and ritual objects of fiber, bronze, ivory, wood, and fired clay transport you to the heart of Africa.

Founded in 1964, this is the only museum in the United States dedicated exclusively to the collection, exhibition, and study of the traditional arts of sub-Saharan Africa. Since 1979, the museum has worked to build a strong permanent collection of works of outstanding aesthetic quality. About a hundred works from the permanent collection are on exhibit.

To assist you in appreciating and understanding the diverse cultures of sub-Saharan Africa, works are grouped according to the major geographical and cultural regions. These include the western Sudan, Guinea, and the eastern, southern, and central regions, plus the coast of Africa.

Highlights:

- *Woman and child figure.* Congo and Zaire. This figure, one of six known examples of this style, was probably carved in the nineteenth century.
- *Muzamba-style mask.* Zaire and Angola. This ancestor mask depicts a young woman of great beauty. Note her delicate narrow nose, her head, which tapers to a well-rounded chin, and her elaborate raffia coiffure.
- *Divination basket.* Zaire and Angola. This basket of fiber and various materials contains objects from the animal, vegetable, and mineral worlds. A diviner shakes out the contents and interprets the meaning of the configuration.
- *Cup.* Zaire. The wooden cup features geometric designs derived from woven cloth. Depicting a human head with ram horns, it displays the carver's skill and innovation.
- *Headrest.* Zaire. This richly carved headrest, used to protect an elaborate coiffure, probably belonged to a person of rank and importance.
- *Seated male and female figure.* Ghana. Carved figures like this are given to girls and women to ensure their fertility and the health and beauty of

their children. Double images are rare; this one may have been kept in a shrine.

• *Vessel.* Malawai. This handmade, fired-clay vessel is used for storing water or for the maize beer that is consumed at funerals and initiation ceremonies.

• *Female and children figure.* Nigeria. This wood sculpture depicts a female devotee, accompanied by children, bearing a bowl for kola nuts or other offerings.

FREER GALLERY OF ART

Few other rags-to-riches stories rival that of the benefactor of this gallery, Charles Lang Freer. A high school dropout who began work in a cement factory, Freer had made a fortune as a railroad car manufacturer by age 46. In 1899, he retired to spend the rest of his life traveling around the world and collecting art. By the time he died, he had collected 9,400 works. He offered them to Franklin Roosevelt in 1904, together with the money needed to build the museum that would house them.

In 1992, after a three-year renovation, the great Renaissance palace that Freer built on the Mall is open again. Inside, around a courtyard filled with shrubs and blossoms, you can tour 19 galleries filled with Asian and Amer-

61.34—Chinese painting; Chin Dynasty (1122–1234); by Lin Shan, *Wind and Snow in the Fir Pines;* ink and light colors on silk; 29.7 × 79.2 cm. (*Courtesy of the Freer Gallery of Art, Smithsonian Institution, Washington, D.C.*)

ican treasures. Oriental ceramics, porcelains, and bronzes; fine art scrolls, panels, and screens; and the finest collection of Islamic paintings in North America head the list. Because Freer believed that James McNeill Whistler was the American artist who best synthesized Western and Oriental art, he bought 1,235 of his works. The Freer's Whistler collection is the largest in the world.

Of all the Whistler works, however, one stands out. It is the Peacock Room, considered the finest room in a museum in America. Whistler created the room as the fitting backdrop to a painting. Later the room, designed for a London townhouse, was dismantled and moved to Freer's home, and then to the gallery. As in an ornate tapestry, the elements of the Peacock Room work together. Gilded leather walls embellished with turquoise peacocks, a gilded shelf holding blue and white porcelains, a red-bordered rug, gilded fireplace andirons, and decorative motifs on shutters and sideboards produce a stunning visual impression.

HIGHLIGHTS:

American, Eighteenth and Nineteenth Century

• James McNeill Whistler, *Harmony in Blue and Gold: The Peacock Room.* 1876–77. The room, decorated with painted leather, canvas, and wood, was designed by the artist to show off *Rose and Silver: The Princess from the Land of Porcelain,* which hangs over the fireplace. An extensive conservation project has restored the room to its original splendor.

Asian Art

• *Cong.* China, circa 3500–2000 B.C. Jade. This important ritual object from one of the earliest Neolithic cultures of China is remarkable for the labor and care taken in working the hard material into perforation and surface decoration.

• *Fanq yi.* China, Western Zhou period, circa 1000 B.C. Bronze. This ritual vessel, bearing a 187-character inscription inside the body and lid, serves as an extremely important historical document of the period.

• *Belt buckle.* China, 400 to 350 B.C. Bronze. This elegant object epitomizes its period in the lavish use of colored inlays and gilded bronze surfaces.

• *Mirror.* China, Tang dynasty, 618–907. Bronze and gold. When new, the undecorated side of the mirror was a looking glass of smooth and highly polished metal. The back side is exquisitely decorated with a thin sheet of gold that carries a repoussé design.

• Gong Kai, *Zhong Kui Traveling.* China, Yuan dynasty, 1279–1368. Handscroll. Few figure paintings from this period can match the artist's spontaneous brushwork and vivid colors.

• Zou Fulei, *A Breath of Spring.* China, Yuan dynasty, dated 1360. Handscroll. Working entirely in ink, the artist has used extraordinarily delicate yet powerful brushwork. The painting is one of the most effective renderings of the flowering plum in Chinese art.

• *Incense box.* Japan, Muromachi period 1334–1573. Lacquer on carved wood. This is one of the earliest surviving Japanese examples of Kamakura-bori, a distinctive type of Japanese lacquerware.

• Tawaraya Sotatsu, *Waves at Matsushima.* Japan, Edo period, early seventeenth century. Ink, color, gold, and silver on paper. One of three screens by the artist. The gallery collection of painting and calligraphy by Sotatsu, Koetsu, and their followers is one of the most important in the world.

• *Nyoirin Kannon.* Japan, Heian period, twelfth century. Ink, color, silver, and gold on silk. This painting on silk embellished with applied cut gold and silver leaf is rare among surviving Buddhist paintings of the period. The artist is unknown.

• *Maebyong.* Korea, Koryo dynasty 935–1392. Gray stoneware with translucent green glaze. A masterpiece from this period.

• *Queen Sembiyan Mahadevi.* India, Tamil Nadu, Chola dynasty, tenth century. Bronze. This sculpture is considered the finest south Indian bronze outside India.

• *Pillow in the form of a tortoise.* Vietnam, Tran dynasty, fourteenth century. Pale gray stoneware with iron or cobalt pigment under translucent white glaze. The only known example of a ceramic pillow from Vietnam.

Near and Middle East

• *Head of a king.* Egypt, Old Kingdom, circa 2522 B.C. Stone. This is a rare and beautiful example of royal sculpture.

• *Plate.* Iran, Sassanian period, fourth century. Silver and gilt. This plate, depicting the great Sassanian king Shapur as a royal hunter, is one of the world's finest examples of Sassanian work.

• *Silver-inlaid brass canteen.* Syria, mid-thirteenth century. Brass, silver, and inlay. This extraordinary piece is decorated with Arabic inscriptions and scrolls as well as scenes from the life of Christ; it reflects the multifaceted artistic motifs of the period.

Hirshhorn Museum and Sculpture Garden

To encourage interest in contemporary art, in 1938 Congress introduced legislation to create a new gallery within the Smithsonian Institution. Almost thirty years later, Joseph H. Hirshhorn, an immigrant from Latvia who had made a fortune in uranium mining, donated his art collection to the American people. In 1974, the Smithsonian Institution opened the modern structure and a five-acre sculpture garden to exhibit the works.

Today over 600 pieces from Hirshhorn's collection of 12,500 paintings, sculptures, and works on paper, plus new acquisitions, are on exhibit. The lower level is used primarily for special exhibitions, with the second and third floor galleries devoted to the permanent works. Inner galleries lit by natural light, plus an extensive garden, show the sculpture collection.

The permanent collection focuses on international modern artists. It illustrates diverse trends, ranging from paintings by nineteenth-century and early twentieth-century Americans George Bellows and Thomas Eakins to the innovative works of contemporary artists. Since Hirshhorn himself was an immigrant, it is appropriate that the museum shows representative works of immigrant artists, including Josef Albers, Willem de Kooning, George Grosz, and Max Weber.

The museum also boasts one of the world's major sculpture collections—over 3,000 works. The Sculpture Garden, one of the few of its kind in the country, exhibits mostly figurative works in bronze. Most famous among these is *The Burghers of Calais,* the 1886 bronze statue by August Rodin.

HIGHLIGHTS:

American, Eighteenth and Nineteenth Century

- Thomas Eakins, *Mrs. Thomas Eakins.* 1899. Although the artist's wife was a warm, witty, and congenial woman, he created an intense, deeply introspective portrait of stark simplicity.

Twentieth Century

- Constantin Brancusi, *Torso of a Young Man.* 1924. The bronze and wood sculpture by the famous Romanian-born artist is one of his most extraordinary works.
- Henry Moore, *King and Queen.* 1952–53. This bronze sculpture is the jewel of the museum's collection of Moore's sculptures—the largest in the country.
- Willem de Kooning, *Queen of Hearts.* 1943–46. This is an important early painting by one of the major post-war American painters.
- Jean Dubuffet, *The Soul of Morvan.* 1954. The French sculpture uses mostly cast-off or decayed natural materials: broken seashells, dead leaves, and, in this case, grapevines he gathered in the vineyards of Morvan.
- Francis Bacon, *Triptych.* 1967. Nearly 60 works by this British artist were shown at the gallery in 1989, from daring figure studies to hallmark diptychs and triptychs.
- Anselm Kiefer, *The Book.* 1979–85. Kiefer is one of the most important artists to emerge from post-war Germany. His evocative landscapes contain buried words and portraits of people from Germany's past.

• Jasper Johns, *Untitled*. 1987. A veritable catalogue of the artist's brush strokes and images, the painting abounds with allusions and references to the recurring motifs in Johns's work.

National Gallery of Art—West Building

In this Roman temple modeled after the Pantheon, it is only fitting that Mercury still serves as a messenger in the twentieth century. The bronze statue in winged hat and sandals fairly flies off his perch beneath the rotunda of this marble palace. With a gesture that lightens the spirit of the weary traveler he is said to serve, Mercury seems to say, "Follow me to the treasures contained here."

A journey begun at the feet of Mercury will take you through 600 years of Western art. Beginning in the two halls that open from the West Building rotunda and continuing to the East Building, you'll see landmark works from the Renaissance through the twentieth century.

The collection of the National Gallery of Art grew from a totally unrealistic idea: that in the twentieth century, it is possible to form a collection of masterpieces equal to those in European museums. Although luck played a part in the ultimate success of this quest, it was really the wisdom and generosity of one man that created what critics have called "an amazing approximation of an impossible standard."

In 1931, billionaire industrialist Andrew Mellon had the opportunity of a lifetime. To help finance its new government, the Soviet Union decided to sell treasures from the Hermitage museum. For only $7 million, Mellon was able to purchase 21 works, among them paintings by Botticelli, Van Eyck, Raphael, Titian, and Rembrandt. These works, combined with Mellon's private collection, added up to 126 paintings and 26 sculptures, which he donated to the nation. He also offered the funds to build the National Gallery of Art.

When the museum opened in 1941, the Mellon collection plus 375 paintings and 18 sculptures donated by philanthropist Samuel Kress made up the collection. Since then, three other collections have been donated, by Joseph E. Widener; Lessing J. Rosenwald and Chester Dale; and Ailsa Mellon Bruce and Paul Mellon. Hundreds of other individuals have also donated artworks.

Today the National Gallery of Art is one of of the world's great museums. Over 4,000 works fill 100 galleries. To aid the visitor in appreciating the wealth, works are divided chronologically into ten periods and countries. There are also separate halls for sculpture, prints and drawings, and decorative arts. The photography collection is world-famous, including 1,600 works of Alfred Stieglitz, 28 works by Paul Strand, an archival collection of Robert Frank's work, 76 images by Ansel Adams, and an impressive Walker Evans collection.

HIGHLIGHTS:

Southern Renaissance

• Duccio di Buoninsegna, *The Nativity with the Prophets Isaiah and Ezekiel*. 1308–11. This panel is from the great altarpiece *Maestà* painted by the artist for the Cathedral in Siena.

• Giotto, *Madonna and Child*. 1320–30. The artist, who broke with the Byzantine painting tradition, reveals here the expression of human form and feeling.

• Fra Angelico and Fra Filippo Lippi, *The Adoration of the Magi*. 1445. This wooden tondo, or circular painting, once the prized possession of Lorenzo de' Medici, shows the grand procession of the Wise Men to the place of Christ's birth.

• Leonardo da Vinci, *Ginerva De' Benci*. 1474. The only painting by the master in the Western hemisphere.

• Botticelli, *Adoration of the Magi*. Early 1480s. This graceful and linear Adoration, set among classical ruins, emphasizes the devotional aspect of the scene rather than the festive.

• Raphael, *Saint George and the Dragon*. 1506. Painted for an emissary of the King Henry VII of England, this is the smallest work in the collection and also one of its most costly.

• Giovanni Bellini and Titian, *The Feast of the Gods*. 1514 and 1529. Painted in 1514 by Bellini, the greatest of fifteenth-century Venetian painters, for the study of the duke of Ferrara; Titian repainted the mountainous landscape at the left, probably in 1529.

• Titian, *Venus with a Mirror*. 1555. Among the many versions of the painting, this canvas is the only one fully accepted as being by the master's hand.

Northern Renaissance

• Rogier van der Weyden, *Portrait of a Lady*. 1455. A superb work by one of the most influential fifteenth-century Dutch painters.

• Jan van Eyck, *The Annunciation*. 1425–30. One of the few paintings in America by one of the "founding fathers" of Dutch painting.

• Albrecht Dürer, *Madonna and Child*. 1505. A major work by the best-known German artist.

• Matthias Grünewald, *The Small Crucifixion*. 1510. The only picture by this emotionally powerful artist in the United States.

• Gerard David, *The Rest on the Flight into Egypt*. 1510. This beautiful painting may be "the earliest tonal symphony with a dominant color in the history of art," according to John Wilmerding, writing in *American Masterpieces from the National Gallery of Art*.

Northern Baroque

• Rembrandt, *A Polish Nobleman*. 1637. Dramatic accents of light and dark, bold brushwork, and dense application of paint all contribute to the powerful presence of the figure, painted during the period of the artist's greatest popularity.

• Jan Vermeer, *Woman Holding a Balance*. 1664. As in most of Vermeer's paintings, a timeless, poetic quality pervades this scene.

• Peter Paul Rubens, *Daniel in the Lion's Den*. 1615. This picture, executed entirely by the artist's own hand, displays Rubens's mastery of the dynamic baroque style that he helped invent.

Southern Baroque

• El Greco, *Laocoön*. 1610–1614. One of the artist's great masterpieces from his late period, and his only surviving mythological painting.

• Orazio Gentileschi, *Lute Player*. 1610. Certainly a masterpiece of Roman baroque painting. The portrayal of the young girl in her twisted pose arrests our attention.

• Annibale Carracci, *Landscape*. Circa 1630. This great baroque artist was the first to paint landscape as an independent subject.

• Bartolomé Esteban Murillo, *Two Women at a Window*. Circa 1655–1660. One of a small number of seventeenth-century Spanish genre scenes, the meaning of which continues to be debated.

• Giovanni Battista Tiepolo, *The World Pays Homage to Spain*. 1762. A Venetian painter of international reputation, Tiepolo was commissioned to decorate the throne room of the Royal Palace at Madrid. In this study for the ceiling, we see him working out details of color, light, balance, and subject matter.

• Jean-Baptiste-Siméon Chardin, *Soap Bubbles*. 1733–1734. An astute observer of everyday life, Chardin imbues mundane activities and idle pleasures with purpose and meaning.

• Goya, *The Marquesa de Pontejos*. 1786. One of Goya's early aristocratic portraits. The fluid brushwork exhibits those qualities that are characteristic of the artist.

Modern European

• Jean-Auguste-Dominique Ingres, *Madame Moitessier*. 1851. The painting shows the artist's mastery of detail and perfection of form.

• Edouard Manet, *The Old Musician*. 1862. Note the objective presentation of a modern subject, the urban poor.

• Edouard Manet, *Gare Saint-Lazare*. 1873. Manet captured the charm of everyday life with a timeless beauty and intensity.

• Paul Cézanne, *The Artist's Father*. 1866. Of his three paintings of his father, this is the most overwhelming, a masterful evocation of the physical presence of the man who dominated the painter's life.

• Pierre-Auguste Renoir, *Pont Neuf, Paris*. 1872. Renoir used light and color to capture the freshness of a sunny day in Paris.

• Claude Monet, *Rouen Cathedral, West Facade, Sunlight*. 1894. In 30 canvases of the subject, Monet showed how the appearance of the cathedral changes depending on light and weather conditions.

• Edgar Degas, *Four Dancers*. 1899. Degas experimented with the effects of garish artificial illumination falling on the carefully arranged limbs of dancers.

• Vincent van Gogh, *La Mousme*. 1888. Exaggerated color and forceful brushwork give the work its vital, expressive quality.

British

• George Stubbs, *Captain Pocklington with His Wife and Sister*. 1769.
• Sir Joshua Reynolds, *Lady Elizabeth Delme and Her Children*. 1781.
• Thomas Gainsborough, *Mrs. Richard Brinsley Sheridan*. 1785–86.
• John Constable, *Wivenhoe Park, Essex*. 1816.
• Joseph Mallord William Turner, *Keelmen Heaving in Coals by Moonlight*. 1835.

American, Eighteenth and Nineteenth Century

• John Singleton Copley, *Watson and the Shark*. 1778.
• Gilbert Stuart, *The Skater (Portrait of William Grant)*. 1782.
• Rembrandt Peale, *Rubens Peale with a Geranium*. 1801.
• Thomas Cole, *The Voyage of Life: Youth*. 1842.
• George Inness, *The Lackawanna Valley*. 1855.
• Albert P. Ryder, *Siegfried and the Rhine Maidens*. 1888.
• Winslow Homer, *Breezing Up (A Fair Wind)*. 1876.
• Thomas Eakins, *Baby at Play*. 1876.
• James McNeill Whistler, *The White Girl: Symphony in White, No. 1*. 1862.
• George Bellows, *Both Members of This Club*. 1909.

National Gallery of Art—East Building

With the opening of the East Wing of the National Gallery of Art in 1978, twentieth-century American and European art got a fitting showcase. In contrast to the classical West Building, the modern East Building provides a new world for a new decade of art. Just as the Italian palace ambience of the one suits the paintings of Botticelli and Titian, so the glass and steel construction of the other complements the works of Klee and Picasso.

When, in 1963, the board of directors decided to add works of contemporary artists to the collections, there were two reasons for a new building:

the demand for additional space and the conviction that the art of the past and the present should be set apart. A new building used for a new purpose called for a new design. Architect I. M. Pei's design answered that need: an innovative structure where sunlight plays through a honeycombed glass roof on a complex system of triangular spaces. As you move between the building's various levels, space relationships change; as your perspective changes, you see the art not only from different angles but also in a different way.

This is particularly true of the commissioned artwork on display beneath the glass roof of the main court. Among these specially selected works by contemporary artists are Alexander Calder's monumental mobile, Henry Moore's *Knife Edge Mirror Two Piece*, Anthony Caro's *Ledge Piece*, and Joan Miró's large tapestry *Woman*, which is put on display only periodically because of its fragile fibers.

HIGHLIGHTS:

- Pablo Picasso, *Family of Saltimbanques*. 1905.
- Frantisek Kupka, *Organization of Graphic Motifs II*. 1912–13.
- Wassily Kandinsky, *Improvisation 31 (Sea Battle)*. 1913.
- Joan Miró, *The Farm*. 1921–22.
- Piet Mondrian, *Diamond Painting in Red, Yellow and Blue*. 1921–25.
- Georgia O'Keeffe, *Jack-in-the-Pulpit Nos. II-VI*. 1930.
- René Magritte, *La Condition Humaine*. 1933.
- Arshile Gorky, *One Year the Milkweed*. 1944.
- Jackson Pollock, *Number 1 (Lavender Mist)*. 1950.
- Henri Matisse, *La Negresse*. 1952.
- Mark Rothko, *Red, Black, White on Yellow*. 1955.
- Barnett Newman, *The Stations of the Cross–Lema Sabachthani*. 1958–66.
- Roy Lichtenstein, *Look Mickey*. 1961.
- Barnett Newman, *Be II*. 1961–64.
- Wayne Thiebaud, *Cakes*. 1963.
- Anselm Kiefer, *Zim Zum*. 1990.
- Constantin Brancusi, *Maiastra (Bird Before It Flew)*, 1911; *Bird in Space*, 1925; *Agnes E. Meyer*, 1929.
- Alberto Giacometti, *No More Play*. 1931–32.
- David Smith, *Cubi XXVI*. 1965.

ARTHUR M. SACKLER GALLERY

A new era began for the Smithsonian Institution when this gallery opened in 1988. With this addition to its crown, the Smithsonian has become a world center for the study of Asian cultures. Like a university open to the world's use, the gallery attracts scholars, collectors, students, artists, and art lovers.

The new $73 million underground museum complex is home to 1,000 pieces collected by its benefactor, Dr. Arthur M. Sackler. Sackler, a medical researcher, publisher, and art collector from New York City, began collecting in the 1950s. To build his collection, Sackler called on the director of the Freer Gallery, Thomas Lawton. Being familiar with the Freer holdings, Lawton was able to select significant works of art and sculpture for the Sackler Gallery that would complement the world-renowned works of art at the adjacent Freer Gallery.

The Sackler collection includes ancient Chinese bronzes, jades, paintings, and lacquerware; Japanese ceramics, and works on paper; and Near Eastern works. In addition, the Sackler Gallery owns the Vever collection of Indian and Persian arts of the book and is expanding its collection of Japanese art, including modern prints and ceramics.

HIGHLIGHTS:

Asia

- *Owl "you" vessel.* Shang dynasty, 1300–1200 B.C. Bronze. The elegant shape and detailed ornamentation of this ritual piece combine naturalistic motifs with fantastic ones, a characteristic of the best Shang bronzes.
- *Deer.* Early Western Zhou period, 1050–1000 B.C. Jade. An important piece because the representation of deer helps to identify the Western origins of the Zhou people, thus verifying China's early contact with the people of the Central Asian steppes.
- *Polylobed altar dish.* Tang dynasty, A.D. 618–907. Gilt and bronze. Fine bronze objects like this one, associated with Buddhist ritual, often reflect foreign influences: the shape of this dish draws on Iranian motifs, while the use of lions as a Buddhist symbol comes from India.
- *Round, tricolored lacquer dish.* Southern Song dynasty, 1127–1279. Lacquer and wood. This is one of the earliest known examples of marbled lacquer, made by making V-shaped grooves and cutting through the strata of yellow, red, and black lacquer.
- *Green jade dragon head.* Yuan dynasty, 13th–14th century. This powerfully sculpted dragon head was originally used as a finial on a staff. A perforation in the sweeping mane of the dragon probably was used to attach colored silk streamers.
- Qui Ying, *A Donkey for Mr. Zhu.* Ming dynasty, 1550. Handscroll, ink on paper. One of the "Four Great Masters" of the Ming dynasty demonstrates his genius for pure line in this amusing figure painting.
- Shitao and Mr. Jiang, *Landscape and Portrait of Honq Zhenqzhi.* Quing dynasty, 1706. Handscroll, ink and color on paper. In creating this painting, great individualist painter Shitao purposely abandoned the proper relative scale to dramatize the lofty personality of his subject.

• Pair of six-fold screens with scenes from *The Legend of the Drunkard Boy of Oeyama.* Edo period, early 17th century. Ink, color and gold on paper. The narrative of the famous legend of the demon of Oeyama is portrayed with exceptional finesse in an unusual circular sequence that encompasses both screens.

• *Palanquin.* Edo period, early 19th century. Silk. With its lacquer and gold decorations and hundreds of gilt ornaments, this is a fine example of a ceremonial palanquin. It was commissioned for the wedding of a noblewoman to a relative of the shogun.

• Shimizu Uichi, *Jar.* Kyoto, 1988. Gray stoneware with iridescent iron glaze. A major work by one of the foremost Japanese ceramic artists of the present day.

• *Head of a Bodhisattva.* Afghanistan, 3rd–5th century. Stucco with pigment. This colossal head of a Buddhist teacher was originally part of a sculptural program of a *stupa,* or Buddhist burial mound.

• *Yogini.* India, Tamil Nadu, 10th century. Stone. A powerful image of a fearsome goddess. This sculpture is one of a set of 64 originally worshiped by kings for their magical properties.

• *Goddess.* Cambodia, 10th century. Stone. This representation of a Hindu goddess, despite the loss of her arms, is a powerful, dignified example of Cambodian figure sculpture at the height of the classical phase.

Near and Middle East

• *Gazelle rhyton.* Iran, 4th century. Silver and gilt. This horn-shaped drinking vessel tapering off to the head of a gazelle is one of the only two known examples of its type from the period.

• *Hemispherical bowl decorated with figured scenes.* Probably from Iran, 7th century. Silver and gilt. Although a few other examples of Sassanian silver and gilt bowls in this shape are known to exist in other collections, this piece is exceptional in its detailed scenes of life of the Sassanian nobility.

• *Shah Zav Enthroned.* Illustration from the *Shahnama* of Firdausi, Iran, 1335–40. Opaque watercolor, ink, and gold on paper. The painting is from one of the earliest and most spectacular copies of the *Shahnama,* the epic history of Iran and Turan.

• *Entertainment of a Prince.* Illustration from the *Mathnawi* of Jalaluddin Rumi, Iran, 1458–59. Opaque watercolor, ink, and gold on paper. The illustration depicts the performance of the Mavlavi dervishes, whose mystic sect was founded by Jalaluddin Rumi in the 13th century.

• *Illuminated page from an album.* India, 1650. Opaque watercolor, ink, and gold on paper. The folio, from an album made for the Mughal emperor Shah Jahan, contains a poem transcribed by Mir Ali-al-Sultani, a famous 16th-century Iranian calligrapher.

Downtown

National Museum of American Art

Most art museums offer the chance to walk across time, to look through the windows into another culture or period that paintings create. For the person exploring his or her American roots, the National Museum of American Art provides a unique opportunity. By touring the galleries here, which are laid out chronologically, you can track the story of the emergence of America's character and philosophy.

Your visual exploration of our nation's history begins in galleries exhibiting Colonial portraits and continues through halls filled with images that illustrate changing perspectives on the American citizen and the country's land. Images shift from scenes of the grandeur of the American wilderness to the frontiers and the American Indians, then to the cities, where technology reigns.

The museum's beginnings go back to 1841, when it became custodian of the U.S. government's art holdings—mostly gifts donated by citizens. Those early works were first exhibited in the Patent Office Building, the same building that houses the museum today. Over the course of more than 150 years, the location of the institution that became the National Museum of American Art has been shifted four times. The collection made a full circle back to this site after temporary venues at the Smithsonian Castle, the Corcoran Gallery of Art, and the balcony of what is now the National Museum of American History.

Although some might argue that the museum does not have the most or the best American art in Washington, it offers something more: As the only museum concentrating exclusively on American art, it presents the more than three-century panorama of our nation's art. Rather than walking through halls filled with works from many nations, here you're served only American fare.

Only a small percentage of the museum's 27,000 holdings are exhibited at one time in the dozens of galleries that cover three floors. Amidst the treasures you'll see a good collection of African-American art. Of particular note is James Hampton's *Throne of the Third Heaven,* considered by some critics to be the greatest work of visionary art in America.

In addition to its paintings and sculptures, the museum also boasts a superb collection of American folk art.

Highlights:

American, Eighteenth and Nineteenth Century

• Washington Allston, *Hermia and Helena.* Before 1818. The subject for this intimate painting of two young women comes from Shakespeare's *A Midsummer Night's Dream. Thomas Cole, Subsiding of the Waters of the Deluge,*

1829. This, one of Cole's most haunting early paintings, evidences the deeply felt romantic symbolism approaching Civil War victory. The icebound, immobile ship, perhaps a metaphorical ship of state, is offered the hope of rescue by an approaching dogsled.

• Albert Bierstadt, *Among the Sierra Nevada Mountains, California.* 1868. The grandeur of this spectacular and poetic painting is enhanced by a sense that time has been suspended; we glimpse a nineteenth-century version of Eden.

• Thomas Moran, *Grand Canyon of the Yellowstone.* 1872. The artist's magnificent depictions of the great chasms and gorges of the Yellowstone and Colorado rivers helped convince Congress to save the nation's wilderness and to establish the National Park Service.

• Eastman Johnson, *The Girl I Left Behind Me.* 1870–1875. More than a genre painting, this work presents a complex psychological image. The title refers to an old Irish song popular during the Civil War; the hazy landscape may allude to the smoke of battle that Johnson saw while fighting.

• Albert Pinkham Ryder, *Jonah.* 1885–1896. The painting unites Ryder's favorite themes of damnation and redemption with his love of the sea. Despite the embracing arms of God, Jonah's terrifying ordeal is palpable as the whale approaches and the waves roil.

• Henry LaFarge and August Saint-Gaudens, *Apollo with Putti.* This decorative panel, designed for the dining room ceiling of the New York mansion of Cornelius Vanderbilt II, is the only one of four that is known to have survived.

• Thomas Wilmer Dewing, *Summer.* 1890. The artist's paintings of women in ethereal landscape settings are among the most highly refined creations of the late nineteenth century. This, one of his finest, reflects his reverence for the highest form of human endeavor: contemplation.

• Winslow Homer, *High Cliff, Coast of Maine.* 1894. The forces of nature are an abiding theme in Homer's art. The tiny figures set against the powerful waves symbolize the concern that pervaded his work during the 1890s: humanity's place in the universe.

Twentieth Century

• Childe Hassam, *South Ledges, Appledore.* 1913. Taking his inspiration from Monet, Hassam studies the subtlety of light on solid and liquid form to create this glittering impression of light on the ocean.

• Robert Henri, *Blind Spanish Singer.* 1912. An influential teacher, Henri focused on urban subjects, advocating a realism that valued the humble and deprived. Fluid, loosely brushed paint, the frontal pose, and carefully described facial structure contribute to the immediacy of the portrait.

• H. Lyman Sayen, *The Thundershower.* 1917–1918. A student of Matisse, this artist who studied both engineering and painting absorbed elements of cubist design, and perhaps art nouveau as well.

• Morris Kantor, *Synthetic Arrangement.* 1922. Kantor's exploration of the possibilities offered by the intersection of prismatic, jagged forms marks a profound understanding of the nature of artistic space.

• Romaine Brooks, *Self Portrait.* 1923. Painted when the artist was 49, the portrait presents a proud, self-contained woman. The ribbon of the Legion of Honor in her lapel subtly proclaims her achievements as an artist.

• Marsden Hartley, *Yliaster (Paracelsus).* 1932. Named for the sixteenth-century mystic who believed that everything evolved from a base matter called "Yliaster," the painting reveals Hartley's concern for the spiritual power of nature.

• Helen Lundeberg, *Double Portrait of the Artist in Time.* 1935. The double portrait, a surrealist meditation on aging, contrasts and links the vitality of childhood with maturity. The flowers, clock, and toy globe symbolize life's irretraceable passages.

• Ralston Crawford, *Buffalo Grain Elevators.* 1937. The clear, clean lines of Crawford's grain elevators offer up a world of rational order, despite the Great Depression and a war that seemed imminent. Symbols of industrialization linked to nature, the elevators stand as icons against the clear sky.

• Edward Hopper, *Care Cod Morning.* 1950. Through contrasts of light and by framing the solitary woman in the window, Hopper creates tension, posing questions that the painting does not answer.

• Stuart Davis, *Memo.* 1956. In the 1920s, the artist introduced imagery from signs, billboards, packages, and other symbols into his art, symbols that tease the viewer to deciper meanings. The syncopation of color and rhythm parallel the energy of daily life.

• Helen Frankenthaler, *Small's Paradise.* 1964. This tour de force of stain painting creates the illusion that colors are lighted from within. By pouring a thin solution of acrylic color onto an unprimed canvas, the artist gets a luminosity not possible with oils.

• Gene Davis, *Raspberry Icicle.* 1967. A leading figure in the Washington Color School of the 1960s, Davis is best known for his strip paintings. In this one, the vertical colored lines reverberate with an almost palpable energy, with a pulsating rhythm akin to music.

• Frederick Brown, *Staggerlee.* 1984. Brown's admiration for the early twentieth-century German Expressionism and the intense spirituality of African art influences his work. In this painting, the subject is really humanity's place in the world, its heritage and commitment.

National Museum of Women in the Arts

"There is no such thing as 'women's' art," say museum founder Wilhelmina Holladay, "but there is a lot of art by women that's waiting to be recognized."

To do something about the sad fact, Holladay bought a building so she could exhibit the 500 works of women artists she had collected over the years. Today, you see the works of these neglected artists displayed in a place that was once owned by the Masonic order.

Upon entering the $5 million landmark, you step into a 90-foot-long hall where two crystal chandeliers (copied from originals in The Hague) light white-marble floors. Climbing the sweeping double staircase, you reach two floors of galleries, displaying both temporary shows and highlights from the permanent collection.

Artworks from the permanent collection date from the Renaissance to the twentieth century. Collected both for their excellence and for their historical significance, paintings, sculpture, prints, and photos include works by some of the world's most famous American, French, and Italian artists. The museum also boasts gems of photography in an extensive collection.

Highlights:

Renaissance

• Lavinia Fontana, *Portrait of a Noblewoman.* 1580. Fontana, the first woman painter to achieve financial success, skillfully depicts the contrasting textures of gauzy silk, embroidered velet, and detailed jewelry.

• Elisabetta Sirani, *Virgin and Child.* 1663. In the subtle differentiation of the child's soft pink skin from his mother's more olive coloring, the painting shows the artist's accomplished technique.

Modern European

• Rosa Bonheur, *Sheep by the Sea.* 1869. The artists made an important contribution to the development of nineteenth-century art. Here, she portrays farm animals in a straightforward, unromantic manner; she captures the essence of a flock of domestic sheep.

• Camille Claudel, *Young Girl with a Sheaf of Wheat.* 1882. Influenced by her ten-year association with Auguste Rodin, Claudel's bronze sculpture replicates Rodin's style; but instead of using unfinished marble as background, as Rodin did, Claudel chose a monumental sheaf of wheat.

• Berthe Morisot, *The Cage.* 1895. One of the significant painters of the period, and an Impressionist, she developed her own style, adapting a brighter palette and applying paint broadly.

American, Eighteenth and Nineteenth Century

• Lilla Cabot Perry, *Lady with a Bowl of Violets.* Perry introduced Impressionism to America. In this painting, the glow of a fire softly reflected in the shining marble mantlepiece demonstrates an Impressionist's concern with the effects of ever-changing light.

Twentieth Century

• Georgia O'Keeffe, *Alligator Pears in a Basket.* 1923. This early period work by the most prominent and successful American artist of the twentieth century shows O'Keeffe's fondness for creating an unexpected viewpoint, for surprising the viewer into a new confrontation with a familiar object.

• Barbara Hepworth, *Figure.* 1962. Hepworth participated in the creation of a revolutionary new sculptural vocabulary by proposing a modern idom of organic and abstracted form.

• Lee Krasner, *The Springs.* 1964. As the wife of Jackson Pollock, Krasner participated in the crucial experiments that led to the evolution of a new mode of abstract painting. In this work, she makes the painting a metaphor for life itself. She invites emotional and intuitive responses.

• Elane de Kooning, *Baccus 33.* 1978. Using a nineteenth century bronze statute for her structure, the artist examines the process and elements of painting. When the image of the sculpture is transferred to the canvas, it disintegrates into fragments of pattern and color. It's a splendid summation of the artist's career.

• Helen Frankenthaler, *Spirtualist.* 1973. The artist began the practice of what is known as stain or color-field painting. This work is a superb example; its contrast of pinks, blues, and yellows give it a provocative and forceful visual edge.

Chapter 3

Gardens

Tudor Place

Nowhere do gardens wear more exotic attire than in the capital city. Gardens here mirror their owners' tastes for things foreign. Many of those who have created world-famous landscapes in Washington first envisioned the gardens they had seen in other lands. Mildred Bliss, who created the garden at Dumbarton Oaks, was the wife of a career diplomat assigned to Venice, Petrograd, Paris, and Stockholm. From her travels she incorporated the French, Italian, and English motifs she had seen. World traveler Marjorie Merriweather Post, wife of an ambassador to Russia, set a Russian dacha on her grounds. She also incorporated into her 16-acre site a Japanese water garden and a French parterre.

Americans who traveled the world brought back impressions that they interpreted into unique landscapes. The gardens hidden behind the Beaux Art Meridian House, for instance, show a French influence: urns, statues, clipped linden trees. In designing the Bishop's Garden of National Cathedral, the wife of the dean drew on her memories of European church gardens. Diplomat Larz Anderson, who built the opulent Anderson House, included a courtyard to show off his sculpture from Japan, France, and Greece. Even George Washington, although he never saw England, worked to create at Mount Vernon a fashionable English garden.

As an international center, Washington also draws foreigners who carry with them memories of the gardens in their native lands. The formal gardens behind the headquarters of the Organization of American States are as Latin as a samba.

If the world travel of their creators shows up in Washington gardens, so does travel of another sort—time travel. Few cities display a broader collection of period gardens: the Victorian Haupt garden behind the Smithsonian Castle, the Federal gardens of Tudor Place, the medieval gardens of the Franciscan Monastery, and gardens as modern as tomorrow at the Federal Reserve Board.

Rounding out this unique mix of gardens from various periods and countries are the landscapes of trees and flowers maintained by the United States government. The National Arboretum, the U.S. Botanical Garden, and the grounds of the U.S. Capitol headline the list. From our government's beginnings, botanical expeditions have brought back exotic species. As a result, we can see an international library of flora from the Asian Valley of the National Arboretum to the tropical rain forest of the Botanical Gardens.

Growing things flourish not only at the famous masterpiece gardens, but also in secret gardens hidden behind brick walls draped with wisteria. You'll discover these and other gardens by following the **Highlight Walk** and by venturing on your own to **More Gardens** in midtown, on Capitol Hill, along The Mall, and beyond.

Highlight Walk
Embassy Row and Georgetown

You'll discover a variety of gardens on this two-mile route that takes you along Embassy Row and to the charming side streets of Georgetown. Garden gates swing open to reveal a world-class garden masterpiece, plus a half-dozen secret gardens.

Among the delights are a Victorian bower, a terrace of flowers and sculpture tucked inside a mansion, twin gardens that unfurl behind two stately townhouses, and a Federal-period flower knot where old roses bloom.

1. Heurich Mansion

Shortly after the keeper unlocks the ornate iron gate at about noon each weekday, office workers and neighbors arrive at the garden of the Heurich Mansion. Whether eating lunch, reading, or simply sitting, people savor the peace and beauty of this Victorian garden, which today looks much as it did almost 100 years ago, when the Heurich family opened their back door to step into it. Lacy clematis shoots and white flowers decorate a trellis. Curving wickets formed into an oversized basket hold beds of flowers. A birdbath set in the middle of a circle of roses welcomes feathered visitors. Honey locust, weeping cherry, magnolia, and other small trees filter the sunlight that dapples a curving brick path.

Incorporating a number of Victorian conventions, the garden was renovated over a five-year period by the New Scotland Garden Club. Before the garden club began work in 1977, the backyard plot was overgrown and crumbling, a victim of disuse. To restore the space in keeping with the historic Romanesque Revival–style residence, the club sought the advice of James R. Buckler, director of the Office of Horticulture at the Smithsonian Institution. Buckler analyzed the existing features, construction, and plants and then offered design concepts for development. The results give us a rare glimpse of Victorian tastes and a delightful reprieve from the bustle of urban life.

For more information on the Heurich Mansion, see **Literature**.

2. Anderson House

French doors off the baroque ballroom of the Anderson House lead to a secluded courtyard arranged with meticulous care. Espaliered magnolias line high brick walls, small yews and pots of flowers dot the flagstone terrace, and two Southern magnolias tower above. Exotic sculptures add interest: a

M Metro

1. Heurich Mansion, 1307 New Hampshire Avenue NW
2. Anderson House, 2118 Massachusetts Avenue NW
3. Textile Museum, 2330 S Street NW
4. Dumbarton House, 2715 Q Street NW
5. Old Stone House, 3150 M Street NW
6. Tudor Place, 1644 31st Street NW
7. Dumbarton Oaks, 31st and R Streets NW

Route

From the Dupont Circle Metro subway station (Dupont Circle Exit), walk west on New Hampshire Avenue one block to the Heurich Mansion. Continue north on 20th Street to Massachusetts Avenue. Turn left and walk one block to the Anderson House. Next, walk east on Massachusetts Avenue, turn right on 24th Street, then turn right again onto S Street to the Textile Museum. Retrace your steps back to Massachusetts Avenue and to Sheridan Circle; follow the street that bisects the circle that leads to Q Street. Walk west along Q Street to the Dumbarton House. Continue west on Q Street to a right on 31st Street. Tudor Place is halfway up the block. You can include a detour to the Old Stone House by walking south on 31st Street to M Street and back. From Tudor Place, continue north along 31st Street to the gates of Dumbarton Oaks. To return to the Dupont Circle Metro station, call a taxicab from the Dumbarton Oaks museum; otherwise walk one block east to Wisconsin Avenue and take a bus down the hill to the Foggy Bottom Metro station.

seventeenth-century Japanese Buddha, a lead Hercules, a 2,000-year-old Greek sculpture, two eighteenth-century French sphinxes.

For more information on the Anderson House, see **Antiques**, **Literature**, and **Military**.

3. Textile Museum

Step outside the Textile Museum's French doors and you'll find yourself in a formal garden with a path that follows a boxwood allée to a small classical pavilion. Behind a wisteria-draped trellis, twin gardens unfold. Seeing such a large garden almost hidden behind boxwood and vines parallels the experience of coming upon a full-color spread in an otherwise black-and-white magazine. Brick walls enclose a magnificent lawn that is shaded by towering trees. Flowers of an earlier age abound: lilac, spirea, lilies of the valley, phlox, and iris. Peonies and roses add to the enchantment. From the eastern edge of the Textile Museum garden, you can survey the old trees and flowers in the Wilson House next door. The garden looks much as it did when President and Mrs. Wilson overlooked it from their morning room almost 70 years ago. Flowers planted by a local garden club now add fringes of color to the predominantly green space that combines an English stone wall with an Italian fountain.

4. Dumbarton House

Walk along the driveway to the back of the Dumbarton House to discover another of Washington's secret gardens. Laid out at the same time the house was built, the garden was designed by Fiske Kimball, who also designed the grounds of the Pennsylvania Museum of Art in Philadelphia. The centerpiece is a classical temple–style wall, with statues in its niches. Behind it stands a trellis of fruit trees. A swath of greenery bordered by boxwood, large trees, myrtle, and flowers completes the scene. A stairway leads from this terrace garden to a handsome metal gate that opens into a new upper garden, which was added in the spring of 1992. The beautifully designed garden features benches under old trees and meandering flower-lined pathways.

For more information on Dumbarton House, see **Antiques**.

5. Old Stone House

The old-fashioned flowers that you hurried out to smell in that garden of your childhood bloom again at Old Stone House. Beyond the white picket fence with the creaking gate lies a bower just inches from the traffic honking down Georgetown's busy corridor, M Street.

You can reach the garden from the street or by stepping out the back door of this pre-Revolutionary house with its Colonial furnishings. The large garden with its old fruit trees, roses creeping up stone walls, seasonal blooms, and carpet of soft, green grass lures romantics. Some take off their shoes while eating picnic lunches, others sprawl in the sunshine or read. A neighboring deli sells sandwiches and fruit.

6. Tudor Place

It's one thing to mislay a pair of gloves, but when you lose a garden you're bound to be truly frustrated. So imagine the joy when the the plan of the boxwood parterre, or flower knot, planted at Tudor Place in the 1800s was rediscovered a half century after it had disappeared.

Tudor Place is the Georgetown estate purchased in 1805 by Martha Custis Peter, the granddaughter of Martha Washington. Prior to the Civil War, Martha Peter's daughter Britannia, the mistress of Tudor Place, left the city. When she returned in 1862, she found that the flower knot had been damaged by intruders. To salvage what remained, she moved plantings to a lower garden. By doing so, however, she erased the evidence that had defined the layout of this original garden element. It took the determination—and luck—of Britannia's grandson, Armistead Peter III, to re-create the flower knot almost 70 years later.

Armistead had no physical evidence with which to work, and he came upon the information he needed in an unexpected way. In 1923, the James River Garden Club published a book showing the plan for the box parterre at Avenel estate. Avenel, as Armistead knew, had been designed by his cousin and was patterned after Tudor Place. Thus, by examining the Avenel plans, Armistead rediscovered the long-lost flower knot of Tudor Place.

Today you discover his flower knot, the rectangular bed trimmed with boxwood that stretches like a colorful patchwork quilt under ancient trees. Once again the original flowers planted here bloom: jonquils, Canterbury bells, sweet william, lavender, and roses. In addition, a number of early nineteenth-century plantings of flowers, shrubs, and trees have survived on the five-acre grounds. They provide an invaluable record of the horticultural taste of that period. Most important of these is the large collection of old roses. Stars are damask and moss roses and the old-fashioned dark pink China rose "Old Blush," planted by Martha Peter.

In exploring the gardens, you also enter a variety of settings: woodland areas, grassy terraces, a circle of seven-foot boxwood, a brick fountain, a wooden pergola, and a bowling green. Among the garden sculpture is a statue by Paul Bartlett, cast from the design he created for the U.S. Capitol. To the west of the south lawn, with its specimen tulips, poplars, and holly, the weeping boxwood originally brought from Mount Vernon in two-inch pots still thrive.

One of the most delightful features of the antique-filled mansion is its conservatory. This room, with three large windows overlooking the sweeping lawn, displays such exotic plants as hibiscus and gardenia. Most prized is the third generation of the sago palms originally nurtured by the Peters in 1813.

Armistead Peter III deeded his family home to a foundation he created. After his death, Tudor Place became a private museum under the auspices of the Tudor Place Foundation. It opened to the public in 1988. On tours of the mansion, visitors see a wealth of antiques and George Washington memorabilia.

For more information on Tudor Place, see **Antiques**.

7. Dumbarton Oaks

If fairies really do exist, they're living in the gardens of Dumbarton Oaks.

How could they resist such a secluded, improbably beautiful setting? From a fairy's point of view, Dumbarton Oaks has it all: stone garden walls with a creaking gate, winding brick paths, grassy knolls shaded by tulip trees, carpets of lilies of the valley, Italian urns embellished with sculptured flowers, fountains glistening in niches, gnarled old trees, and a pebble pool where mockingbirds flutter and splash. Real, live people find enchantment here, too, especially when they understand what it took to carve the 16-acre terraced garden out of the wilderness.

The effort began in 1921, when owner Mildred Bliss dreamed of creating a garden to match the beauty of those she had seen in Europe. She commissioned one of the greatest landscape architects of the era, Beatrix Farrand, to turn her dream into reality. Farrand, a charter member of the American Society of Landscape Architects who had designed gardens for such clients as J. Pierpont Morgan, Mrs. John D. Rockefeller, and Mrs. Theodore Roosevelt, spent 25 years creating the 10-acre formal gardens, which she would call the greatest of her 50 years' practice. With Bliss, she agonized over just the right proportions, colors, and sites for every detail.

The greatest challenge was to accommodate the steep bank that slopes from the mansion to the ravines of Rock Creek Park. Creative genius triumphed as Farrand planned a series of interlocking terraced gardens resembling giant steps. These gardens progress gradually from formality to informality; the gardens closest to the house are confined in rectangular spaces, but as one moves away the landscape gradually expands.

As you walk between these two extremes, you pass through a series of garden rooms. Since Bliss and Farrand both believed that gardens should be places to live, they planned various separate areas with individual themes. Among these are the Green Garden, featuring only greenery as a foil for the colorful dresses of female guests; the Rose Garden, with 1,000 roses grouped by color; the Star Garden, a tiny garden enclosed by white azaleas; the Fountain Terrace, featuring an eighteenth-century lead fountain and seasonal flowers; the Arbor Terrace, named after the wisteria-covered arbor; and Mélisande's Allée, a brick walk that winds through a grassy meadow abloom with flowers.

Like rooms in a house, these gardens are furnished. A charming collection of benches provide just the right perch for panoramic views or intimate studies. Among your choices for sit-down garden viewing are benches of Italian rose marble, a garden seat beneath a graceful lead canopy, and gray stone sofas reminiscent of those in the garden of Villa Palagonia near Palermo, Sicily.

Other human-made pieces decorate the gardens: copies of a columned monument from Naples, gates with Italian-style finial vases filled with wrought-iron flowers, paving of baroque scrolled Doria stone from Italy, a mosaic of pebbles from a Mexican beach, a copy of a French eighteenth-century terra-cotta urn, and a fountain patterned after one in the little Italian town of Nervi.

Beyond the garden rooms lie the Ellipse, with an antique Provençal fountain as centerpiece, and three hillsides, each named after the flora they feature: crab apple, forsythia, and cherry.

Behind the fence at the foot of the garden lies Dumbarton Oaks Park, a 27-acre preserve of natural growth that was once part of the estate but now belongs to the National Park Service.

Note: Washington National Cathedral is about three-quarters of a mile from Dumbarton Oaks. Take any metro bus headed north. See the **Beyond** section for information about the cathedral. The new Kahlil Gibran garden about one mile from the Textile Museum features a bronze bust of the Arabian poet, inscribed quotations, and a walkway bright with rhododendrons and azaleas in season.

More Gardens

Capitol Hill

Folger Shakespeare Library

Daffodils, rosemary, thyme, lavender, and boxwood color and scent Washington's newest garden. Set behind a wall on a corner of the land occupied by the Folger Library building, this small garden features the plants that Shakespeare mentioned in his plays, and others that most likely were known to him.

The charm of the garden is twofold. The flowers, shrubs, and trees are artfully planted, and they inspire fascinating commentary about their history and lore. On regularly scheduled tours, you hear details about many of the plants—with a Shakespearean line or two sprinkled in. You'll hear, for instance, about the creeping thyme that became the base of an unguent sold in the 1600s to enable the user to see fairies. No wonder Shakespeare refers to a "bank where the wild thyme blows" in *A Midsummer Night's Dream*. Your guide will tell you, too, about the "gillyvore," or pinks (a precursor of the modern carnation), mentioned by Shakespeare in *A Winter's Tale*. Pinks were used to flavor wine; the Crusaders drank pink-flavored wine to control fevers and plague.

Information like this helps you focus on the individual plants, but to see the flower knot and its bordering garden as a whole you're led to an upstairs balcony. From this perch, you look down on two large areas of lawn, the serpentine-shaped boxwood, and gravel walkways that set off the diamond-shaped plantings in the knot. The shape echoes the pattern in the wrought-iron fence and in the terrace railing. Other features of the small garden invite inspection and repose: the teak English benches, a sundial, an arbor of white roses, a shady linden, and magnolia trees.

U.S. Capitol

If you're like most people, you've explored the U.S. Capitol and the treasures that lie inside its walls. But have you also discovered the rarest of leafy green ornaments that decorate its grounds?

Few realize that when they visit the Capitol building, they reach it by walking through one of the finest arboretums in the world. Over 3,000 trees from 33 states, Europe, and Asia grow on the Capitol grounds. In addition to one of the most varied collections of trees in the country, the 155-acre grounds also boast 100 species of wooded plants.

Even before you reach the grounds, you can appreciate how the trees have been planted to show the Capitol to best advantage. Landscape designer Frederick Law Olmsted of New York City's Central Park fame, chose trees that would provide the best frame for the Capitol dome. Like a jeweler cutting a gem, Olmsted arranged trees to leave six open views. To create dramatic views from other vantage points, he planted low trees to produce the effect of the Capitol rising out of banks of foliage. His care and skill can also be appreciated during a walk along the curving paths that lend a natural feeling to the grounds. Olmsted's naturalistic approach to garden design contrasts with the aesthetic approach of Pierre-Charles L'Enfant, who designed the city of Washington. L'Enfant's city is one of straight lines; Olmsted's gardens curve.

Although only half of the 229 varieties of trees and shrubs that Olmsted planted remain, the ones that do are unusual. These include a cherry tree that blooms not only in spring but also in December (if the weather cooperates), a 55-foot tree registered with the American Forestry Association as a national champion, a silvery beech, a bald cypress, and a redwood.

A tree labeling program, begun by Olmsted in 1882, has continued. In recent years, old labels have been replaced with metal plates that list both the common and scientific names of each tree.

Most famous of the trees is the Washington elm in front of the Senate entrance, believed to have shaded our first president when he laid the Capitol cornerstone. Some of the oldest trees are two English elms and a spreading American elm. The American elm, known as the Cameron elm, stands near the southwest corner of the House wing. The tree is named in honor of Senator Simon Cameron, who, in 1875, saw workers about to uproot it to put in a sidewalk. The senator hurried to the Senate floor, where he pleaded that the tree be saved. His efforts were successful: Instead of demolishing the tree, the workers laid the sidewalk around it.

On your tour of the Capitol grounds, don't miss the north side, with its spring grotto and gardens; at the foot of the west front terrace, note the Victorian lampposts and walls carved with flowers and leaves.

For more information on the U.S. Capitol, see **Technology**.

Library of Congress

In Washington, with its many government buildings, you sometimes find gardens of potted flowers filling courtyards. One of the surprises is the atrium in the Madison wing of the Library of Congress. Marble benches are almost hidden in the thick foliage of palms, ficus trees, philodendron, and Chinese evergreen. The sound of fountains splashing into three dark pools provides the perfect soundtrack.

Foggy Bottom

Federal Reserve Board

Washington's most modern garden shimmers and sways on the grounds bordering the site of the Federal Reserve Board. With this one-acre garden, landscape architects Wolfgang Oehme and James van Sweden started a revolution in landscaping. Here, as at their other important public sites—including Pershing Park and International Center—Oehme and van Sweden have substituted a rich landscape of decorative grasses and colorful perennials for rolling lawns. Instead of concentrating only on spring blossoms, the landscapers have planted for year-round color. A landscape that cherishes the natural and the romantic replaces eighteenth-century ideals of formality and spaciousness.

The hallmark of the new American-style gardens are the ornamental grasses Oehme and van Sweden imported from the American prairies and the mountainsides of China and Japan. These 6-inch to 12-foot exotic newcomers introduce contrasting color and texture. In addition to greeny greens, there are grayed greens, blue-greens, and orangey greens that turn purple in the shade. In each season, the scene changes: In the fall the purple grasses turn golden; in the winter the color shifts to silver. Perennials massed by single color change, too. The daffodils exit and the daylilies arrive; the bright yellow black-eyed Susans fade in autumn as the sedum turn rust; and black seed heads of flowers bob above the winter snow.

The Mall

U.S. Botanic Garden

In the nineteenth century, when scientists returned from expeditions to foreign lands they needed a place to deposit the exotic plants they brought with them. At first, temporary buildings were constructed at the foot of the U.S. Capitol to hold these collections. Then, in 1938, the present conservatory was constructed.

Today, that aluminum- and glass-topped greenhouse shelters a rare collection of 8,000 species of tropical and subtropical plants. Many were brought to the United States in 1842 from the Wilkes Expedition in the South Seas. Most spectacular are the 200 varieties of blooming orchids displayed each week, which are drawn from the Botanic Garden's collection of 10,000 plants. As impressive are three collections that experts rate as the finest on earth: the 90 varieties of American azalea, the 900 varieties of chrysanthemum, and the 12 varieties of cycad.

But seeing these incomparable collections is just one of many reasons for a visit. If you're like most people, you'll also feel as if you've been transported into the heart of a tropical rain forest or exotic jungle. You walk beneath banana palms, breadfruit, and cacao trees; cross bridges beside ponds where tropical fish swim, and emerge in a valley of ferns. You see bright flowers, hear a tumbling waterfall, and breathe the humid air perfumed with a medley of scents. Especially in the heat of summer or chill of winter, the Botanic Garden offers instant escape. Steam-warmed air, which is as nurturing to humans as to plants, remains at a constant temperature no matter what the weather does outside.

In addition to permanent displays, the Botanic Garden features seasonal exhibits. In the summer, 300 baskets of hanging plants and topiary animals decorate the entrance terrace. Other seasons bring a profusion of hyacinths, Easter lilies, tulips, gladiolus, dahlias, roses, acacias, primroses, chrysanthemums, and poinsettias. Also a part of the Botanic Garden is the ornamental garden south of the greenhouse, across Independence Avenue. This park of lavishly varied flower beds features an exquisite fountain designed by the sculptor of the Statue of Liberty, Frédéric-Auguste Bartholdi. Among the plantings, which are labeled, is a banana tree that bears fruit each autumn, and three flowering cherry trees.

Enid A. Haupt Victorian Garden

The Victorian garden that opened in 1988 behind the Smithsonian Castle looks as if it has been there for years. Over 50 mature trees, one a towering 40-foot weeping beech, shade fully grown shrubs and lush flower beds. Entering through the lacy iron gate off Independence Avenue or from the Mall, you feel as though you've stepped into a long-established garden.

The truth is, the garden was only recently planted; except for a venerable linden tree that has stood on the grounds for 100 years, the plantings were moved fully grown to the site. That's because benefactor Enid Haupt gave the $3 million to develop the garden, with the stipulation that it be an "old" garden from day one.

Haupt's new "old" garden grows on a 4.2-acre site on top of the underground Sackler Gallery and Museum of African Art. Covering the site behind the Castle and the Arts and Industries Building is an ornamental area with three themes: a central Victorian parterre, an Oriental garden with moon gates inspired by Beijing's Temple of Heaven, and an Islamic garden of fountains and pools.

If you like to do your garden sightseeing while sitting down, you'll be happy to find a wealth of strategically placed garden benches. Like the urns and wickets, the garden furnishings are Victorian-period antiques. Nineteenth-century street lamps decorated with flower-filled baskets add to the old-fashioned mood.

Note: Several gardens border the Smithsonian museums. Most notable is the richly planted garden that lines the spiral walkway between the Hirshhorn Museum and the Arts and Industries Museum. The Smithsonian's horticultural division also exhibits choice plants from its greenhouse inside the Constitution Avenue entrance to the National Museum of Natural History. The courtyard of the newly restored Freer Gallery of Art displays seasonal blooms.

MIDTOWN–SEVENTEENTH STREET

THE WHITE HOUSE

No trees and flowers have more historic stories to tell than those on the grounds of the White House. The 18 acres of grounds bordering the executive mansion abound with living links to the presidents who have lived here during the past two centuries.

Presidents planted many of the trees and created some of the gardens we see today. Although the men are gone, their shady, colorful, scented memorials tell us about them and their families:

- Andrew Jackson planted a pair of Southern magnolias between the Rose Garden and South Portico so he would have "something green" by which to remember his wife, Rachel, who had died shortly before his election.
- John F. Kennedy had the Rose Garden redesigned as a traditional American garden, complete with bluegrass, crab apple and pink saucer magnolia trees, shasta daisies, and geraniums. He loved his new garden, walking through it to and from the Oval Office and using it as a setting to greet guests.
- Lyndon B. Johnson donated the Children's Garden, a hideaway behind American holly trees on the south grounds. Adding to the appeal for his own grandchild and all those who would follow, Johnson included an apple tree for climbing, a lily pond stocked with goldfish, and child-sized tables and chairs.

- Grover Cleveland, who married his 21-year-old bride in the White House, commemorated the event by planting two delicate Japanese maples on the south lawn. One survives today, just to the west of the central fountain.
- Harry Truman planted a magnolia tree and thus changed the White House scene depicted on the back of the $20 bill. Now instead of just one magnolia tree to the east of the South Portico, which the bill shows, there is Truman's second tree to the west. Truman enjoyed pointing out that with the addition of the new tree, the U.S. Treasury engraving was wrong and thus the $20 bill was "a counterfeit."

In addition to the trees planted by every president from John Quincy Adams to Ronald Reagan, the White House grounds contain many others. There are 80 varieties in all. Some are exotic and found almost nowhere else in Washington. These include the cedar of Lebanon, native to Asia Minor, and the weeping silver linden, a native of southeastern Europe.

For more information on the White House, see **Antiques**.

Octagon House

Although nothing except the smokehouse remains of the service yard that once extended for acres behind the Octagon House, the re-created garden falls into the "secret" category. As you step through the stone gate on 18th Street, you'll probably be surprised to find a tiny garden tucked between the residence and the towering offices of the American Institute of Architects building. On warm days, office workers sit on the garden wall eating their lunches. In the spring, particularly when the cherry and crab apple trees bloom, it's a delight.

Organization of American States

Inside this palace of a building, beneath the largest sliding-glass roofs in the country, a tropical forest flourishes. Coffee, banana, date, and breadfruit trees grow luxuriantly beside flower beds filled with plants from all over the Americas. Most famous of the trees is a fig-rubber tree graft planted by President Taft in 1910 as a symbol of inter-American unity. In the center of the patio floor, a pink marble fountain splashes. Fascinating pre-Columbian ornamentation and designs copied from Mayan, Aztec, Inca, and Zapotecan ruins add interest.

Behind the building's west terrace lies one of Washington's most beautiful secret spaces, the exotic Aztec Garden. This handsomely laid out garden features a blue-tiled pool guarded by a statue of the Aztec god of flowers, Xochilipilli. In season, the blooms of tropical water lilies and yellow irises add color. Two green plots edged with boxwood and ivy line a magnificent

Organization of American States Building

collection of old trees: a sycamore, a black spruce, an American beech, a pine oak, a magnolia, a blue spruce, a horse chestnut, and a green ash. A marble balustrade surrounds the garden. At its western boundary, the garden ends at the doorstep of the Museum of Art of the Americas. See **Art** for more information.

Constitution Gardens

Just 100 feet from one of the busiest traffic corridors in Washington lies a willow-shaded island reached by a wooden footbridge. Wild ducks congregate on the seven-acre lake surrounding it. Five thousand trees, a network of bike and walking paths, benches, and a small concession stand add to the charm. For sightseers there's a memorial to the 56 signers of the Declaration of Independence: their names engraved in stone.

BEYOND

WASHINGTON NATIONAL CATHEDRAL

Stepping through the Norman arch that leads to the Bishop's Garden you travel back 800 years in time. Suddenly you're in a medieval church garden. The scent of boxwood, herbs, and tea roses pervades. You feel uneven paving underfoot, as you follow the stone path that curves beside a weathered wall. Peonies, iris, columbine, and tulips bloom amidst ruins: a column from the Abbey of Cluny, a thirteenth-century Gothic capital, an old baptismal font from a French monastery. Ivy frames a bas-relief on a garden wall. Water in an ornamental pool shaped like a cross reflects clouds. Old trees stand guard: yews, cedar, a rare medlar, a pear surrounded by dwarf boxwood.

The Bishop's Garden, set on the 57-acre grounds of Washington Cathedral, has for more than half a century offered refreshment from the pace of the bustling capital. For happily, unlike most other American and European cathedral gardens, this one is open to the public.

Designed by Frederick Law Olmsted, Jr. (son of the famed landscape architect of New York Central Park), the Bishop's Garden was based on medieval garden plans developed by Florence Brown Bratenahl, the wife of the cathedral's second dean. To create a garden to complement the Gothic-style cathedral, Mrs. Bratenahl studied old manuscripts, rare herbals, and primitive woodcuts.

We see the result of her devotion today. A medley of small gardens play against each other in contrasting colors, masses, and light-dark patterns.

Most noteworthy from a historic perspective is the Hortulus (Little Garden), designed to look like a ninth-century herb garden. The plants were selected from Charlemagne's list of plants for his imperial garden.

Other period gardens include the Rose Garden of hybrid tea roses; the herb bed where the single "Peace" rose planted by Haile Sellasie, Emperor of Ethiopia, blooms amid the thyme; and two perennial gardens planted with flowers found in English church gardens.

A recent addition is the 1955 woodland path that winds among wildflowers planted each spring and fall by local garden clubs. The footbridge that crosses a ravine along the way received the American Institute of Architects Award for Design in 1977.

Artfully placed at the head of the path is an equestrian statue of George Washington by sculptor Herbert Hazeltine. You get the impression that the General has just ridden out of the woods into the clearing. Entries in Wash-

Meridian House

ington's own diary tell us that in fact he did ride across this site (long before it was Cathedral grounds) en route to dine with friends at Rosedale. (The farmhouse Washington visited still stands in adjacent Cleveland Park.)

The free brochure "The Bishop's Garden," available at the Herb Cottage gift shop, describes more things to see. Ideally, you'll read the brochure and do some initial touring while seated on a garden bench, perhaps sheltered in the charming gazebo.

While you're in the Herb Cottage note the dried herbs, seeds, and cookbooks. In addition, a greenhouse on the grounds sells a unique variety of growing herbs and other plants.

For more information on Washington National Cathedral see **Art, Literature**, and **Music**.

Meridian House
Northwest Washington

Short of climbing into a tree house, few experiences put you more in touch with nature than stepping onto the terrace of the Meridian House. For as you do, you enter a room of linden trees whose branches form a lacy canopy. Thanks to a rare pollarding (cutting-back) technique, these trees, which usually demand 30 feet of growing space, thrive within only 10 feet. The result is a charming miniature forest that is sure to be unlike anything else you've seen.

But that's just the beginning. Beyond, in the gardens behind the elegant Meridian and Meyers-White houses, you discover trees and shrubs planted in the early twentieth century. Seventy years ago, when these gardens were created, a landscape design that favored the formal and symmetrical was in vogue: Shrubs and trees were carved, clipped, and pollarded. The gardens were planned to be less formal and more wild as they extended beyond the residences. Thus, trees like the 60- to 70-foot willow oaks, Southern magnolias, and weeping hemlocks were planted to add contrast to the formal garden areas.

Today, the gardens have been not only restored but enhanced. Many of the flowers that bloom today were popular in the period when the gardens were originally planted. The new additions include native roses, crepe myrtle, butterfly bush, and Indian azaleas that show off their unusual pale lavender blooms in the fall.

The gardens that cover a half city block hold surprising variety. In addition to the linden terrace, there are formal walkways lined with statuary, a rock garden, an expansive lawn, a greenhouse, and the city's most beautiful parking lot. In place of asphalt or gravel, this lot is landscaped. Squares of grass with paving between make up an innovative checkerboard that in its geometry echoes the formality of the bordering gardens.

Hillwood
Northwest Washington

Much like her former residence-turned-museum, Marjorie Merriweather Post's garden shows off her wealth. Just as in her home Russian icons, jewel-encrusted chalices, and a glory of porcelain and Fabergé treasures overwhelm the eye, so on her grounds rare trees and flowers proliferate. The gardens tell us something about their owner and the life-style of the rich and famous that the heiress enjoyed. Rarely will you see more varied plantings or a more eclectic collection of garden settings.

More than 3,500 different kinds of plants and trees grow in the 25 acres of gardens that make up the Hillwood estate. The gardens were designed

Hillwood Museum. Stairs leading to Japanese Garden

by Perry Wheeler, of White House Rose Garden fame. Winding paths lined with laurel, rhododendron, boxwood, and ivy from Mount Vernon lead to numerous gardens.

A miniature Japanese garden, complete with waterfall, moonbridge, and stone lanterns, awaits discovery. There are also formal French gardens of boxwood parterres, white stones, and glistening blue-water canals. A vine-covered gate leads to a rose garden. A stone poodle holding a basket of flowers in his mouth stands guard at the entrance to a pet cemetery, where markers testify to the affluent dog days of Rags, Tiger, Crème de Cocoa, Lassie, and Bobo.

One garden path leads to a dacha, a Russian-style country house, that is filled with oil paintings, crystal, and tapestries. Nearby, at the end of a stone walkway lined with wildflowers, stands an Adirondack-style lodge. Inside are displays of North American Indian handiwork, on extended loan from the Smithsonian Institution.

A high point for horticulturists is the greenhouse, which houses one of the country's most extensive collections of orchids. The star of the collection is the green *Cattleya* and the upside-down-blooming *Stanhopea* from Central America.

For more information on Hillwood, see **Antiques**.

Franciscan Monastery
Northeast Washington

Like a historic European shrine, the Franciscan Monastery of Mount Saint Sepulchre rises on a wooded hillside in northeast Washington. Replicas of principal shrines and chapels found in the Holy Land dominate the 45-acre site. A lavish assortment of flowers, trees, and shrubs add color and texture. In the spring, thousands of daffodils dance on hillsides while tulips and Easter lilies nod beneath blossoming cherry and dogwood trees. During warm months the tropical perennials are moved from the greenhouse to the outdoors: hibiscus, lantanas, tiger lilies, and palm and banana trees.

Every June, 600 rosebushes burst into bloom. This incomparable spectacle can be credited both to the loving care lavished by the monastery brothers and to their use of the most up-to-date methods for developing hybrids.

Even in winter, the gardens are worth visiting. If you're lucky, you'll arrive at that rare moment when snow is on the ground and the red Christmas roses bloom. Even if you're not on hand for that spectacle, a winter visit offers a good opportunity to appreciate the leafless deciduous trees and shrubs as well as the dwarf maples, cherry, and dogwood trees of the Oriental garden.

No matter what time of year, "God's garden" becomes the ideal place to muse. If you follow the woodland path, you may find meditation assisted by the religious sites along the way: a replica of the stone Grotto of Lourdes, a portico of hand-carved stone pillars that looks out on old Italian boxwood, and a Byzantine-style church. Whether on a spiritual quest or simply out to relish the beauty of a peaceful garden, you won't be disappointed by the Franciscan Monastery.

Kenilworth Aquatic Gardens
Northeast Washington

The only original marshland in the area survives here on the banks of the Anacostia River in northeast Washington. Divided into 44 ponds, the gardens boast what may be the most distinguished collections of aquatic plants anywhere. Over 100,000 of the rarest water lilies and lotus brighten this Monet landscape.

The gardens were begun in 1882 by Walter B. Shaw, a disabled Civil War veteran. Shaw first imported a few species of water lilies from his home state of Maine. Later, he expanded the gardens into a family business. In 1938, the Department of the Interior bought the gardens, which are now administered by the National Park Administration.

Most of the ponds are devoted to a single species. Among the enchanting blooms, the extraordinary *Victoria amazonica* from South America displays leaves that look like six-foot platters. In another pool, the Nelumbo lotus, whose waxy leaves shed raindrops, unfurls its petals to reveal seedpods that look like shower heads. Another variety of pink-tinged East Indian lotus was grown from seeds believed to be at least 350 years old.

Interesting trees, including the bald cypress, Japanese resin trees, the Carolina laurel, and saw-toothed oaks, surround the ponds. Animal life, too, abounds in and around the ponds. Green heron, hooded merganser ducks, snapping turtles, bull frogs, and spotted salamanders cavort.

In 1991, Congress appropriated funds for the construction of a boardwalk that will stretch from the Anacostia River across the Kenilworth grounds via two islands. Eventually, ferryboat service will provide a link with the National Arboretum.

In addition to following the present earthen trail to see the ponds, don't miss the exhibits in the newly renovated visitor's center. Displays show water lily propagation and a "living wall" of wetland animals.

U.S. National Arboretum
Northeast Washington

After 25 years of existence, the U.S. National Arboretum opened its gates to the public in 1948. It was a simple case of flower power—glorious clouds of azaleas. Once word got out about the spectacular hybrids being grown for research purposes at the National Arboretum, people wanted in. Because so many requested permission to enter, Arboretum administrators changed their policy and opened the site to the public permanently.

Now the Arboretum attracts a steady stream of visitors; in the spring, during azalea season, the stream becomes a flood. Although off the beaten track—a 20-minute drive from downtown Washington—the Arboretum has turned into one of the garden-lover's most popular sightseeing destinations. Especially from mid-April to late May, hillsides and valleys turn into festivals of azaleas in shades of pink, rose, scarlet, orangy-red, and pure snowbank white. Over 70,000 plants festoon walls, mountain walks, and formal gardens. The most popular spots for viewing are the Morrison and Lee Gardens, Mount Hamilton, and Azalea Valley.

But azaleas are just the beginning. The National Arboretum, created by an act of Congress in 1927, is part of the Agricultural Research Service. As such, it conducts research to develop woody plants that will grow in various zones of the United States. Thousands of specimens grow in 47 separate gardens and collections that dot the 444-acre preserve. Following nine miles of paved roads, you ramble along byways with names like Crabtree Road and Holly Spring Road to destinations such as Beech Spring Pond, Fern Valley, and Dogwood Circle. You could spend days wending your way along the network of trails that lead to gardens and arbors of azaleas, daylilies, wildflowers, hibiscus, maples, crepe myrtles, bald cypress, and more. Simply follow the signs. Or, if you'd like to discover the arboretum systematically, pick up a map at the Administration Building, where you can see ponds filled with aquatic plants and rare Japanese koi fish, including a red, white, and blue specimen that was presented during the American bicentennial celebration.

Next to the Administration Building, at the end of the entrance path, you'll find the National Bonsai and Penjing Collections (which close at 2:30 P.M.). A specially designed pavilion was constructed to house the $4.5 million Japanese bonsai collection. The six-acre site now also displays bonsai of two additional styles: the Chinese penjing and the North American bonsai. You reach them by walking through a ceremonial gate along a path lined with Japanese cedar, ferns, and wildflowers. At the end of the path you come to a sunny garden that includes several bonsai as well as plants collected by botanists in Japan. Then, stepping inside a pavilion, you see the miniature trees. When presented by the Japanese for the bicentennial, the collection included 53 trees. More have since been added.

The miniature bonsai, standing only two to three feet high, are dwarfed and shaped trees and shrubs arranged in shallow pots. Like ordinary trees and shrubs, the 34 varieties of bonsai represented in the collection change with the seasons; the red maple turns to flame in the fall, the cherry and crab apple trees burst with blossoms in the spring. Most prized in the collection is the two-foot high, 180-year-old red pine from the Imperial household.

In the near future, a new permanent pavilion will be built to house the 31 penjing given to the American people in 1986 by Dr. Yee-sun Wu. These dwarfed potted plants differ from the bonsai in that they are tray landscapes depicting miniature scenes. Some of the specimens are planted in notable containers; one on display is three centuries old. Outstanding among the penjing trees are the Fukien tea tree planted in an antique pot, a small-leafed banyan, and a Guandong fir. Next to the temporary facilities showing the Penjing Collection is the American Pavilion, which was built to display American bonsai. Included in this collection, which may be the largest of its kind in the world, are bonsai species found only in America, including the bald cypress and coast redwoods.

Beyond the Bonsai Collection, roads lead to dozens of sites. Among the most popular are the dwarf conifer collection; the Asian Garden, with its lacquered vermilion pagoda; Fern Valley; and the National Herb Garden, which includes a rare collection of old roses.

The National Herb Garden, across the road from the National Bonsai Collection, basks under the sun and in the distinction of being the largest designed herb garden in the world. The fragrant collection, spread over 2½ acres, shows off several thousand plants from around the world. The fragrant medley of annuals, perennials, woody trees, and shrubs is grouped into three areas: the Knot Garden, the Historic Rose Garden, and the Specialty Garden.

The plantings in the Knot Garden form an intricate design inspired by ancient Greek and Roman patterns. You can best appreciate the intricate design by surveying it from the elevated Administration Building. From this vantage you see the patchwork of greenery—beds of herbs, an English boxwood allée, trellises and vine-covered fences—contrasting with the red brick terrace and pathways. Hedges of dwarf evergreens circle a round pool where water splashes from a single spout. During the summer, plants in pots, mostly from the Mediterranean, are set out: colorful oleander, jasmine, pomegranate, and dark green olive trees.

The Historic Rose Garden is part of the National Herb Garden because roses were grown primarily for their medical attributes in the sixteenth century. Even today, rose fruits or hips are used in the manufacture of vitamin C tablets. The rose garden contains more than 80 types of old roses, chosen not only for their beauty but also for their historical interest and value to society as food, medicine, or perfume. Among the rose garden highlights are the Alba, Gallica, and French roses, which are among the oldest in cultivation; damask roses, with their distinctive fragrance; centifolia, or cabbage roses; the old-fashioned moss rose, and the China rose popular in Victorian times for its soft shade of rose pink.

The Specialty Garden features plants that have been arranged in ten different categories, based on their use or historic interest:

- *Dioscorides Garden.* Named after a physician who lived in A.D. 60; displays a representative selection of the 400 ancient plants Dioscorides listed in his reference book on botany, pharmacology, and medicine.

• *Dye Garden.* A variety of plants used to color fabrics until the mid-nineteenth century: goldenrod, marigold, indigo, madder, the saffron crocus, and others.

• *Early American Garden.* Medicinal and culinary plants used by the colonists, including both those brought from the Old World prior to 1840 and those native to America: nasturtium, marjoram, oregano, teasel, May apple, chicory, wild fennel, valerian.

• *American Indian Garden.* Herbs used by the Native American Indians for food, medicine, smoking, baskets, home construction, dyes, and poisons: wild strawberry, wintergreen, cucumber, partridge berry, blueberry, goldenrod, bergamot, wild tobacco, bloodroot.

• *Medicinal Garden.* Plants currently synthesized for medicinal use or those with potential for future use: red periwinkle, castor bean, opium poppy, ginseng, autumn crocus, Japanese peppermint.

• *Culinary Garden.* The familiar plants used in cooking for centuries: parsley, thyme, basil, chives, coriander, dill, savory, garlic, rosemary, and various mints.

• *Industrial Garden.* Economically important plants in current use or with a potential for future use as sources of fuel, fiber, natural rubber, dyes, medicines, and oils: flax, rape, jute, marigold, soybean, jojoba, sorghum, saffron, sesame, goldenrod.

• *Fragrance Garden.* Plants historically grown for their scent for aromatics, air fresheners, perfume, and cosmetics: lavender, geraniums, mints, lemon balm, clary, carnations.

• *Oriental Garden.* A selection of herbs cultivated and used in Japan, Korea, and China for centuries. Some are almost unknown as herbs in America: horsetail, iris, balloon flower, cinnamon fern. Labels provide information about how the plants are used.

• *Beverage Garden.* Teas and other plants used to make beer, wine, liquor, and liqueurs: licorice, lemon balm, juniper, hops, pomegranate, and fig.

Beside the entrance gate at one end of the Herb Garden you come upon the New American Garden, designed by Wolfgang Oehme and James van Sweden (see Federal Reserve Board entry). In contrast to the traditional expanse of grass, this front-yard garden is planted for maximum year-round interest. Trees, shrubs, and flowers were chosen to provide contrast in leaf size, shape, color, and texture: the blue fruit and coarse evergreen foliage of the leather-leaved holly grape, the tall evergreen Foster holly with its red berries, the fine silky-smooth calamagrostis. Of particular interest are the seldom-used native plants that grow here, including the gay feather, with its bright lavender flower, and yellow masses of coreopsis.

From the New American Garden you get a good view of the arboretum's newest attraction, the National Capital Columns. Atop a knoll dotted with wildflowers stand the 24 columns that once graced the East Front of the U.S. Capitol. The columns, which date back to the early 1800s, were removed in the 1950s as part of the east portico expansion. In 1984, the columns were transferred to the arboretum for display. Today, they stand on a simple stone platform with a fountain at its center. Water from the fountain flows across the platform in channels and cascades down a gentle slope to a reflecting pool. The pale white columns stand out dramatically against the forest backdrop.

More flowers and trees await discovery at the National Arboretum. No matter when you arrive, beauty abounds. From late March to early April, the camellias, pears, magnolias, witch hazels, and tulips bloom. In mid-April, more color appears with early azaleas, rhododendrons, daffodils, and flowering cherries. Later in spring come the dogwoods, mountain laurels, peonies, and old roses. Summer brings the water lilies, daylilies, crepe myrtles, hibiscus, and herbs. Fall colors include the yellows of tulip poplar and hickory and the reds and bronzes of the dogwoods. In all seasons the holly, ferns, conifers, boxwood, and herbs add interest.

Special events scheduled throughout the year include lectures, classes, workshops, guided walks, and films. Picnicking is permitted in designated sites. For detailed information about the arboretum's major gardens and collections, get a copy of the 72-page color-illustrated guide, "The United States National Arboretum: America's Living Museum," available in the Arbor House Gift Shop next to the main entrance gate.

Mount Vernon
Mount Vernon, Virginia

Of all gardens, few better reflect the taste of their owner than George Washington's gardens at Mount Vernon. Whether you're walking in the flower garden or the kitchen garden, or beneath arbors of shady trees, you're likely to know the father of our country a little better by the time you leave.

The plantings that Washington knew and loved still flourish here. Sixteen of the trees he planted grace the estate—two tulip poplars, three white ashes, seven hollies, and a hemlock, a buckeye, a chestnut oak, and a mulberry. Other trees and plants that Washington noted in his own writings still bear fruits, vegetables, and herbs. Boxwood hedges planted in 1798 define walkways. His handsome greenhouse, demolished in an 1835 fire, has been reconstructed.

Washington's gardens flourish thanks to a sophisticated preservation program begun in 1926. Every effort possible is made by the Mount Vernon

The upper gardens at Mount Vernon. (*Courtesy of Mount Vernon Ladies' Association*)

Ladies' Association to preserve original plantings. If a tree dies, however, it is replaced with a species of the same type—often an offspring of the original.

Garden research also plays an important role. Using eyewitness accounts, a designer team consisting of a horticulturist and a landscape historian have recently replanted the one-acre upper garden to better reflect Washington's own preferences. Following a practice of the period, Washington mixed different flower varieties in beds centered by a fruit tree. Instead of great beds of intertwined roses—which dominated the gardens previously—the roses now mingle with flowers of many types. New varieties that Washington might have used also have been introduced, including foxglove, larkspur, bluebells, cornflower, heliotrope, hollyhocks, and nasturtiums.

Today, the replanted upper garden is a highlight of any garden lover's tour. The ideal time to visit Mount Vernon is in mid-April or early May, since that is the time flowers bloom and trees flower. The loveliest sight today, as it undoubtedly was in Washington's time, is the contrasting blooms of the white dogwood and the rose-colored redbud. These trees bloom profusely on the estate, but nowhere more dramatically than beside George and Martha's gravesite.

Mount Vernon offers docent tours of the residence, where you can view some outstanding antiques. See **Antiques.**

Brookside Gardens Wheaton, Maryland

Although young, Brookside Gardens, which opened in 1969, have already gained national recognition. In 1971 the 50-acre site won the National Award for Landscape Design and was named one of the best-maintained gardens in America by the Professional Grounds Maintenance Society.

The botanical gardens, named after the brook that borders them, are set in woodlands in the heart of Maryland's Wheaton Regional Park. You will enjoy a variety of experiences as you explore the beautifully laid out gardens. Just off the parking lot stands a greenhouse where tropical trees bloom in a landscape complete with stream, waterfall, and wooden bridge. Next to it lies a rose garden displaying "All-America Rose Selections," and a fragrance garden composed of plants selected for their scent and texture.

Walking up the hill through a garden of ornamental grass, you reach a gazebo. Beyond that perch you can follow paths carpeted with pine needles, leading to acres of rhododendrons and azaleas. The path becomes a bridge as it crosses a series of water lily ponds, culminating in a Japanese teahouse and garden on a tiny island.

Positioning itself as a community garden, Brookside offers a wealth of public programs. Among these are tours especially designed for schoolchildren, apartment dwellers, and horticulturists. Brookside also provides a diagnostic center for plants, puts on a lecture series, publishes a bimonthly newsletter of gardening hints, and offers a research library of 1,000 books and 40 periodicals.

Meadowlark Gardens McLean, Virginia

This new 95-acre park in the Virginia suburbs features three ponds, a formal garden, woodlands of azaleas, wildflower-strewn hillsides, topiary, a boxwood maze, and four miles of hiking trails. The $3-million property, once a farm, was bequeathed to the Northern Virginia Regional Park Authority. Clearing the land and otherwise transforming the farmland into a world-class garden has been the park authority's most ambitious project in its 27-year history.

Thanks to the birdhouses provided by the National Audubon Society, the eastern bluebirds are joining the geese, ducks, and songbirds that now inhabit the park.

River Farm
Alexandria, Virginia

Considering his love of flowers, George Washington undoubtedly would be pleased with how his former property looks today. The 27 acres of River Farm, purchased by Washington in 1759 as part of a larger land holding, burst with blooms. In spring, especially, the meadow fronting the Potomac River property turns Technicolor with bright red wallflowers and yellow daisies. Artists set their easels beneath the 200-year-old walnut trees Washington may have planted.

In the garden, pathways wind beneath arbors to three rose gardens. The collection boasts over 450 hybrid teas, grandifloras, floribundas, climbers, and miniature roses. In the official All-America Rose Selection Display Garden, award-winning cultivars are displayed a year before they reach the market.

And as if roses aren't enough of a sensual feast, River Farm also features one of only nine dahlia test gardens in the United States. These flowers mingle with a wealth of cultivated blooms, set against a backdrop of boxwood and espaliered pears and oranges. River Farm is a garden for all seasons: Winter brings Christmas and Lenten roses, and in early spring the hillsides turn to color with bluebells, tulips, and begonias.

The earliest English colonists settled on this site over 350 years ago. In the eighteenth century, the operator of a ferry-boat that ran between Virginia and Annapolis lived here. George Washington bought the property in 1789, and it stayed in his family for 100 years. Now, it's headquarters for the American Horticultural Society, which continues to plant and tend the gardens.

You can enjoy the spectacle from behind the picture windows of the manor house, in the restored period parlor that may go back to the Washington era. An impressive collection of eighteenth-century English and Scottish antiques enhances historic musing. If the day is bright, you'll want to enjoy a picnic lunch on the perfectly placed wooden tables and benches. Afterward, allow plenty of time to smell the roses.

The American Horticultural Society offers seasonal festivals at River Farm with such activities as crafts, wine tastings, garden tours, plant seminars, and music. The society also offers a program of workshops that include gardening and flower arranging.

Chapter 4

Literature

A statue of a Roman scholar, by Robert Aitken

If Washington were a walled city, its walls would be lined with books.

Washington's love affair with books and authors began over 200 years ago. Shortly after the founding of the capital, Thomas Jefferson sold to Congress his own collection of 6,700 books. Jefferson's books, mostly hand-picked from Parisian bookstalls, became the foundation of the Library of Congress.

Since those early days, Washington has become one of the world's greatest repositories of books. Over 500 libraries dot the landscape of downtown and suburban Washington. Government agencies like the departments of Commerce, Transportation, and Agriculture support their own libraries. In addition, myriad other public and private institutions boast impressive collections. Think of any field of study—geography, medicine, textiles, theater, Shakespearean England, the Middle East—and you'll find a library that caters to that special interest.

Abundant resources, opportunity, power, and impressive sights draw countless authors to this highly literate city. From the earliest days, people have come to write about politics and leaders, to be part of the literary scene, and to enjoy the pleasures of a great city. Some of the most famous authors have written about Washington: Walt Whitman described the White House by moonlight; Carl Sandburg poetically spotlighted the Washington Monument; Pulitzer Prize–winning poet William Meredith cast a twentieth-century perspective on the U.S. Capitol. Others have written novels and works of nonfiction while living in or visiting the capital. Today, one can see the sites they lived in or frequented.

These sites, the rich libraries, and the poetry and prose that describe Washington landmarks—all combine to create literary Washington. You'll discover the best of it as you follow the **Highlight Walk** and venture on your own to **More Literary Sites** on Capitol Hill, along 17th Street, and in Dupont Circle, Foggy Bottom, and beyond.

Highlight Walk
Pennsylvania Avenue

As it is today, Pennsylvania Avenue was Washington's main street in the early 1800s. The broad avenue linked the first two public buildings—the U.S. Capitol and the White House. As such, the thoroughfare was the best known to literary visitors. Most of the words written about the city in those early years were of scenes along the avenue or at the great public buildings at either end.

You can still see sites along the avenue that early literary figures knew. Many of the remaining buildings preserve their rich associations with noteworthy authors and poets. On other sites, where historic structures once stood, majestic government buildings have risen. Today, like the notes of a trumpet, they herald the star at the summit of the avenue: the U.S. Capitol, topped by its gleaming dome.

Among the literary sites you'll see as you walk are the square that has been Washington's cultural heart for 200 years, a library of unsurpassed ornamentation, the hotel known to such literary greats as Mark Twain and Charles Dickens, and a plaza inscribed with 39 quotations describing Washington, D.C.

1. Lafayette Square

For 200 years, Lafayette Square has reigned as the political, cultural, and social center of the capital. The primary magnet, of course, has been its neighbor to the south, the White House.

As you stand in the square, you see around you the structures and the reminders of former residences where famous writers lived or visited. Among them:

• *Dolley Madison House.* At the southeast corner of the square, this was once the headquarters for the Cosmos Club. One famous visitor at the club was Rudyard Kipling, author of *Kim* and *The Jungle Book.*

• *Rogers House.* This Federal-period house on Jackson Place was once the residence of James Kirke Pauling, who collaborated with Washington Irving on *Salmagundi.*

• *Hay Adams Hotel.* The twin residences of John Hay and Henry Adams, which once stood on this site, were called "the Little White House." The two friends entertained the literary greats of the day at their salons, which were unrivaled then and since.

Both were prolific writers. Hay collaborated with John G. Nicolay to write a ten-volume biography of Lincoln. Adams wrote numerous books, including *The Education of Henry Adams,* a classic today that won a Pulitzer Prize in 1919, and the first Washington novel, *Democracy,* published in 1879. Exposing financial and political scandals of the Grant administration, *Democracy* captured in a timeless way the real people of the city of Washington:

> In February a delicate haze hangs over Arlington and softens even the harsh white glare of the Capitol . . . youthful diplomats, unconscious of their danger, are lured into asking foolish girls to marry them. The

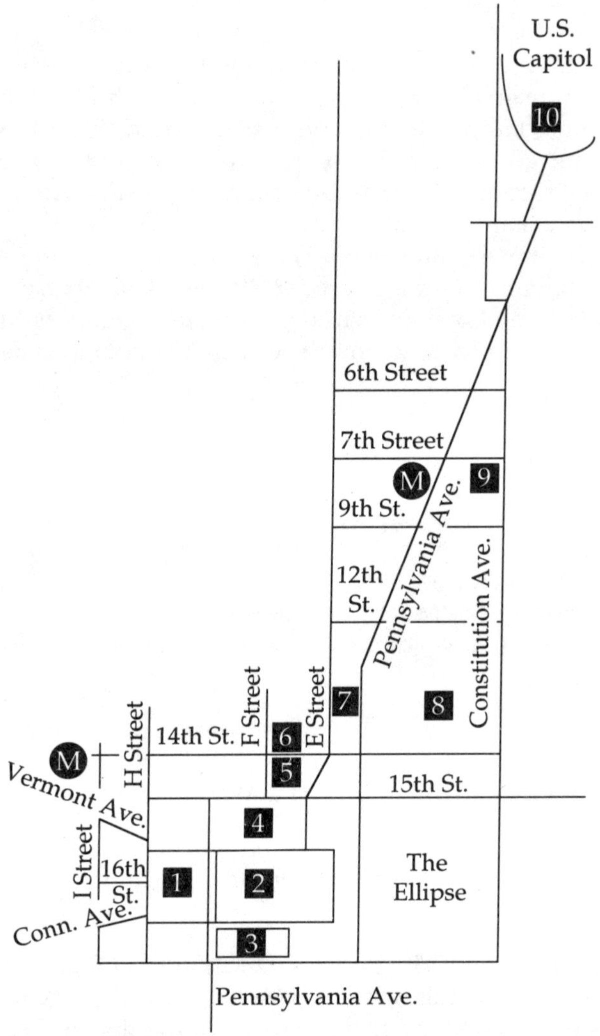

M Metro

1. Lafayette Square, Pennsylvania Avenue and 16th Street NW
2. White House, Pennsylvania Avenue and 16th Street NW
3. Old Executive Office Building, Pennsylvania Avenue and 17th Street NW
4. U.S. Treasury, 15th Street and G Street NW
5. Willard Hotel, E Street and 14th Street NW
6. Newspaper Row, 14th and F Streets
7. Freedom Plaza, E Street between 13th and 14th Streets
8. Federal Triangle, Pennsylvania Avenue between 15th and 9th Streets
9. National Archives, Pennsylvania Avenue and 9th Street NW
10. U.S. Capitol, Capitol Hill

Route

Begin your walk at the McPherson Square Metro subway station (White House exit). Walk one block south on Mt. Vernon Avenue to Lafayette Square. Cross the square and detour one block west to the Old Executive Office building. Then walk past the White House and turn right on 15th Street. Climb the steps of the south entrance of the U.S. Treasury building for a sweeping view of Pennsylvania Avenue and the U.S. Capitol. Next, walk along E Street to the Willard Hotel, then walk around the corner on 14th Street to see the onetime site of Newspaper Row, now dominated by the National Press Building. Go back to E Street for a stop at Freedom Plaza, across from the National Theater. Cross the plaza and continue your walk along Pennsylvania Avenue, past the buildings that make up the Federal Triangle. Stop to see the exhibit gallery at the National Archives. Then, with a nod to the west front of the U.S. Capitol, end the tour at the Archives Metro station.

> blood thaws in the heart and flows out into the veins like the rills of sparkling water that trickles from every lump of ice and snow . . .

For more information on Lafayette Square, see **Military**.

2. The White House

The White House has been inhabited by a number of presidential authors, including some who made a substantial contribution to the literature of America: Teddy Roosevelt was the author of numerous books, including the four-volume *The Winning of the West;* Woodrow Wilson wrote three books, including the five-volume *History of the American People.*

Famous writers have also called at the White House. Among them were Edgar Allan Poe, Charles Dickens, and Thomas Paine, author of *The Age of Reason* and *Common Sense.* Visitor Walt Whitman, in his book *Specimen Days,* observed the White House by moonlight:

> The white portico—the palace-like tall, round columns, spotless as snow—the walls also—the tender and soft moonlight, flooding the pale marble, and making peculiar faint languishing shades, not shadows—everywhere a soft transparent hazy, thin, blue moon-lace, hanging in the air . . .

For more information on the White House, see **Antiques**, **Art**, and **Gardens**.

3. Old Executive Office Building

This Victorian masterpiece, completed in 1888, contains within its ornate walls one of Washington's earliest libraries. The State Department Library, now the White House Law Library, once was home to such important national documents as the Declaration of Independence and the United States Constitution. In addition to its historic significance, the library also warrants attention as a decorative masterpiece; the design and execution of the metal ornamentation is unsurpassed.

For more information on the Old Executive Office Building, see **Military**.

4. U.S. Treasury Building

From the terrace, take in the spectacle of Pennsylvania Avenue, where President Grant liked to stroll and President Arthur relished a sleigh ride following a snowfall. Other presidents have galloped down the avenue on horseback and ridden in carriages and cars. Walt Whitman wrote about Abraham Lincoln following his second inauguration:

> I saw him on his return, at three o'clock after the performance was over. He was in his plain two-horse barouche, and look'd very much worn and tired; the lines, indeed of vast responsibilities, intricate questions, and demands of life and death, cut deeper than ever upon his dark brown face, yet all the old goodness, tenderness, sadness and canny shrewdness underneath the furrows . . .

Writers have captured in words the life on Pennsylvania Avenue in many ways. Among the gems are Whitman's descriptions of the avenue during the Civil War: the "bronz'd and bearded young faces" of the soldiers and "the officers' horses tied in front of drinking or oyster saloons." Mary Clemmer Ames, a chronicler of Washington of the 1880s, noted the colorful mingling of people:

> A distinguished senator or member who has been making the halls of the Capitol ring . . . a fine lady, attired in a rich velvet dress most elaborately trimmed . . . Chinese of high rank in native dress . . . ragged negro boys . . . the office-seeker—one of the peculiarities of the streets of Washington . . .

5. Willard Hotel

A hotel has stood on this site since 1818, and from the beginning, Washington society mingled here. Nathaniel Hawthorne, who visited Washington during the Civil War, wrote of the Willard:

Willard Hotel

> [It] may be much more justly called the center of Washington and the Union than either the Capitol, the White House, or the State Department. It is the meeting place of the true representatives of the country—not such as are chosen blindly and amiss by the electors . . . governors of sovereign states . . . illustrious men . . . generals . . . statesmen and orators . . . office-seekers, wirepullers, inventors, artists, poets, prospers . . . diplomatists, mail contractors, railway directors . . .

At the Willard Hotel, Hawthorne adopted "the universal habit of the place," calling for "a mint-julep, whiskey-skin, gin cocktail, brandy smash, or glass of pure old rye." Perhaps he raised his glass to Walt Whitman, whose "sumptuous Willard bar" was a favorite.

Other literary greats walked the great halls of the hotel, including Mark Twain, who visited the Willard in 1867 while making publishing arrangements for his book *Innocents Abroad*. Twain, so the story goes, wanted to present himself to his admiring public with the proper flourish. So, upon seeing a crowd gathered in the lobby, he ran around to the rear entrance so he could make a grand entrance down the sweeping stretch of carpeted luxury know as "Peacock Alley."

Less flamboyant, in fact unknown to the public, was Emily Dickinson's 1855 visit to the Willard Hotel. She came during the term of her father, a member of Congress and the Whig party. She wrote only the briefest observations about Washington. This, the richest record, describes her trip to Mount Vernon:

> . . . on one soft spring day we glided down the Potomac in a painted boat, and jumped upon the shore . . . hand in hand we stole along up a tangled pathway till we reached the tomb of General George Washington . . . we paused beside it and no one spoke a word . . . then hand in hand, walked on again, not less wise or sad for that marble story . . .

Another famous woman, Julia Ward Howe, visited the Willard in 1861. Haunted by the sights of the Civil War and with the melody of the old English song marching troops sang, she composed new words. From her room looking down on Pennsylvania Avenue, she wrote the song that became the anthem of the Union army, "The Battle Hymn of the Republic." A plaque at the main entrance of the Willard marks Howe's visit and the creation of her immortal anthem. When Martin Luther King wrote his "I Have a Dream" speech, he stayed at the hotel in the room Howe had occupied.

6. Newspaper Row

With the outbreak of the Civil War, about 60 important newspapers set up bureaus on 14th Street between E and F Streets. Today the National Press Building, the center for national and international news, stands at the northern end of this same block.

7. Freedom Plaza

Thirty-nine quotations about the city of Washington are inscribed on the surface of the large plaza. Reviewing the words of major historical, political, and literary figures, several academic and government committees narrowed the initial 500 entries down to the final selections.

Here are a few of the quotations that the judges felt best capture the character, aspirations, and intentions of the nation:

> No nation has ever before had the opportunity offered them to deliberately decide the spot where their capital city should be fixed. (Pierre-Charles L'Enfant, 1789)

> A century hence if this country keeps united it will produce a city though not so large as London yet of a magnitude inferior to few others in Europe. (George Washington, 1789)

> . . . it is mean in detail but the outline has a certain grandeur about it. (James Fenimore Cooper, 1838)

> The Capital of the great republic gathered its people from the winds and so the manners, faces and fashions presented a variety that was infinite. (Mark Twain, 1874)

> Wherever the American citizen may be a stranger, he is at home here. (Frederick Douglass, 1877)

> Washington is no place to carry out inventions. (Alexander Graham Bell, 1887)

> With the World War Washington changed its character forever. In a moment it became the heart of the world, the world counting every pulsation. (Marietta Minnegerode Andrews, 1928)

> Washington was planned by men of imagination who stood amidst the swamps and briar patches and the head of navigation on the Potomac and visualized a city of half a million population. (George Rothwell Brown, 1930)

8. Federal Triangle

The row of neoclassical government office buildings that line Pennsylvania Avenue make up the northern arm of a triangle of buildings that stretches for eight blocks. Constitution Avenue forms the southern side of the triangle, which has its base on 14th Street and its apex at 6th Street. Walking along Pennsylvania Avenue you see the buildings that house the Department of Commerce, the U.S. Postal Service, the Internal Revenue Department, the Justice Department, the National Archives, and the Federal Trade Commission.

From the beginning, many writers came to Washington not to pursue their literary careers, but rather to find work with the government. One of the most famous writers who did just that was Walt Whitman, who worked in the Patent Office, the Interior Department, and the Attorney General's office, where he wrote his famous poem "When Lilacs Last in the Dooryard Bloomed."

Whitman's friend, author John Burroughs, worked as a clerk in the Treasury Department. Washington scenes inspired his two famous nature books, *Wake Robin* and *Winter Sunshine*.

Contemporary authors also have been drawn to government jobs in Washington, writing books while here. One of the most famous examples is Rachel Carson, author of *The Sea Around Us* and *Silent Spring*, who worked at the Department of Interior in the 1960s. Another is Louis Halle, who wrote his best-selling book *Spring in Washington* in 1945, while serving as an official at the State Department. "I took to monitoring the seasons when the government wasn't looking," his opening words explain. He goes on to describes the arrival of birds and budding flowers in a rich mixture of speculation and philosophy. Referring to two violets he noted blooming between the cracks in the pavement of Rock Creek Parkway:

> I could view the crumbling of our civilization with equanimity if violets were to spring up in the cracks. They would, too.

9. National Archives

This repository of the records of government is best known as the place that permanently displays the Declaration of Independence, the Constitution, and the Bill of Rights. The archives also safeguard billions of documents, photos, and motion picture films that writers use in researching their books. Some of the leading authors who use archive documents speak at monthly author and booksigning events. Among the well-known writers who have lectured are Carl Bernstein, columnist Jim Brady, McGeorge Bundy, Archibald Cox, Taylor Branch, Hendrick Smith, and Alex Haley.

10. U.S. Capitol

Like other tourists, writers and poets have visited the symbol of America that crowns Capitol Hill. City planner Pierre-Charles L'Enfant, who laid out Washington in 1791, saw the site of the U.S. Capitol as "a pedestal awaiting a monument." He linked the Capitol with other important government buildings by diagonal boulevards that cut through the grid of streets.

But L'Enfant's city, planned for 300,000, had under 3,000 inhabitants when Charles Dickens visited Washington in 1842. The great English novelist climbed to the top of the Capitol for a bird's-eye view and derided "the vast designs of its projector, an aspiring Frenchman":

> It is sometimes called the City of Magnificent Distances, but it might with greater propriety be termed the City of Magnificent Intentions . . . Spacious avenues, that begin in nothing, and lead nowhere; streets, milelong that only want houses, roads, and inhabitants; public buildings that need but a public to be complete; and ornaments of great thoroughfares, which only lack great thoroughfares to ornament—are its leading features.

Since Dickens's appraisal, other poets and writers have seen a different city spread beneath their feet as they stand on the west terrace. The eyes of poet May Miller saw a "cool magnificence of space." Poet Greg Orfalea, watching people flying kites on the Mall between the Ellipse and Constitution Avenue, saw:

> . . . essence
> of magnolia join the waltzing
> wind that tosses these figures
> Of generals senators
> students and street cleaners
> onto the soft green shoulder of this woman
> undulation
> across the Ellipse
> from the Constitution . . .

Perhaps the same view from the terrace of the Capitol, looking toward the Mall to the Washington Monument, inspired Carl Sandburg's poem "Washington Monument by Night."

When poets turn their gaze to the Capitol itself, they see the symbol in various ways. The title of Josephine Miles's poem "Softly the Capitol Hill Surveys Its Scene" hints at her perspective.

Modern authors turn the Capitol into a backdrop for their tales of government and politics. Among them are Robert A. Caro, whose book *The Path of Power* describes the rise of Lyndon B. Johnson, and Allen Drury, who wrote about the Senate in *Advise and Consent*.

In "On Jenkins Hill" (the old name for Capitol Hill), Pulitzer Prize–winning poet William Meredith ponders the dome "heavy with reference." Poet Lawrence Lee, in his poem "The Dome," uses the monument as a symbol of the city where "marble is a dream designed."

For more information on the U.S. Capitol, see **Gardens** and **Technology**.

More Literary Sites

Capitol Hill

Folger Shakespeare Library

Shakespeare's characters and plays come to life in this unique combination of theater, library, and exhibit hall. Devoted to Shakespeare and his time, the Folger features the world's largest collection of his plays and poetry. It also includes works by his contemporaries that show us life in England in the sixteenth and seventeenth centuries. In the oak-paneled Elizabethan Great Hall, you can see one of the 79 First Folios that the library owns. Also on display are pieces from its collection of Shakespeare-related prints, playbills, rare books, and theatrical artifacts.

But seeing an exhibit is just one reason for a visit. The Great Hall itself, a re-creation of a Tudor long gallery, is another. The impressive room stretches the length of the building beneath high vaulted ceilings. Along the edges of the polished tile floor the titles of Shakespeare's plays are inscribed. Handsome standards—the shield and eagles of the United States and the coat-of-arms of Elizabeth I—decorate opposite ends of the hall.

The feeling that you've stepped back four centuries into Renaissance England persists as you pass through a richly carved door into the foyer of the Shakespeare Theater at the Folger. Once a year in April, on the Saturday closest to the Bard's birthday (April 23), the doors to the Reading Room open. Carved tables stretch for the length of this Tudor-style room paneled in white oak. Around the perimeter, in carved vaults and shelves, lie the rarest manuscripts and books. At one end of the room a bust of Shakespeare reigns; it is a copy of the one in Stratford-upon-Avon's Trinity Church, where the Bard is buried. Colored light streams through a stained glass window that pictures the seven ages of man described in *As You Like It*.

On the exterior of the marble building, note the nine bas-relief sculptured panels that illustrate familiar scenes from Shakespeare's plays. Along the roof line are carved quotations that praise the poet. On the corner is a statue of Puck, with the inscription "Lo, what fools these mortals be."

For more information on the Folger Library, see **Gardens** and **Music**.

Library of Congress

When book lovers go to heaven, they probably end up in a place that looks a lot like the original Library of Congress building. Nowhere will you find more books in a more beautiful setting.

Built to portray American culture, this Italian Renaissance palace boasts 112 murals and 22 sculptures. Fifty craftsmen took seven years to create a

Neptune Fountain, Library of Congress

wonderland of mosaics, stencils, medallions, lunettes, metal castings, and marble sculpture. At few other sites will you see decorative elements executed with richer materials by finer craftsmen on such a grand scale. Opulence reaches its peak in the central Great Hall, where you stand as if inside a Fabergé Easter egg, surrounded by baroque splendor. Countless details vie for attention. Among them are literary allusions in the paintings and inscriptions.

The Great Hall, which is undergoing renovation, will probably be closed for most of 1992. But when it reopens—or is shown on specially arranged tours—you'll see again a wealth of literary high points, concentrated in two areas of the Great Hall: First, in the east corridor, see the glass-case exhibits of the Gutenberg and Mainz Bibles. The Gutenberg Bible, which is one of three perfect vellum copies in existence, marks the invention of printing by movable metal type. Ninety copies of the Gutenberg Bible were printed sometime before 1456. In contrast, only one copy of the hand-illuminated Mainz Bible was created.

Above the two books, note the six paintings that illustrate "The Evolution of the Book."

- *Cairn.* Primitive men raise a heap of stones, perhaps as a memorial or to commemorate an event.
- *Oral Tradition.* An Arabian storyteller relates a tale.
- *Egyptian Hieroglyphics.* A worker cuts an inscription over a temple door.
- *Picture Writing.* A Native American Indian paints a tribal story on deerskin.
- *The Manuscript Book.* A monk in a cell laboriously illuminates the pages of a great book.
- *The Printing Press.* The inventor Gutenberg examines a proof sheet.

Second, savor the allusions to poetry embellishing the south corridor. The large painting on the east wall, *Lyric Poetry,* introduces the subject of the surrounding lunettes—a series of crescent-shaped paintings in which artists have represented the work of American and English poets. In the first three, the figure of a young boy suggests the poet's words:

> Tennyson: "Flushed Ganymede, his rosy thigh half-buried in the Eagle's down."
> Keats: Endymion lying asleep on Mount Latmos, with the moon shining down on him.
> Wordsworth: "There was a boy; ye knew him well, ye cliffs and islands of Winander!"

For Emerson's poem "Uriel," an angel is depicted retiring in scorn from the anger of his companion upon hearing his proposition:

> Line in nature is not found;
> Unit and universe are round;
> In vain produced, all rays return;
> Evil will bless, and ice will burn.

To represent Milton, Comus in the guise of a shepherd is shown as he responds to the song of the Lady:

> Can any mortal mixture of earthy's mould
> Breathe such divine enchanting ravishment?

Although no specific lines are illustrated, Shakespeare's poem "Venus and Adonis" is depicted by the dead body of Adonis, killed by the boar, lying naked in the forest.

From the Great Hall, continue your exploration of the Library's literary allusions with a visit to the Rotunda Reading Room. From the balcony of the visitors gallery you can survey the reading room below and get a close look at the decorated rotunda.

Allegory abounds. Between the dome and the lantern in the collar of the rotunda stretches a 150-foot mural depicting the evolution of civilization. In it, a dozen 10-foot-high figures represent the epochs or countries that have contributed most to American civilization. Set on 8 marble piers are symbolic figures in plaster, and between them, on the balustrades, stand 16 bronze portrait statues. Among the 8 statues that represent characteristics of civilized life and thought, note "Philosophy," who carries a book. Also in this group, "Poetry" wears a heavy garment that symbolizes the seriousness of drama (she stands next to "Law," with a robe drawn over her head). Of the larger bronze statues that circle the rotunda, look for William Shakespeare in his Elizabethan garb, toga-draped Homer, and historian Edward Gibbon, who carries a book.

Other books and artifacts from the library's collection are on display in the exhibit hall in the Madison Annex, across the street from the main building. If you're lucky, you may see such treasures as the original copies of Walt Whitman's poems, original books from Thomas Jefferson's library, Abraham Lincoln's first draft of the Gettysburg Address, the papers of 23 presidents, and the compositions of Beethoven or Mozart. There is a rooftop cafeteria in the Madison Building with a spectacular view.

For more information on the Library of Congress, see **Gardens** and **Music**.

Union Station

The walls of Washington's public buildings fairly sing with the poetry and prose of the famous. Poetry in stone reaches its zenith at Union Station. The great beaux arts masterpiece, completed in 1908, wears a half-dozen quotations chosen by a president of Harvard University, Charles William Eliot. Eliot borrowed from such sources as the Bible, Shakespeare, and Ralph Waldo Emerson. Most visible on the entrance facade is Boswell's quote:

> He that would bring home the wealth of the Indies
> must carry the wealth of the Indies with him.
> So it is in traveling, a man must carry knowledge
> with him if he would bring home knowledge.

Note: Union Station offers an array of restaurants and a fast-food court. For more information on Union Station, see **Technology**.

THE MALL

NATIONAL MUSEUM OF AMERICAN HISTORY

In addition to its system of research collections, the Smithsonian Institution houses rare books in the Dibner Library of the History of Science and Technology. Located in the National Museum of American History, this collection includes the books given to the library in 1976 by Dr. Bern Dibner, an electrical engineer who had collected some of the most important works on the history of science and technology. Among the treasures—some in handsome bindings of wood and leather—are a first edition of Darwin's *Origin of Species*, a fifteenth-century edition of the works of Aristotle, early editions of the Bible, and even a microscope from the laboratory of Louis Pasteur.

The library staff draws from the collection for the books it displays in a new exhibition gallery adjacent to the library. In the seven cases, you can see rare books that carry out an exhibit theme. In the past the library has mounted exhibits related to major exhibits elsewhere in the museum complex. For instance, in connection with the 500th anniversary of Columbus's arrival in the New World, the library exhibited copies of books the explorer used to make his calculations, and other scientific books from the fifteenth century.

By special arrangement, groups can visit the library to see such examples of the book-making art.

Note: You can lunch or enjoy snacks in the museum cafe or the old-world Palm Court restaurant. For more information on the Smithsonian Institution's museums, see **Art**, **Gardens**, **Music**, **Science**, and **Technology**.

NATIONAL AIR AND SPACE MUSEUM

Most people don't realize that by making a request ahead of time, they can visit a specialized library at the National Air and Space Museum. Browsers with an interest in air and space will find delights among the 500,000 photographs on videodisc and 4,000 aerospace films.

EMBASSY ROW–GEORGETOWN

ANDERSON HOUSE

Hidden downstairs in the Anderson House lies a library of 10,000 volumes devoted to the Revolutionary War. Among the treasures brought out for specially arranged tour groups is a sheepskin document signed by George Washington, a map created by Thomas Jefferson's father around 1750, and books of exquisite engravings.

For more information on this opulent mansion, see **Antiques**, **Art**, and **Gardens**.

Textile Museum Jenkins Library

This handsomely furnished room overlooking a garden contains more than 10,000 books and periodicals covering textile arts. Particularly beautiful are the lavishly illustrated books on the art of lace making.

For more information on the Textile Museum, see **Art** and **Gardens**.

Washington National Cathedral

For the lover of old and rare books, the National Cathedral's Rare Book Room shouldn't be missed. Tucked away in a corner of the cathedral, the room features treasures from a 10,000-volume collection of religious works. About 40 are displayed in glass cases.

Although most of the books on exhibit change, one masterpiece remains on permanent view: the first printing of the King James Bible, which James I gave to his second son, Prince Henry. The volume still has its original silk ties. Other books can be appreciated from both a historic and an aesthetic viewpoint. If you love beautiful books, you'll delight in a fifteenth-century choral book printed on sheepskin parchment, a choral book from 1470 with woodblock illustrations, and examples of books with painted forepages.

To see the books at close range outside their cases, you can visit the book vaults downstairs by joining a group (and by special arrangement). From the library's adjacent book vault, the librarian lays a dozen or more special volumes on the library table for inspection and discussion. With urging, the librarian may show you colorfully illuminated works and a potpourri of other visual feasts: a 1716 missal in silver and red, bound with hinges; a Pilgrim's Bible from 1600, bound in copper fittings; a Bible with French steel engravings and marbled paper; the Queen of Portugal's diary, in a leather case with an embroidered cover; a manuscript Book of Esther scroll with an ivory turning pin.

For more information on Washington National Cathedral, see **Art**, **Gardens**, and **Music**.

Note: Nearby Georgetown University boasts one of the few remaining cast iron library buildings in the United States. The Riggs Library, built in 1891, served as the university's main library until 1970, when the Lauinger Library was completed. A portion of the university's periodical collection is still housed here. Visitors are admitted by special request.

Dupont Circle

Historical Society of Washington Library

The collection includes 70,000 photographs, 3,000 glass-plate negatives, and 1,500 other pieces, such as sketches and engravings, relating to the history

Middle East Institute

of the District of Columbia. The library is part of the Victorian Heurich Mansion.

For more information on the Heurich Mansion, see **Gardens**.

Middle East Library

Housed in a renovated Victorian stable and set in a leafy courtyard, this library offers a rare book collection that includes accounts of nineteenth-century journeys to the East. Some feature fascinating sketches and photos of India and Turkey.

National Geographic Society Library

The reading room, filled with Society magazines that go way back, features one of the city's best examples of cartography. Displayed in the entrance hall is a 1530 masterpiece by Venetian cosmographer Guiseppe Rosaccio. The rare map was recently discovered rolled up in a Tyson's Corner warehouse.

For more information on the National Geographic Society, see **Science**.

Note: At lunch or teatime, soak up literary ambience at the Tabard Inn, the onetime home of novelist Edward Everett Hale, author of the famous story "The Man Without a Country." His house was later incorporated into this Dupont Circle haunt of writers, which is now a country inn.

Foggy Bottom

Kennedy Center Library

This airy room on the terrace level of the theater complex holds biographies about film and theater people, dance journals, costume books, review collections, and over 200 periodicals covering theater, dance, opera, music, film, and broadcasting about the theater and entertainment. Several machines are available for listening to and viewing records and tapes from the library's collection. There is also a restaurant and a cafeteria on the roof. Outside, near the outdoor lot and walkway, see the statue of Don Quixote, a gift from the government of Spain.

For more information on the Kennedy Center, see **Art** and **Music**.

17th Street

DAR National Headquarters Library

This unique collection features extensive genealogical holdings, plus books relating to the American Revolution, American Indians, American women, and states' history. Intricate ironwork, moldings, and a frosted skylight make the room one of the area's prettiest.

For more information on the DAR, see **Antiques**.

Beyond

F. Scott Fitzgerald's Gravesite
Rockville, Maryland

To pay your respects to novelist F. Scott Fitzgerald, drive out to his gravesite at St. Mary's Cemetery in Rockville, Maryland. The words etched on the gravestone echo the final lines of *The Great Gatsby*, "So we beat on, boats against the current, borne back ceaselessly into the past."

Joaquin Miller's Cabin
Rock Creek Park

Inhabiting a domicile of a different sort was California poet Joaquin Miller. Miller, famous for his book *Songs of the Sierras,* lived in a log cabin on Meridian Hill. In 1912 the cabin was moved to Rock Creek Park, where it can still be seen. Occasionally poetry groups hold readings in the cabin.

Scottish Rite Temple, Robert Burns Library
Northwest Washington

With its 3,411 volumes by and about the eighteenth-century Scottish poet, the library boasts the world's second-largest collection, given to the Temple in 1912 by the Carnegie Institution. A bust of Burns overlooks the wood-paneled library, with its impressive walls of books.

Chapter 5

Military

Display ship *Barry*, Washington Navy Yard (*Courtesy of U.S. Navy Photo*)

As the seat of government, Washington, D.C., has from its earliest days been the defense command post of America. Those who control the nation's military arsenal come together here to develop the strategies that defend our country.

Evidence of Washington's 200-year military history begins with the War of 1812. Because of the capital's location on the water, the founding fathers were concerned about its defense and constructed Fort Warburton (now named Fort Washington) upriver from Mount Vernon. However, the British simply circumvented this naval block. Approaching the capital from its "back door" via Bladensburg, Maryland, they marched into the city, burning the U.S. Capitol and other government buildings in August 1814.

Reminders of that war fought within the city remain. Even coats of paint have not fully disguised the scorched stone that testifies to the British burning of the White House. At the Smithsonian, the flag that flew over Fort McHenry in 1814 can still be seen. The flag, which survived those "bombs bursting in air," inspired Francis Scott Key to write the words that would become our national anthem.

"The Civil War transformed the city from a provincial capital of an emerging nation into the veritable nerve center of a major nation," writes historian Benjamin Franklin Cooling in *Swords and Shields*. An extensive system of forts and batteries was the physical symbol of the realization that Washington was vulnerable and had to be protected.

A 37-mile ring of 68 forts was built around the city. Richard M. Lee writes in *Mr. Lincoln's City* that by 1865, the military forts were "the marvel of their time." This elaborate system of forts supported over 800 heavy fortress cannon. Twenty miles of trenches for infantry troops connected the forts, with 93 prepared artillery positions in between. As a result, Lee notes, Washington behind its forts grew "into the most powerful base the Union had."

Civil War forts and other remnants abound. The major centers of Union activity in Washington can still be seen today: the Navy Yard, the Army Arsenal (Fort McNair), the Potomac wharves at 6th and 7th Streets, and the Maryland Avenue railroad yards. Most of Foggy Bottom was covered with supply storehouses, barracks, army camps, a depot for as many as 30,000 horses and mules, plus harness repair and blacksmith shops. The area also contained camps for wagon trains, mess halls, a large bakery, and a commissary warehouse.

In addition to these historic sites, Washington boasts over a dozen statues and memorials dedicated to Civil War officers. Most outstanding of these is the colossal memorial to Ulysses S. Grant and the monument to William T. Sherman. The Sherman monument stands on a tree-lined knoll overlooking Pennsylvania Avenue, where the general supposedly stood to review the triumphant return of his troops on May 24, 1865.

A good part of his immense army marched into town toward the end of a parade of victorious troops that had filled the avenue for two days. Walt Whitman estimated that he viewed more than 200,000 men, "their wide ranks stretching clear across the Avenue . . . I watch them march, or ride along, at a brisk pace through two whole days." That parade, probably the greatest military parade in American history, celebrated the end of the Civil War. Not again until the ends of World War I and II would Pennsylvania Avenue see such throngs of celebrants.

At the outset of World War I, shortly after the Declaration of War against Germany in 1917, tens of thousands of workers swarmed into the city to staff the war bureaus. Buildings sprung up seemingly overnight, and men in uniform filled the streets. As a writer in the WPA Guide noted, "Washington was the center not only of an embattled nation but to some extent of an embattled world. Statesmen, military experts, financiers, business executives came to consult with U.S. officials on various phases of the war."

But long after World War I ended the temporary buildings erected during the war remained: People knew the "war to end all wars" had not yet been waged. Thus, when World War II began, people had the feeling that they were simply picking up where the country had left off in November 1918.

Each war in U.S. history has left its mark on Washington. Reminders of the wars Washington has witnessed dot the city. Dozens of memorials, museums, the Pentagon, and Arlington National Cemetery entice the military buff. Some are within an easy walk of a Metro subway station, while others are best reached by car. You'll see the best of military Washington if you follow the **Highlight Walk** and venture on your own to discover **More Military Sites** along Embassy Row and the Mall, in Foggy Bottom, and beyond.

Highlight Walk
Pennsylvania Avenue

This one-mile-plus walk uses both shoe leather and the Metro subway to show you the sights. On a stretch of Pennsylvania Avenue and a jog via subway to Massachusetts Avenue, you'll see some of the city's newest and most impressive sites and cover at least 200 years of military history. On the itinerary are memorials to foreign military heroes who helped America win its war of independence; the ornately embellished building that was the hub of World War I military operations; elaborately detailed monuments to a Civil War hero; the stunning new memorial to Navy servicepeople; and

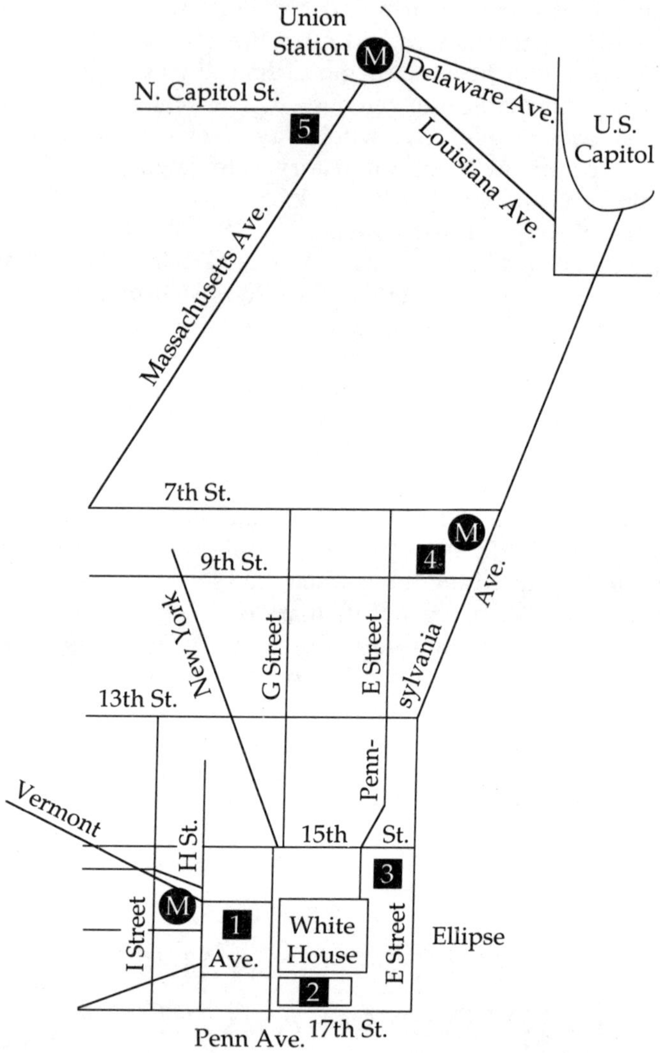

M Metro

1. Lafayette Square, 16th Street and H Street NW
2. Old Executive Office Building, 17th Street and Pennsylvania Avenue NW
3. Sherman Memorial, E Street and 15th Street NW
4. Navy Memorial, Pennsylvania Avenue between 7th and 9th Streets NW
5. Museum of the National Guard, One Massachusetts Avenue NW

Route

From the McPherson Square (White House exit), follow Vermont Avenue south to Lafayette Square. Cross the square and walk west one block to the Old Executive Office Building, following 17th Street south to E Street. At E Street, turn left and walk east past the White House to 15th Street and the Sherman Memorial. Continue on Pennsylvania Avenue, walking toward the U.S. Capitol. After a stop at the Navy Memorial, board the Metro subway at the Archives Station to the east of the memorial. Transfer to the Red Line and ride to the Union Station Metro subway station. Walk one block west on Massachusetts Avenue, past North Capital Street, to the National Guard Museum. Complete the tour by returning to the Union Station Metro subway station.

a museum devoted to the 350-year history of the militia and the National Guard.

1. Lafayette Square

Since Washington, D.C., was founded decades after the Revolutionary War, there are not many reminders of that war here. Unlike Boston, New York, and Philadelphia, where the actual sites of military encounters can be seen, in the capital city only artifacts and statues remind us of the struggle.

Among these, none more dramatically tell the story of our war for independence than the statues of four foreign heroes that stand on the corners of Lafayette Square. They are Comte de Rochambeau, Major General Friedrich Wilhelm von Steuben, the Marquis de Lafayette, and Brigadier General Tadeusz Kościuszko. These memorials make the point that without the assistance of foreign friends, the Colonies may not have won their independence. The subjects of the memorials also suggest a broader truth: that since our ancestors were immigrants (or we ourselves are), our roots can be found in foreign lands.

In addition to honoring individuals, the memorials tell a larger story. When read together, the details in bronze suggest some of the most important events that made up the Revolutionary War: Kościuszko holds a map of the fortifications at Saratoga; Rochambeau plans the battle of Yorktown; von Steuben inspects American troops at the great maneuvers of 1778; and Lafayette petitions the French National Assembly to assist the Americans in their struggle. Where most statues are single portraits of the honored individual, these memorials stand as galleries of bronze pictures because they also illustrate episodes from the lives of their subjects.

The centerpiece of Lafayette Square commemorates a military hero from another war: Major General Andrew Jackson at the Battle of New Orleans. At the base of the statue, four cannon captured from the British by Jackson salute the victor.

2. Old Executive Office Building

Until World War II, the Old Executive Office Building (OEOB) held within its seven acres the departments that later would grow to fill the 3-million-square-foot Pentagon—and the State Department headquarters in Foggy Bot-

Old Executive Office Building

tom. The world's largest office building when it was completed in 1888, the OEOB held 4,500 employees at its peak in 1918. Made up of four wings joined by corridors, it was constructed to house the State, War, and Navy departments. Overcrowded almost from the beginning, the Navy Department moved out in 1918. The War Department coped with the space problem until 1938; in that year it also moved out of the OEOB, scattering to 17 facilities before moving into the Pentagon in 1943. The State Department followed suit in 1947.

Before those moves, OEOB was for over 60 years the capital's military and diplomatic nerve center. Twenty-five secretaries of state, 21 secretaries of war, and 15 secretaries of the navy served on the site. Among the famous who have worked here were several men who would go on to become president: Theodore Roosevelt, William Howard Taft, Franklin D. Roosevelt, Lyndon B. Johnson, Gerald Ford, and George Bush. In addition, John Hay, Admiral George Dewey, and General John J. Pershing had offices here.

Over 1,000 treaties were signed here, including the document that ended the Spanish-American War. Of all the historic dramas played out on the OEOB stage, none surpassed the meeting on December 7, 1941, following the bombing of Pearl Harbor, between Secretary of State Cordell Hull and the Japanese envoys.

Now, on regularly scheduled tours, you can walk the halls that military leaders of World Wars I and II have walked. You can even see the 26 flower-filled urns set in place by one enterprising building superintendent, Douglas MacArthur, who served in that position in 1913.

Equally important, in touring the OEOB you gain unique insight into American military history. Carved, molded, and painted into the ornamentation of the building, both inside and out, are the symbols around which our military tradition has grown. For instance, you can spot the Indian Treaty room doors, carved oars, carved anchors decorating the room's upper balcony, and tridents embellishing the column capitals.

The ornate pediment at the pavilion over the entrance caps the portico that leads to the old War Department. It is a 30-foot-wide, 8-foot-high metal sculpture depicting an Americanized version of a classical memorial to captured arms. From ancient times onward, the victorious have displayed their military trophies, hanging captured arms and booty first from trees and later in memorials. The memorial above the OEOB entrance features a central figure—actually an empty medieval suit of armor—wearing a helmet topped by an American eagle and tasseled flags. The figure is bracketed by cannon. Two United States shields stand as backdrops. Fasces, spears, cannon, cannonballs, a pikestaff, and laurel and oak leaves complete the trophy. Many of these symbolic additions appear inside the building as well. One of the most frequently used symbols is the fasces, bundles of sticks enclosing an ax. The fasces dates to Roman times, when it was carried in procession ahead of the consul to signify his authority.

Although the ornamentation features classical subjects, its lavish style speaks of a more recent time. Begun during the administrations of Ulysses S. Grant, the OEOB stands as an expression of the exuberance and optimism that swept the country following the Civil War. Completed in 1888, the structure has been called America's answer to a baroque palace.

Driven by a desire to avoid the monotonous building that characterized the capital, the architect designed a facade of supreme complexity: 1,572 windows and 900 columns dot the OEOB's jigsaw puzzle of pavilions, balconies, mansard roofs, chimneys, and tier upon tier of sculptured detail. Inside, European craftsmen painstakingly embellished walls, ceilings, and floors. Their efforts are preserved. Today you see floors of exquisite marquetry and English Minton tile, stenciled walls burnished with gold leaf, lacy metalwork that resembles brass and bronze, and lavishly carved pilasters and moldings.

This opulence links an old world with a modern one. When the artisans so richly decorated the new OEOB, the Civil War had only recently ended. By the time all the original tenants had moved out, our nation's modern military machine had been born and had grown to adulthood.

3. Sherman Monument

One of Washington's most elaborate memorials stands on the site where General Sherman supposedly stood to review the victorious Union troops returning from their march through Georgia.

An equestrian statue of Sherman stands on a pedestal set on a large terrace. At its base, inscriptions, eight bas-reliefs, and statues read like a textbook. The memorial depicts Sherman's military career and expresses both the terror he introduced to warfare and his love of peace.

One bronze grouping, *War*, portrays a woman with bound hands standing atop a dead soldier who still clasps his rifle. The other, *Peace*, shows a boy feeding birds and a woman holding an olive branch. The inscriptions and bas-reliefs are presented on tablets at the base of the statue. An inlaid mosaic lists the names of Sherman's battles and the chronology of his military assignments. A bronze tablet lists the names of the generals who served under him, and relief medallions depict favorite generals under his command and show Sherman and his staff planning the Battle of Missionary Ridge. Life-size soldiers stand guard on the corners of the terrace, each representing a branch of the army: infantry, artillery, cavalry, and engineers.

The memorial, dedicated in 1903, has stimulated controversy over the years. As James M. Goode writes in *The Outdoor Sculpture of Washington,* "the elaborate nature of the structure is often cited by peace groups as an unjustifiable glorification of one of America's cruelest military leaders. Defenders insist it is actually a memorial to peace, Sherman's main objective."

4. U.S. Navy Memorial

Washington's newest military memorial differs from the others. Rather than being simply a site to see—a memory in bronze—this one invites participation.

It helps that the memorial is located in the heart of a neighborhood that since 1975 has been undergoing a multimillion-dollar redevelopment. As you travel along Pennsylvania Avenue, you can't miss seeing the tall ship masts that mark the location of the memorial. The flags hanging from the masts seem to wave you into the amphitheater that, together with a visitor center, makes up the memorial.

By stepping beyond the low wall that partially encloses the amphitheater, you begin a lively interaction with the memorial. First, you see the 100-foot-round granite map of the earth laid out on the floor of the amphitheater. As you walk over and around it, you get a unique perspective. In addition to seeing the vastness of the oceans as compared to land mass, you also view the earth as if you were in outer space, the Navy's newest frontier. The perspective is due to the map's scale; one inch equals twelve miles on earth. Carrying out that ratio, by standing five to six feet above the map you get the view you would get from 700 to 800 miles above the surface of the earth.

Moving back down to earth from outer space, you next come face to face with the life-size statue *The Lone Sailor*. Rather than looking down from a pedestal, this bronze sculpture, wearing the classic blue jacket, meets you at eye level. Like *The Homecoming* inside the visitor center, it was created to stir your feelings and involve you with this living memorial. You'll sense the strength of the sailor but also his yearnings for home. Looking at *The Homecoming*, you'll feel both the sadness of parting and the joy of reunion.

In a different way, you're invited to become actively involved as you view the displays and the movie in the visitor center. Interactive monitors engage you as you learn about classes of ships and the history of the U.S. Navy. In the 250-seat movie theater you're asked to run away to sea as you watch the state-of-the-art film produced by the creators of the National Air and Space Museum's popular feature film *To Fly*.

If you visit on a Thursday evening during the summer months, you'll also *hear* this living memorial. That's when the U.S. Navy Band performs a concert of classic and patriotic music. Visitors sit on the steps of the amphitheater as the band plays and the banners on the masts wave.

5. Museum of the National Guard

At last the minute man stands historically correct. No more does the Revolutionary War's citizen-soldier wear leggings, which didn't come into vogue until after the Revolution. Nor does he carry a percussion-cap gun instead of the correct flint-lock musket. He doesn't lean on the wrong plow either. Instead of a plow from Virginia, the one that completes the scene now is the correct New England model.

The old representation of a minute man was based on the Concord, Massachusetts, statue executed by Daniel Chester French. The details of French's original sculpture, which Felix W. deWeldon interpreted for the National Guard Association building in 1966, were historically inaccurate. Those errors have been corrected in the new *Minute Man* by Philadelphia sculptor Evanglos Frudakis, part of the new facilities for the National Guard Association that opened in 1991. "Since we're a historical society, we really should get it right," explains museum curator John Listman.

It looks as if the organization is getting a number of other things right, too. Rather than featuring only the Revolutionary War period, as it had in the past, the museum has expanded its focus to encompass American militia history from pre-Revolutionary times to Desert Storm. Five additional wars have been represented in six diorama: the Civil War, the Spanish-American War, World War I, the Pacific and Atlantic theaters of World War II, and the Korean War.

These dioramas form the centerpiece of the "Medals of Honor Gallery." The gallery, with state-of-the-art audio and visual components, tells the story of Medal of Honor recipients. Exhibits also dramatize the part each state and territorial militia has played in American history. Every state is represented with at least one artifact, such as a uniform, medal, weapon, photo, document, or portrait of a prominent person.

Adjacent to the museum is a research library that displays select books and other documents relating to militia history.

More Military Sites

Embassy Row

Anderson House Museum

As General Washington and Major General Rochambeau prepare for battle, the drummer boy beats a tattoo, soldiers march, and horse-drawn caissons rumble. On the river, French navy officer Comte de Grasse commands his fleet of warships.

In this museum house, one of the country's finest collections of miniature soldiers continues to play out the most dramatic moments of the Revolutionary War. Over 2,000 pieces are displayed in dioramas in the Reception hall of the opulent Anderson House. Collected from many sources over a 40-year period, the individual pieces were made by the best American, English, and French craftsmen in the field.

Many of the miniatures were created by an artist who referred to family portraits and other pictorial sources. Rather than being mere toys, these are actual sculptures. Among the most outstanding are those representing American heroes, including George Washington, Lightfoot Harry Lee, Alexander Hamilton, and Henry Knox.

Most of the scenes depicted in the miniature displays illustrate the role French officers played in helping us win in our struggle against Great Britain. This focus on the French stems from the fact that the Anderson House serves as headquarters of the Society of The Cincinnati, made up of lineal male descendants of commissioned officers who served in the Continental Army or Navy during the Revolution. When the society was founded in 1783, the first members invited the officers in Rochambeau's army and de Grasse's fleet to join. The French contingent continues to be part of the society today.

A national museum of relics of the American Revolution, the Anderson House also displays an outstanding collection of portraits. Among these are paintings by Gilbert Stuart, including his portrait of Captain Jacob Shubert, and John Trumbull's portrait of George Washington. Related artifacts on display include swords, medals, and historically important works of glass, silver, and porcelain.

For more information on the Anderson House, see **Antiques**, **Gardens**, **Literature**, and **Music**.

The Mall

National Air and Space Museum

Although many of the air and space craft displayed at the Air and Space Museum demonstrate America's technological prowess, some artifacts can also be considered military successes. The aircraft are located in four different galleries:

World War II, Gallery 205

- *North American P-51 "Mustang."* Because of their range, Mustangs were among the first to escort heavy bomber missions deep into Germany during World War II. Primarily used for reconnaissance and ground support missions, the plane came in at low altitudes to strafe train troops and enemy installations.

• *Mitsubishi A6M5.* The primary Japanese naval fighter throughout the war.

• *Macchi C.202 Folgore.* The primary fighter for the Italian Regia Aeronautical.

• *Martin B-26B Marauder Flak Bait.* The fast and rugged U.S.A.A.F. medium bomber, which flew 202 missions, the greatest number of any Allied bomber in Europe.

World War I Aviation, Gallery 209

• *Albatros D va.* The main German fighter from 1916 until Armistice Day, this aircraft was built in greater numbers than any other German fighter. It is one of two in existence.

• *Fokker D-VII.* The famous German fighter plane that could hold a steep climb without stalling. This made the plane a lethal weapon in rear attacks from below, since it could attain and maintain a high altitude from which to drop down on unsuspecting Allied aircraft. The Allies specified that the aircraft be turned over to them as part of the armistice terms.

• *SPAD XIII.* One of the most documented World War I aircraft in existence. The aircraft XIII was flown by many Allied aces, including Eddie Rickenbacker. This particular plane was assigned to Captain A. Raymond Brooks of the U.S. 22d Aero Squadron and is credited with three kills.

Jet Aviation, Gallery 106

• *Messerschmitt Me 262 Schwalbe.* The world's first operational jet fighter, powered by two Junkers Jumo 109-004 1,980-pound thrust engines. Of the 1,443 built, only 330 became operational.

• *Lockheed XP-80 "Lulu Belle."* A prototype of the P-80 "Shooting Star," which was the first operational jet fighter to be produced in full quantity in the United States.

• *McDonnell FH-1 "Phantom."* The first regular shipboard jet fighter powered by two Westinghouse J-30-WE-20 1,600-pound thrust engines.

Looking at Earth, Gallery 110

• *Lockheed U-2C.* The high-altitude (70,000 foot) reconnaissance aircraft first flown in 1955.

• *de Havilland DH-4.* The only U.S. plane to serve in combat as a bomber and observation plane, with the U.S. Army Air Service.

In November 1991 the exhibit "Legend, Memory and the Great War in the Air" opened. Five fighters and a bomber flown during World War I have been painstakingly restored. Included among the treasures is a Fokker D. VII, Pfalz D.XII, SPAD XIII, Voison VIII LA.P, Albatros D.Va, and the Sopwith 7F.1 SNIPE. Four aircraft engines, a dozen airplane models, and a fascinating collection of equipment and material complete this historic account of the first widespread military use of the airplane.

National Museum of American History

Thanks to its expansion program, begun in 1991, the Military Hall of the museum now exhibits artifacts from each of America's great wars. Where previously the collection covered the American Revolution, it now includes the Civil War, World War I, World War II, and the Korean and Vietnam wars.

Although most of the weapons, uniforms, and other artifacts are displayed behind glass, some objects are within reach, with ropes discouraging hands-on contact. Because of this accessibility, you get the feeling that you can step into history. This is particularly true with the gunboat *Philadelphia,* and the various American Revolutionary War cannon.

Highlights from the Revolutionary War:

- *Gunboat Philadelphia.* Part of the fleet Benedict Arnold had hastily constructed to contest Britain's plan to isolate the colonies by capturing Lake Champlain.
- *12-pound carronade.* Illustrates a different concept in warfare. In contrast to long-range cannon, this short-range piece of artillery was used to fight at close range. To compensate for the fact that colonists couldn't shoot well, this weapon allowed them to deliver heavy wallops to enemy ships, battering and knocking down their masts.
- *Seventeenth-century bronze cannon.* Cast in the Netherlands in 1631. Since the colonists got their weapons from various countries, it's typical of those used during the Revolutionary War.
- *George Washington's Yorktown tent.* Probably made in 1776. The general used the tent at Valley Forge before huts were built. Occasionally it was displayed on the grounds of the Custis-Lee Mansion in the early nineteenth century. Washington's adopted grandson Custis gave it to the United States in 1844.
- *George Washington's uniform, camp stool, camp kit.* His sword is on display in the Ceremonial Court.

Foggy Bottom

Vietnam Veteran's War Memorial

Years from now, when historians study the impact of the Vietnam War on twentieth-century America, one of their sources will be the offerings to the dead left at the Vietnam Memorial.

Vietnam War Memorial

The objects, gathered from the base of the granite slabs that bear the names of those killed or missing in action, are being preserved by the National Park Service. Stored already in metal drawers and cabinets are tens of thousands of offerings: medals, candles, statues of saints, dog tags, stuffed animals, combat boots, flags, letters, and poems.

When the Vietnam Veteran's War Memorial was dedicated in 1982, no one had any idea that it would have such an impact. Millions of people have since made their pilgrimage to what has become a national shrine. Many come to locate one special name from among the 58,132 engraved on the two 246-foot-long walls of the V-shaped monument. Some make a rubbing of the name as a memento. If the name is positioned too high on the wall for them to reach, Park Service employees give a hand. Climbing on tall ladders, they make the rubbing, framing the name on a page that is printed with information about the memorial. Included is an explanation of why the names are not in alphabetical order: they are inscribed in "the order they were taken from us."

Although popular, the monument is not without controversy. When the design of the young architectural student Maya Ying Lin was selected, some objected, calling the abstract black monument a "black gash of shame and sorrow." Unlike traditional memorials that make patriotic statements about war, this memorial, critics felt, made a nihilistic statement. By doing so instead of bestowing glory on those who had died in the war, critics argued, it degraded the dead. The objectors asked that the memorial be constructed above ground instead of embedded in it, and that the stone be white and not black.

A compromise was reached. Patriotic, realistic, and heroic elements—a 50-foot pole for an American flag, and a realistic statue of three soldiers on patrol—were added at the site, and the memorial itself was built as planned.

Often at the memorial you'll see Vietnam War veterans looking up the names of comrades killed or missing in action. To help them cope with their powerful emotions, veterans groups have set up tents nearby. These groups, which provide information about soldiers who remain missing in action, also conduct a 24-hour vigil at the memorial.

Beyond

Arlington National Cemetery
Arlington, Virginia

Arlington National Cemetery was created because of the need to bury those who died in the Civil War.

Shortly before that war, the Union Army commandeered the Custis-Lee estate, which had been the home of Robert E. Lee, who married Mary Anne Randolph Custis, the great-granddaughter of Martha Washington. Arlington House became the headquarters for the defense of Washington.

Under an act of Congress, a commission was set up to assess insurrectionary property and to tax it. Regulations required that title holders pay tax personally. Since General Lee was serving in the Confederate Army, this meant that Mrs. Lee was required to travel behind enemy lines to Alexandria to pay the taxes.

Mrs. Lee, however, was an invalid confined to a wheelchair. An agent was sent in her place, but the payment was refused and the estate was offered for sale at a public auction. The tax commissioners, the only bidders, purchased the property for government use. Owned by the government and used as a military installation, Arlington came under the jurisdiction of the quartermaster general, Brigadier General Montgomery Meigs.

Some suggest that Meigs, who considered Southerners who left the Union to be traitors, was determined to wreak his revenge on General Lee. When Meigs was given the task of surveying sites for use as a national burial ground, he chose the land immediately surrounding Arlington House, though there were many better-suited plots on the 1,100-acre tract. "It was clear that Meigs's intention was to bury soldiers in the immediate proximity of Arlington House, rendering the mansion uninhabitable should the Lee family ever attempt to return," writes James Edward Peters in *Arlington National Cemetery: Shrine to America's Heroes.*

To further doom the property as a residence, Meigs ordered that a ten-foot-high burial vault be constructed in Mrs. Lee's rose garden. Into this vault were put the remains of 2,111 unknown soldiers found in trenches and battlefields. This memorial to "the Unknown Dead of the Civil War" can be seen today among the roses that Robert E. Lee picked each morning for flowers to place beside his daughters' breakfast plates.

In addition to this famous memorial at Arlington National Cemetery, Civil War buffs can see other sites that relate to the war. Foremost is Arlington House itself, the Robert E. Lee Memorial. Restored in 1925, the mansion shows something of how life was lived just prior to the Civil War. Some of the original furnishings have been returned, including a ceiling lantern, china, silver, glassware, serving tables, marble mantels, Victorian parlor furniture, and paintings, including the Revolutionary War scene *The Battle of Monmouth, New Jersey.*

For 35 years after the end of the Civil War, Arlington was considered a Union Cemetery. Although many Confederate soldiers had been buried on the tract, their graves could not be decorated, and family members were sometimes even denied entrance.

At the dedication of the Confederate Monument by President Woodrow Wilson in 1914, 3,000 veterans of both the Union and the Confederacy place wreaths on graves to symbolize the reconciliation between North and South. The remains of Confederate soldiers who had been buried elsewhere in Arlington and at national cemeteries in Alexandria and at the Soldiers' Home in Washington were reinterred in circles around the Confederate Monument.

The monument, created by renowned sculptor and war veteran Moses Ezekiel, is rich in symbols. The 32-foot female figure at its top, which represents the South, dramatizes the biblical passage inscribed at her feet: "And they shall beat their swords into plowshares and their spears into pruning hooks." In one hand she holds a laurel wreath and in the other a pruning hook and plow stock.

Friezes contain more symbols: One re-creates in bronze 14 shields, depicting the coats of arms of the 13 Confederate states and Maryland, which supported the South during the war. Below, another frieze depicts Confederate soldiers leaving for and returning from war. One section shows loved ones bidding them farewell, another relays the wounded returning. Elsewhere, a frieze depicting life-size figures of mythological gods and Southern soldiers dramatizes the effect of war on Southerners of all races.

Other monuments to Civil War heroes include the superb equestrian monument to Major General Philip Kearney, the tomb effigy of Major John Rodgers Meigs, and the bronze female figure that marks the grave of Brigadier General Richard L. Hoxie. The McClellan Arch, which was constructed as a tribute to the general whose wartime headquarters were at Arlington House, stands south of the main gate to the cemetery. (He is not buried at Arlington.) It bears two gold inscriptions of the general's words. In addition to these memorials and monuments, you'll find the gravesites of numerous Civil War heroes and heroines.

Among the most noteworthy gravestones:

- *John Leonard Clem.* He began his military career as a drummer boy at age nine and retired as a Major General 56 years later.
- *George Crook.* The tombstone of this veteran of Civil War and Indian campaigns depicts in bas-relief Apache chief Geronimo surrendering to the general in 1883.
- *Oliver Wendell Holmes.* Civil War veteran and Supreme Court Justice.
- *Juliet Opis Hopkins.* Florence Nightingale of the South.
- *David Dixon Porter.* Rear Admiral of the Navy, Civil War hero.
- *Philip Henry Sheridan.* Civil War general, General in Chief of the U.S. Army.
- *John Wheeler.* Confederate general, congressman, U.S. Army General.

At the end of the Civil War, 16,000 were buried at Arlington Cemetery. By 1957, the number had grown to 93,000, and by 1986, 200,000. Land holdings increased from the original 200 to 612 acres.

Arlington's stature also grew over the years. With many national heroes or their families choosing the cemetery as a final resting place, only limited space remains, and burials are controlled by government regulations.

The ceremonies held at Arlington Cemetery have contributed greatly to its honored status. Memorial Day observances, which began in 1868, continue today with programs that include wreath-laying, oratory, and music. In 1920, the Memorial Day crowd that had overflowed in the old amphitheater moved to the new Memorial Amphitheater for the day's programs. But of all ceremonies, none surpassed the 1921 interment of the unknown soldier of World War I in the Tomb of the Unknown Soldier.

The tomb, a simple 50-ton block of white marble, is inscribed with the words "Here rests in honored glory an American soldier known but to God." Reliefs carved on the side of the tomb depict the symbolic figure of Victory offering a palm branch to Valor while gently holding the hand of Peace.

Following the armistice, Americans commemorated their dead at local services throughout the country. But more was needed to adequately memorialize those who had been lost, especially the unidentified dead. Catering to this public sentiment, Congress in 1921 approved a resolution to symbolically bury all unknown soldiers. One unknown soldier would be chosen to represent all the others.

In elaborate ceremonies in France, one body was selected at random from among four bodies exhumed at Châlons-sur-Marne. This body was placed in a special casket, put aboard Admiral Dewey's flagship, the *Olympia*, and carried to America. In Washington, the unknown soldier lay in state in the U.S. Capitol, and 100,000 mourners paid their respects. Then, with full military honors, the remains were buried forever in the specially constructed Tomb of the Unknown Soldier. At the ceremony at Arlington prior to burial, representatives from the Allied nations paid tribute by awarding their country's highest medals. The medals are displayed in the adjacent trophy room.

Following the armistice that ended World War II, plans were made for the interment of another unknown soldier. But that action was delayed because of the hostilities in Korea. Finally, in 1956, unknown soldiers from both World War II and the Korean War were interred. On Memorial Day in 1984, the tomb received the body of an unknown soldier from the Vietnam War—again symbolizing all the unidentified casualties.

Guarding the tomb on a 24-hour basis is a single soldier from the Army's 1st Battle Group, Third Infantry Division, known as the Old Guard. He paces in precise steps back and forth before the tomb: he marches ten steps in one direction, stops for 30 seconds, and then shifts his rifle from one shoulder to the other and changes directions. Each hour on the half hour the guard is ceremoniously changed as one soldier goes off duty and another comes on.

Among other major monuments to twentieth-century heroes is an impressive equestrian statue of Field Marshal Sir John Dill, of England. Dill served in France during World War I and was sent to the United States in 1941 to serve as chief officer on the newly formed British-American Joint Chiefs of Staff. Upon Dill's untimely death in 1944, Congress authorized that he be buried in Arlington, an extraordinary honor for a foreign soldier.

Also of note are the memorials to more recent heroes: one for the servicemen killed in Beirut and another for those who died during the attempt to rescue American hostages held in Iran in 1980.

Gravesites of World War I and II heroes include those of:

- *Henry Harley "Hap" Arnold.* American military aviation pioneer.
- *Omar Nelson Bradley.* Five-star general, World War II's "GI General."
- *George Scratchley Brown.* World War II fighter pilot.

- *Claire Lee Chennault.* Commander of the Flying Tigers of World War II.
- *Jacob Loucks Devers.* World War II Sixth Army Commander.
- *William Joseph "Wild Bill" Donovan.* World War I hero, World War II spymaster.
- *William Frederick Halsey, Jr.* Fleet Admiral of the United States Navy.
- *William D. Leahy.* Five-star fleet admiral of the Navy during World War I.
- *John Archer Lejeune.* World War I field commander.
- *George C. Marshall.* Five-star general.
- *Audie Murphy.* World War I's most decorated soldier, later an actor.
- *John J. "Black Jack" Pershing.* General of the Armies, the only man besides George Washington to hold the rank.
- *Hyman G. Rickover.* Admiral and "Father of the Nuclear Navy."

Garber Facility
Suitland, Maryland

This facility, which serves as storehouse for the National Air and Space Museum, preserves veteran aircraft from both world wars. Many rare planes, some the only remaining examples of their type, fill 14 warehouses. On specially arranged tours, visitors see the highlights.

The planes here have been preserved and reconditioned. For some visitors, that makes a trip here like stepping back into the action—or newsreels—of the war years.

Each aircraft at the Garber Facility has a story behind it. Some played historic roles or are noted for a particular accomplishment. Others represent a technological milestone in aeronautical development. These are important from a military viewpoint:

- *Boeing-Stearman N2S-5 "Kaydet."* The last standard biplane produced for the U.S. armed forces. Thousands of military pilots in the 1930s and 1940s got their first taste of flying in a Kaydet. More than 10,000 were supplied to the U.S. Army Air Forces, the Navy, and to foreign nations for training purposes between 1936 and the end of World War II.

- *Grumman F6F-3 "Hellcat."* The plane that downed more than 75 percent of Japanese aircraft destroyed in aerial combat by Navy carrier pilots was introduced to the Pacific fleet in late 1943 and became the standard fighter of the Navy's fast carrier force. An unusual mechanism allows the wings to fold back against the fuselage. This feature allowed a greater number of airplanes to fit on each carrier.

- *Vought F4U-ID "Corsair."* One of the most successful piston-engine fighters, and the last produced for the United States. The plane, with its

Boeing B-29 "Enola Gay," Garber Facility (*Courtesy of National Air and Space Museum*)

distinctive inverted gull wing, rolled off production lines for 13 years. It entered combat service in the Solomon Islands in 1943 and served throughout the rest of World War II as well as the Korean War.

• *Boeing B-29 Superfortress "Enola Gay."* The most famous aircraft at the facility, it represents the pinnacle of World War II bomber technology and symbolizes the birth of the nuclear age. On August 6, 1945, the "Enola Gay" dropped the first atomic bomb used in war.

• *"Hawker Hurricane" Mark IIC.* Britain's first multi-gun, single-set monoplane fighter. During the dark days of 1940, the "Hawker Hurricane" bore the brunt of Britain's defense against the Luftwaffes's aerial armada. It is the first combat aircraft with retractable landing gear, and the first to exceed 300 m.p.h. in level flight.

• *Lockheed P-38J "Lightning."* One of the most versatile fighters of World War II. First flown in 1939, the unique twin-boom, twin-engine craft was produced throughout the war and fought in every theater.

• *Messerschmitt Me 163B "Komet."* The first operational rocket-powered aircraft to see combat in World War II. While it could approach 600 m.p.h. in level flight, it burned its dangerously volatile fuel so fast that it could fly under power for only about ten minutes. Once its fuel was exhausted, it would glide home. And with no room for landing gear, it made a hard landing that often caused remaining traces of fuel to explode. Of about 350 built, this is one of the few that remains.

• *North American F-86A "Sabre."* The first U.S. sweptwing jet fighter. When it was introduced, the plane ended the contest for air superiority during the Korean War. By the end of the war, F-86s had shot down nearly 800 Migs and established a victory ratio of better than ten to one.

• *Republic P-47D "Thunderbolt."* The heaviest and most powerful single-engine fighter of World War II. Fighting in virtually every theater of the war from 1943 to the end, the "Thunderbolt" served as a fighter bomber and bomber escort. Strong and fast, it was deceptively maneuverable in a roll and could outdrive any opponent.

• *Grumman TBF-1 "Avenger."* One of the best torpedo bombers of World War II. Introduced during the Battle of Midway in 1942, it was the first U.S. Navy aircraft to carry a torpedo load within its fuselage. The "Avenger" could carry a single 2,000-pound torpedo or four 500-pound bombs, and it could land on the smallest aircraft carriers.

Although tours of the Garber Facility are usually by reservation only, once a year the doors open to the public during the annual Wings and Things open house. During the spring, this free weekend event gives visitors a chance to view the collection and to watch and talk with museum technicians who are working on historic aircraft.

Pentagon
Arlington, Virginia

Nowhere can you get a more sweeping perspective of twentieth-century warfare than under the Pentagon's roof. On regularly scheduled tours, you walk some of the 17½ miles of corridors that link the 23,000 employees working in the world's largest office building. Guiding the way is a serviceman or servicewoman who relays a wealth of information on the various ribbons, medals, streamers, flags, photos, paintings, models, and artifacts you see, including the pen Eisenhower used to sign the Japanese surrender documents. There are also endless portraits of famous military leaders, including each Commander in Chief. From this overwhelming abundance of information, organized into exhibits for each of the four service branches, you can add greatly to your understanding of both world wars and of subsequent conflicts.

Probably no display gives a better overview of World War II than the *Life* Collection of Art from World War II. About 100 works from the collection of 1,500 images are exhibited on a rotating basis. The collection grew with *Life* magazine's support when funding for the American War Art Program, established by the U.S. Army, ran out in 1943. In 1960, Time, Inc., presented 1,056 artworks to the Department of Defense.

The *Life* collection is the nucleus of the larger American Collection, which also includes pictures depicting the Army's medical efforts, donated by Abbot Laboratories. Models of ships, submarines, and aircraft also dramatize the war. The aircraft displayed include the Bell XS-1, the SR-Blackbird, the B-29 Superfortress, and the C-5A Galaxy.

In the Navy corridor, you see models of the guided missile frigate USS *Oliver Hazard Perry*; the nuclear-powered USS *Carl Vinson*, and the USS *Tarawa*, and amphibious assault ship. Each model comes with fascinating

Fort Ward, Alexandria, Virginia (*Courtesy of Alexandria Convention and Visitors Bureau, photo by Nina Tisara*)

details, as told by your guide—often with patriotic fervor. The guide's banter, which is packed with factual detail, includes quantities of trivia, too. You can test your knowledge and possibly learn something new. In any event, you'll most likely be entertained, if by nothing else than the fact that for the entire length of the tour your guide walks backward. Without a backward glance, he or she somehow avoids bumping into anything or anyone.

Fort Ward
Alexandria, Virginia

At the end of 1862, Washington, D.C., was the most heavily defended location in the Western hemisphere. A ring of 68 forts, 93 batteries mounting over 900 guns, and 30 miles of trenches and roads circled the city. The fifth largest fort in this defense system was Fort Ward, with its 35 guns mounted in five bastions. A model of nineteenth-century military design and engineering, the fort today offers a rare look into Washington's Civil War history.

About 90 percent of the fort's original earthwork walls remain. As you follow a 45-minute self-guided walk, you'll also see the fort's northwest bastion, restored to its 1864 appearance.

Your walk should begin at the museum, housed in a headquarters building reconstructed by historians with the help of Mathew Brady photographs.

After a visit to the museum, with its Civil War artifacts, look into the adjacent officers' hut, which shows how comfortably some officers lived. Then continue to the ceremonial gate that once stood at the entrance of the fort. The arch of the gate is adorned with a castle, the symbol of the Corps of Engineers who designed the fort. Note the cannonballs on each of the columns.

By following the trail that stretches atop the earthen walls, you'll reach the restored northwest bastion. Part of the original wall that once surrounded the fort has been reconstructed at this site. You can look down 20 feet or more from the parapet to the ditch that surrounds the bastion.

To give you an idea of the armaments, the bastion has been armed with reproductions of the guns listed in the 1864 table of armament for the fort: three 4.5-inch rifles, two 24-pound howitzers, and one 6-pounder gun. Before you return to the ceremonial gate, you'll pass a marker showing where a Parrott rifle once stood; the gun could fire a 100-pound projectile a distance of five miles.

Although the Confederates never came within firing range of Fort Ward, some students of the Civil War believe that had it not been for the Union forts, the South might have won the war. Because of the importance of Fort Ward, the city of Alexandria allocated necessary funds to preserve the historic fort in time for the 1961 Centennial of the Civil War. The Fort Ward Museum and Historic Site are set on 40 acres of woods, verdant with old trees.

U.S. Marine Corps Memorial
Arlington, Virginia

The battle rages below as six Marines plant the U.S. colors on Mount Suribachi, on the island of Iwo Jima, on February 23, 1945. Even with the capture of the 55-foot peak, however, the fighting continues. Before the Americans win control of the strategically important island, one month will have passed and 6,000 Marines will have died.

The memorial adjacent to Arlington Cemetery freezes in bronze one of the most famous moments in World War II. The 100-ton sculpture, which is the largest cast bronze figure in the world, was inspired by the Pulitzer Prize–winning photo of the flag raising taken by UPI photographer Joe Rosenberg. When sculptor Felix deWeldon got the commission to translate the famous photo into bronze, he knew the work would have to be of heroic proportions. Because of its size, every aspect had to be painstakingly detailed—from the expressions on the faces of the men to their clothing and equipment. To create the necessary detail, deWeldon used as live models the three Marines from the picture who had survived the battle. For the other three, who had died on Iwo Jima, he used photos and all available physical data.

At the base of the memorial, burnished on polished black granite, are the names and dates of major Marine Corps engagements. Of the hundreds of battles in which the Marines fought for two centuries, Iwo Jima is but one. However, as author James Edward Peters writes in *Arlington National Cemetery*, the memorial "vividly illustrates the courage, determination, and skill with which Marines have performed their duties."

The flag planted on Iwo Jima almost a half century ago continues to fly today at the U.S. Marine Corps Memorial. Since 1961, when President John F. Kennedy signed a proclamation ordering this observance, the flag has flown for 24 hours a day. In the summer at twilight, you can see the Marine Corps Drum and Bugle Corps marching at the ceremonies held on the parade grounds adjacent to the memorial.

Washington Navy Yard
Southeast Washington

One of the biggest surprises for the military buff is the extensive collection of naval artifacts on view at this museum on the grounds of the Navy Yard. Housed in the nineteenth-century building that served as a gun factory, the Navy Museum brings together under one 600-foot-long roof the highlights of U.S. Naval history.

Since its opening in 1963, the museum has been collecting objects that chronicle the history of the U.S. Navy from the Revolution to the present.

Seen in their entirety, the models, documents, fine art, tools, equipment, and items associated with some of the Navy's greatest heroes give a unique view of our nation's military history. Of 5,000 objects spanning 200 years of history, the most impressive are those associated with the Revolutionary War.

HIGHLIGHTS:

Eighteenth and Nineteenth Century

• *Model of John Paul Jones's ship, the* Bonhommme Richard. It was on this ship, during a bloody four-hour battle with HMS *Serapis,* that Jones said "I have not yet begun to fight."

• *Fully rigged foremast fighting top from the USS* Constitution. The museum got this portion of the vessel that was nicknamed "Old Ironsides" in 1976, when the original top was replaced with a reconstructed one. The figures on the platform dramatize the close range at which battles were fought at sea: A Marine sharpshooter prepares to fire a musket as a sailor gets ready to hurl a grenade.

• *Reproduction of a portion of the* Constitution's *gun deck.* On display on the deck are two 24-pounder cannons with block and tackle, nineteenth-century weapons, and shipboard objects like leather buckets, board pikes, and harpoons.

Civil War artifacts are also on display. One of the most treasured objects is the original half-model of the *Monitor,* the Union's first ironclad vessel. On it, you can see the builder's original plating marks and notations. The *Monitor,* designed by John Ericksson, featured a revolving turret that protected its two guns during its famous battle against the CSS *Virginia* (Merrimac).

A second Civil War highlight is the shell that lodged in the sternpost of the USS *Kearsarge* during the 1864 battle against the CSS *Alabama.* Thanks in part to the fact that the shell did not explode, the *Kearsarge* won the day.

Although the museum at the old Navy Yard boasts a number of outstanding Civil War and Revolutionary War treasures, its greatest strength lies in its twentieth-century collection, which includes guns, bombs, shells, ship models, a gun mount, a bathyscaphe, and a fighter airplane.

Twentieth Century

• *Mark-6 moored contact mine.* One of 56,511 laid by U.S. ships in the North Sea during World War I to neutralize the U-boat threat.

• *14-inch railway gun model.* Designed and built in 1917 to counter the German army's use of artillery mounted on trains. Adapted from the 14-

inch guns used on battleships, the Railway Gun boasted a range of 20 miles. Its accuracy and power severed German railroad and communication lines and thus hastened the end of the war.

• *5-inch 38-caliber gunmount from the cruiser* Reno *of World War II.* This surface and anti-aircraft weapon, designed for use at sea, was noted for its accuracy and rapid firing capability.

• *Corsair Vought F4U.* The first fighter plane to exceed speeds of 400 m.p.h. The gull-winged plane, developed as a carrier plane, has been restored to look like the one Jolly Rogers Squadron's Commander Tommy Blackburn flew. Blackburn shot down 11 planes during World War II; the Corsair is credited with 2,140 kills.

• *Training version of the Japanese "Baka Bomb" used on kamikaze missions.* With the bomb slung under his airplane and the nose of the bomber filled with explosives, the pilot guided his rocket-propelled weapon at speeds up to 550 m.p.h., crashing it into his target.

• *40mm Quad Gunmount.* A rapid-fire anti-aircraft gun used on ships in World War II. Between October 1944 and February 1945, the 40-mm gun was credited with shooting down half of all Japanese aircraft. You can climb aboard to train and elevate the barrels.

• *Bathyscaphe* Trieste. A submersible developed in 1959 to locate the wreckage of sunken submarines. Developed by the famous Swiss hot-air balloonist Auguste Piccard, the *Trieste* descended 36,000 feet into the Marianas Trench, the deepest place on earth. On a subsequent mission in the Atlantic, the *Trieste* discovered the wreckage of the nuclear submarine *Thresher,* which sank in 1963.

Other Military Sites

With numerous military bases in the capital, sightseeing opportunities abound. To see an impressive collection of planes, tanks, machine guns, and more, visit the Marine Corps Air Ground Museum. The Quantico National Cemetery is nearby, with its memorials to heroes.

Over at the U.S. Army Ordnance Museum, you can tour hundreds of exhibits, including tanks of various designs. The museum is actually a laboratory where students from the Army Ordnance School study the evolution of the tools of war.

At the new Jewish War Veterans National Memorial Museum, Archives, and Library, you'll survey the contributions of Jewish war veterans from the 1630s to the present.

In addition to Fort Ward, you can also visit various other Civil War forts in the area. Among these is Fort Washington. Here you can hike for three miles to see the 1808 fort and the eight batteries that surround it. The National Park Service, which maintains the park, offers tours and sponsors historic reenactments of Civil War life at the fort.

Although there are many memorials to Union officers in the parks of Washington, the Confederate Embassy is the only shrine commemorating the Confederacy. In the Victorian mansion that houses the embassy's library and museum you'll see such artifacts as oil paintings of Robert E. Lee and Stonewall Jackson, a marble bust of Robert E. Lee, furniture that once belonged to Jefferson Davis, and numerous battle flags and rare prints. By special arrangement, groups can enjoy mint juleps or a Southern-style dinner in the antebellum ambience of the old mansion.

Chapter 6

Music and Theater

Ivory Figurine from the Miller Collection, (*Courtesy of Library of Congress, Music Division*)

From the beginning, dramas have played on the Washington stage—on both sides of the footlights. Like actors, the capital's colorful characters who perform in courtrooms, chambers, and board rooms often harbor as great an appreciation for the dramatic as those on theater stages. Little wonder that theater has been an important part of the city's life.

Washington's theatrical roots run deep. Shortly after Congress moved to its new capital city in 1800, two theaters opened their doors: The United States Theater, housed in Blodgett's Hotel on Pennsylvania Avenue, staged its first performance in 1800, and the Washington Theater, at 11th and C Streets, sold its first tickets in 1804. When the National Theater came on the scene in 1835, the city's theaters rivaled the best in the country.

Star performers booked for capital theaters included Joe Jefferson III, whose version of *Rip van Winkle* made him America's most beloved actor; Junius Brutus Booth and his son Edwin, famed for their roles in Shakespeare's *Richard III*; Jenny Lind, the Swedish nightingale; and the wildly acclaimed Mademoiselle Celine Celeste, a dancer and pantomimist. In addition, the city welcomed a roster of comedians, rope dancers, hornpipers, magicians, acrobats, lilliputians, giants, tattooed men, clowns, and trained animals, including equestrian acts.

But the luminaries in the audience often rivaled those on stage. Theater managers understood human nature. They invited the best draws in town and seated them where they could best be seen. Music often heralded the arrival of celebrities, particularly the president of the United States. Beginning with President James Monroe, who entertained the visiting Marquis de Lafayette at the Washington Theater in 1819, every president has attended theater at least once in the capital city.

Two theaters remain from the early days. The National Theater was reincarnated six times, having burned to the ground on five occasions. And vintage-1862 Ford's Theater, closed as a theater for over 100 years following Lincoln's assassination, reopened in 1968 after restoration.

At the National Theater, you can relive the night in 1850 when Jenny Lind performed before an adoring audience. Washington's elite—including President Millard Fillmore, his entire cabinet, Supreme Court justices, and a roll call of national heroes—crowded the theater. But of all the luminaries, one stood out: Daniel Webster. To the astonishment and delight of the packed house, the renowned statesman stood up and sang along with the star when she reached the chorus of "Hail Columbia." At the end of the song, Webster bowed and Lind curtsied. As the audience applauded wildly, the two continued exchanging gestures, bowing and curtsying at least ten times.

Although quieter in his appreciation of the theater, Abraham Lincoln was no less enthusiastic. He visited the National Theater and Ford's Theater often. Particularly during the Civil War, Lincoln used the theater as a diversion from his cares.

At the National Theater, Lincoln and his son Tad became acquainted with manager Leonard Grover. In fact, Tad on occasion borrowed props and costumes from Grover, using them for productions in the playhouse he had set up in the White House. Once he even surprised his father, who was sitting in his box, by appearing unannounced on stage.

You may hear the echo of Lincoln's laughter at Ford's Theater, where he and his wife attended the April 14, 1865, performance of the comedy *Our American Cousin*. As we know, his laughter this time was cut short by the sound of a gunshot; then cries, shouts, and wails. The doors of Ford's Theater closed the same year.

Since then, other theaters have come and gone. In 1971, in memory of another assassinated president, the John F. Kennedy Center for the Performing Arts opened on the banks of the Potomac River. Six stages in the edifice offer concerts, plays, ballets, musicals, motion pictures, and other entertainments.

Elsewhere in the capital city, legitimate and small theaters flourish. For a complete listing of the offerings at the 50 or more stages in the city, refer to the *Washington Post* or *Washington Times* weekend editions.

Musical programs outnumber other forms of entertainment. Washington is a city of music: At least 60 organizations present concerts on the stages of the Kennedy Center or in alternative spaces. Few cities boast more ideal locations for concerts. A wealth of public buildings and parks serve as settings, many described at the end of this chapter.

You'll see some of Washington's best music and theater exhibits and scenes by following the **Highlight Walk** and venturing on your own to **More Music and Theater** sites in Dupont Circle, Foggy Bottom, Georgetown–Embassy Row, the Mall, and beyond.

Highlight Walk Downtown–Capitol Hill

Sometimes a theater offers more than a stage for performers. Because of their history or status, some theaters in Washington rank as sightseeing destinations in themselves. Other sites hold surprises for the music lover and the theater lover. With careful timing you can enjoy a rare day that takes you behind the scenes of Washington's theatrical and musical world. Tours of two of Washington's most historic theaters combine with a chance to see an exhibit of Shakespeare folios and an Elizabethan stage. If you're

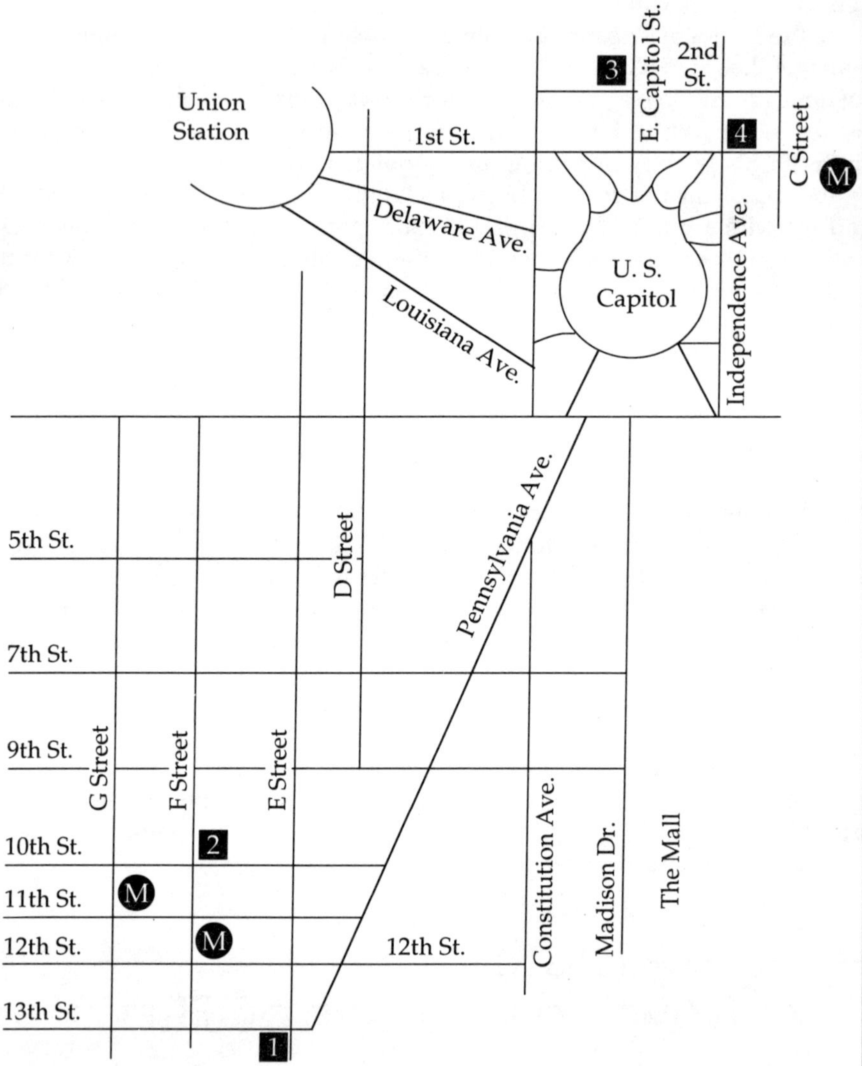

M Metro

1. National Theater, 1325 E Street NW
2. Ford's Theater, 511 10th Street NW
3. Folger Shakespeare Library, 201 East Capital Street SE
4. Library of Congress, Music Division, Madison Annex, Independence Avenue and 1st Street SE

Route

From the Metro Center subway station (12th & F Street exit), walk south on 13th Street to E Street and the National Theater. After your visit, continue along E Street to 10th Street and Ford's Theater. Next head for Capitol Hill via Metro subway from the 11th and G Street station. Get off at the Capitol South station and follow First Street SE to East Capitol Street and the Folger Shakespeare Library. Retrace your steps along First Street SE to Independence Avenue and the Library of Congrèss Madison Annex. Exit via the library's C Street entrance, which is diagonally opposite the Capitol South Metro subway station.

part of a group and make special arrangements, you'll also get a rare look at one of the country's finest flute collections.

1. National Theater

While washing their clothes in the creek that once flowed beneath the National Theater, two actors quarreled. One shot the other, the story goes, burying his weapon in the dirt. Almost 100 years later, in 1974, when the theater was being remodeled, the gun surfaced. It was sent to the Smithsonian Institution, where experts dated it as coming from the late nineteenth century.

This story is but one of many you hear as your guide takes you behind the scenes of Washington's oldest theater. First built in 1835, the theater that now stands in the heart of downtown Washington is the fourth on the site. The current 1885 structure replaces three previous theaters that burned down and one that fell down during a Wild West show.

A slide show gives visitors an overview of the National Theater's long history. Then you explore the house and its unusual decor. New York set designer Oliver Smith lent his expertise during the 1974 renovation. Drawing on a popular Regency-period palette, he chose robin's egg blue, coral, and melon shades for the walls and ceiling. Gilding adds a gleam to the flowers in the ceiling coffers and the frieze of horses' heads.

Continuing behind the scenes, you see the dressing and rehearsal rooms and an old-fashioned fly floor. Instead of relying on hydraulic lifts and cranes, this scenery-changing apparatus runs with manpower and rope.

2. Ford's Theater

This is one theater where the drama played offstage overshadows any performed behind the footlights. For here on that April night in 1865, Abraham Lincoln was assassinated when John Wilkes Booth fired his derringer. Today, 125 years later, you can almost smell the gunpowder. That's because every effort has been made to bring that night to life.

With a budget of $2,000,000 and three years of painstaking effort, the National Park Service oversaw the rebuilding of the theater section by section. The original crimson damask sofa once again stands in the presidential box. The George Washington etching hangs as it did in 1865, amidst the flags that decorate the box. Other pieces were reproduced using numerous sources, including Mathew Brady photographs, scraps of curtain from museum collections, and wallpaper reproduced from the original pattern of the manufacturer. Of all the reproductions, most touching is the rocking chair in which Lincoln sat. On tours, you see the rocker and the stage as he viewed it, framed by Nottingham lace curtains and brocade draperies.

In addition to joining a 15-minute tour that re-creates the fateful night, you can see the theater while enjoying a performance. As part of the interpretive program of the National Park Service, the theater once again stages contemporary plays and musicals.

Don't miss the downstairs museum of objects associated with Lincoln's assassination. The exhibition space, reopened in June 1990 after renovation, shows over 400 objects, including the derringer Booth fired. A display of historic playbills and tickets also shows you more about early theater in Washington.

3. Folger Shakespeare Library

Elizabethan England comes to life as you step inside this re-creation of a Shakespearean playhouse, which is part of the Folger Shakespeare Library. Although not an authentic reproduction, the Shakespeare Theater at the Folger imitates the roofless theater of Shakespeare's day. A charming canopy where a painted unicorn romps adds to the authenticity, as does the wood paneling and benches. From the two-tiered period-style stage, actors perform Shakespeare and other period plays.

The theater occupies only a portion of the Library structure. The Elizabethan-style Great Hall extends from the theater foyer. Here you see a wealth of Shakespearean memorabilia from the Folger Library's vast collection. Founded as a memorial to William Shakespeare, the collection now boasts over 275,000 volumes, plus playbills, costumes, photographs, oil paintings,

Folger Shakespeare Library, the Theatre (*Courtesy of The Folger Shakespeare Library*)

and other artworks, including statuary. But the stars of the collection are the 79 First Folio editions of Shakespeare's work.

For more information on the Folger Shakespeare Library, see **Literature**.

4. Library of Congress

In addition to books, this edifice—designed to reflect the breadth of our cultural ancestry—also shelters one of the greatest collections of music and music literature. Over four million pieces of music, 300,000 publications, and 350,000 sound recordings tell the story of the development of music in Western civilization. International in scope and spanning a millennium, the collection provides researchers with incomparable resources.

One of the music department's most interesting collections consists of 1,600 musical instruments donated by a physicist with a passion for collecting flutes, Dayton Clarence Miller. Miller, who died in 1941, collected not only flutes but related instruments, music, books, and art objects, including pictures and sculptures of flutists and composers.

By special arrangement, groups are sometimes shown Miller's fascinating cache of instruments and *objects d'art*. On such occasions, the curator pulls out drawers filled with flutes: flutes of carved ivory, of blue enamel, of cut glass with silver fittings, of antique metal studded with semiprecious stones. One made by Miller is of silver and gold. There are seventeenth and eighteenth-century jade flutes from China. For history buffs, the biggest thrill is seeing the flute probably given to James Madison by the Marquis de Lafayette during his 1813 visit to America. Others are impressed with the blue-and-white porcelain case that probably belonged to King Frederick II of Prussia.

Also on display in the music division collection is a mahogany violin case with marquetry embellishments made for King Ludwig II of Bavaria.

The Library of Congress boasts at least a dozen other special collections, including those related to George Gershwin, Jascha Heifetz, Geraldine Farrar, Liszt-Rosenthall, and Sergey Rachmaninoff. Groups can make special arrangements to see such treasures as the first printing of *The Star-Spangled Banner* and original manuscripts of Brahms, Mozart, Bach, and Hayden. Although most of the library's collection ordinarily can't be seen by the the casual visitor, some of the most famous holdings can be heard. Several times a year the Juilliard String Quartet plays the Stradivari violins, viola, and violoncello presented to the library by Mrs. Gertrude Clarke Whittail. After her donation, Mrs. Whittail established a foundation to provide funds for chamber music concerts so the general public could hear the instruments played.

For more information on the Library of Congress, see **Literature**.

More Music and Theater

Dupont Circle

Sumner School Museum and Archives

The recently restored 1872 Sumner School, with its peaked Victorian Gothic clocktower holds surprises for music lovers. Behind the weathered red brick walls, you'll discover three antique pianos, the likes of which you'll see nowhere else in Washington: a walnut, Art Nouveau–style upright grand piano with unique upholstered sound-conducting panels; a rare 1861 rosewood grand piano and pump organ; and a square Victorian grand piano dated 1860.

Musical notes of another sort emanate from the 1870 Swiss "Automaton" music box that still plays 25-inch diameter discs. With a little luck you'll get an attendant to play one of the discs from the catalogue of 70 tune sheets.

Foggy Bottom

Kennedy Center

At the Kennedy Center for the Performing Arts, visitors become actors in their own drama as they step inside a series of spectacular rooms. One, the Opera Lounge, rivals a stage set for a Viennese opera. Its Waterford chandelier, hung with 3,000 pieces of crystal, glitters beneath a 22-carat gold leaf ceiling, shedding light on a rich Bukhara rug and reproductions of Goya tapestries. A door off this lounge leads to another lounge, where Oriental lacquer screens and oil lamps from Sri Lanka gleam.

The one-hour tours of the house show participants the insides of three of the center's six theaters. Along the way, you see a museum's worth of tapestries, oil paintings, sculpture, murals, and artifacts. Highlights are the two Matisse tapestries given to the center by the people of France, and an alabaster vase, circa 2600 B.C., from Egypt.

Forty foreign countries presented the center with the treasures you see on the tour: the Great Foyer chandeliers from Sweden, 60-foot tall mirrors from Belgium, planters from India, rugs from Morocco, fiberwork sculpture from Brazil, and more.

Israel contributed the artwork and furnishings of the Concert Hall lounge. The room features a wall of carved musical instruments and words from the 150th Psalm, which begins "Praise Him with the sound of trumpets . . ." Overhead, in the colors of stained glass embellished with gold leaf, a ceiling mural depicts musical scenes from the Bible.

The nations of Africa constructed and decorated the African Lounge in the Opera House. The stunning room features a ceiling of geometric panels, fabric walls, a carpet the color of clay-rich earth, and a door carved by Nigerian artists from a 700-year-old tree. Artwork decorates the walls: Kente cloth from Senegal, tapestry and strip-weave fabric from the Ivory Coast.

The Clark Room, named after General George Clark of the Lewis and Clark expedition, boasts one of the area's finest collections of Boehm porcelain. Nine cases are filled with an aviary of beautifully fashioned birds, with fish, fox, owls, a tiger, and blooming flowers. Spotlighted in one case is a one-third size reproduction of the white swans that President Nixon presented to Chairman Mao on his trip to China.

The free Self-Guided Tour brochure lists other of the center's treasures, including the famous bronze bust of President John F. Kennedy.

For more information on the Kennedy Center, see **Literature**.

Georgetown–Embassy Row

Barney Studio House

With the completion of her Studio House in 1902, millionaire Alice Pike Barney finally had the stage she craved. Barney wrote plays and pageants for what she felt was a culturally deprived city; she directed and produced them on a raised area at one end of her drawing room.

An artist who had studied with James McNeill Whistler in Paris, Barney sought to import to Washington the artistic and intellectual life of Paris. Her husband, an Ohio millionaire, had built homes for her in Bar Harbor and on Rhode Island Avenue in Washington; he disapproved of her plans to build a Bohemian studio outside the city limits in the wilderness around Sheridan Circle. When he died, however, she was free to live the life she dreamed in her offbeat haven.

Today you see her romantic Spanish Renaissance–style studio furnished with heavy dark oak and pine pieces. More a stage set than a home, the studio is made up of a series of dramatic elements: a balcony supported by spiraling black columns festooned with grapes, leaves, and cupids; green quatrefoil windows; a floor-to-ceiling mirror; a reproduction of a German Renaissance marriage chest; and unusual Tiffany glass light fixtures.

You also learn about this theatrical pioneer, who founded the Sylvan Theater on the Washington Monument grounds and supported other artistic endeavors in Washington and Los Angeles. Mementos and artwork testify to the celebrities who visited Barney's studio house: the Barrymores, Caruso, Sarah Bernhardt, and President Theodore Roosevelt.

Dumbarton Oaks

Musical history was made in the Music Room of this Georgetown mansion. In a setting reminiscent of a Renaissance palace, world-famous composers premiered new compositions, renowned pianists serenaded, and dozens of the finest singers trilled and resonated.

The beauty of the room, kept constant over the years, tends to carry one back to the days when music filled the air. In 1938, Nadia Boulanger conducted the world premiere of Igor Stravinsky's *Dumbarton Oaks Concerto* among the fifteenth-century antiques and tapestries here. Aaron Copland conducted his world premiere of *Monet* beside the fireplace that once stood in a French château. Years before soprano Leontyne Price made her Metropolitan Opera debut, she sang while pianist-composer Samuel Barber played. A few years later, on her way to the Met, Joan Sutherland sang Handel as Paul Callaway conducted.

Other voices that echoed here include those of Montserrat Caballé, Eileen Farrell, and Judith Raskin. Tenors, baritones, and basses have included Ernst Haefliger, Hugues Cuenod, Peter Pears, Michel Senechal, Gearad Souzay, Dietrich Fischer-Dieskau, Justino Diz, Donald Gramm, and Doda Conrad. The most impressive memento of the glorious sounds that have filled Dumbarton Oaks is the grand piano that dominates the room. Polish pianist Jan

National Theater

Paderewski autographed the instrument after his performance here during his concert tour of Washington.

For more information on Dumbarton Oaks, see **Antiques**, **Gardens**, and **Literature**.

WASHINGTON NATIONAL CATHEDRAL

Of all concert stages, none outshine the Gothic splendor of Washington Cathedral. In this setting, where the colored light filtered through stained glass windows plays on carved stone, the music of voice, organ, and bell resounds.

On most Sundays, you can hear the 48 voices of the Cathedral Choir of Men and Boys, one of eight organs, a 53-bell carillon, and a 10-bell peal. The bass, tenor, and alto voices of 22 men blend with the treble voices of the 26 young boys. Together, the combined Cathedral Choir of Men and Boys sings the service anthems, motets, canticles, versicles, responses, psalms, and hymns on Sundays and during the week.

When the "thousand voices" of the recently enlarged and renovated Grand Organ sing, most feel the sound reverberating. The mighty Grand

Organ is a synthesis of the very best that all centuries of the finest organ-building experience could offer. Sunday afternoon organ recitals following the 4 P.M. Evensong are scheduled as visiting organists come to the cathedral.

Music lovers also thrill to the sounds of Washington Cathedral's other unique offering: the combination of both carillon and change-ringing bells. The cathedral is the only religious edifice in the world to house both.

The cast bronze bells in the carillon, which are tuned to the 53 notes of four-and-one-half octaves, are played from a keyboard on the floor of the bell chamber. When played Saturdays at 4:30 P.M., the melodies of the carillon sing for miles around. The best place for listening, however, is amidst the flowers of the Bishop's Garden. For more information, see **Gardens**.

On Sunday mornings, following the 11 A.M. service, you'll hear a second set of bells, the ten-bell ring. Unlike the carillon, which is designed to play hymns, the ten-bell ring is a complex system of bell ringing in which bells are rung in the order dictated by mathematical principles. Ringing sequences in which bells sound individually, as struck by the one person assigned to each, can take up to 3½ hours. The effect is musical to the trained ear, because when struck properly the sound is even and the beat becomes evident.

Music of a different sort fills the cathedral during its summer festival, when it presents 12 to 16 evenings of free concerts, ballet, and drama. At other times you can catch the voices of a visiting choir. Choral groups from around the country come to sing, so you can thrill to the sound of their music in this heavenly acoustical environment.

For information on the Cathedral, see **Antiques**, **Gardens**, and **Literature**.

The Mall

National Museum of American History

The Hall of Musical Instruments delights the ear and eye. Here the finest stringed instruments, antique harpsichords, chamber organs, and grand pianos can not only be seen but heard. For their chamber music programs, the staff moves choice instruments into a 180-seat theater, where you can hear quartets, trios, and large groups perform.

Even if you arrive when a performance isn't under way, you'll hear recordings of many of the instruments as you tour the exhibit. The Violin Treasures exhibit shows the work of four of the finest craftsmen of string instruments: Gaspero da Sallo de Brescia, Nicolò Amati, Giuseppe Guarneri, and Antonio Stradivari.

Taking the spotlight are two violins, a viola, and violoncello made by Stradivari between 1687 and 1709. Producing beautiful sounds was just part of the master violin-maker's skill. Stradivari also ornamented his pieces with consummate skill. Note the ivory inlays in the form of grapevines, cupids, and arrows. For contrast, he inlaid ebony sawdust in the cutout portions. The effect of dark and light ornamentations against the rich wood is stunning.

In 1991 a new exhibit opened in the Hall of Musical Instruments. Highlights include a forte-piano made in Salzburg in 1788 by Schmidt, a 1761 Parisian harpsichord by Stehlin, various eighteenth-century wind and brass instruments, stringed instruments by the great Tyrolean maker Stainer, and a pair of kettle drums. A new touch-screen-activated sound system offers visitors the opportunity to hear works by Mozart played on museum instruments by members of the Smithsonian's staff.

Jazz buffs delight in the museum's History of Jazz Collection, which shows some of the 200,000 music manuscripts, photographs, and art in the Duke Ellington archive. The jazz collection also includes trumpets of Dizzy Gillespie, Harry James, and Charlie Shavers; Hymie Schertzer's saxophone; Buddy Rich's drum set; and even the "famous door" of the Famous Door nightclub in New York City.

The museum pioneered in the development and publication of critically based record sets interpreting the history of jazz. More than 20 important albums, including *The Smithsonian Collection of Classic Jazz* and *Big Band Jazz*, have been issued. Books researched and written by staff members are also for sale.

For more information on the museum, see **Military**, **Science**, and **Technology**.

CONCERT STAGES

Among the most popular concert stages are Washington's famous landmarks. During the summer, military bands present musical programs almost every evening at either the Washington Monument, the U.S. Capitol, the Jefferson Memorial, or the Marine Memorial. When the bands strike up with a blare of French horns, tubas, and trumpets, you hear musical history. Some of the bands, established by the U.S. government almost 200 years ago, play the music that Americans have been hearing ever since the country began.

Concerts by four military bands are offered during June, July, and August at 8 P.M. at the sites noted.

- *The Marine Band.* "The President's Own" was established in 1801 by Thomas Jefferson. Performances alternate between the Capitol grounds on Wednesdays and the Washington Monument on Sundays. The band also presents the Evening Parade at the Marine Barracks, 8th Street SE at I Street, on Fridays between mid-May and early September. Reservations are necessary.

• *U.S. Army Band.* "Pershing's Own" grew out of the musical organizations of the American Expeditionary Forces formed by General John J. Pershing in World War I. The band presents a mix of country, blues, Bach, choral music, jazz, pop, and show tunes. The highlight of the season is the July performance of Tchaikovsky's *1812 Overture,* in which cannons are fired. Concerts are on Fridays on the Capitol grounds, Tuesdays on the grounds of the Washington Monument.

• *U.S. Navy Band.* Formed in 1923, it performs on Mondays at the Capitol and on Thursdays at the Washington Monument. The highlight of the season is the Children's Lollipop Concert, with music especially for children plus elaborate sets, costumes, balloons, clowns, and free lollipops. The band also presents a multimedia program on Wednesdays at 8:45 P.M. at the Washington Navy Yard waterfront.

• *U.S. Air Force Band and Singing Sergeants.* "America's International Musical Ambassadors" present concerts on Tuesdays on the Capitol grounds and on Fridays at the Washington Monument. Their Christmas-in-August program, scheduled for the Friday closest to August 25, features carols and Christmas music.

Other popular concert stages include:

• *Anderson House.* Free noontime performances by the United States Air Force Chamber Players, and Saturday afternoon concerts by a variety of musical groups. Refreshments follow some concerts.

• *Corcoran Gallery of Art.* Each year the gallery's "Musical Evening Series" presents chamber music, with concerts performed by internationally known groups. The renowned Tokyo String Quartet and Cleveland Quartet participate regularly, performing on matched sets of Amati and Stradivarius string instruments owned by the gallery. For information, call (202) 638-1439.

• *Hillwood Museum.* Concerts that feature the music of Russia, from balalaika folk musicians to the Yale Russian Chorus, are presented. Some concerts include a reception in the museum cafe. Admission charge. Call (202) 686-8500.

• *Library of Congress.* Summer outdoor concerts the third Thursday of each month at Neptune Plaza, put on by the American Folklife Center. Bluegrass, gospel, and Hispanic musicians perform. The Chamber Music series that runs from fall to spring features the Juilliard String Quartet and the Beaux Arts Trio. Free. For information call the music division at (202) 707-6590.

• *National Academy of Sciences.* A series of free concerts presented by the academy's chamber ensemble in residence; guest artists have included the New Music Concert, Canadian pianist Jane Coop, and the Budapest Chamber Orchestra. Held on Friday or Saturday evenings at 8 P.M. in an auditorium that critics have labeled "acoustically stunning." Free. For information call (202) 334-2436.

• *National Gallery of Art.* More than 2,000 concerts have been presented during the past 50 years. With the fountain and lush foliage of the Garden Court as backdrop, the National Gallery Orchestra and visiting stars perform. Each spring for six consecutive Sundays, concerts feature the works of American composers. In the past these "American Music Festival" concerts have featured pianist George Shearing and vocalist Joe Williams. Free, but passes required. Call (202) 842-6941 for information.

• *Old Post Office Pavilion.* Jazz, folk, bluegrass, pop musicians, dancers, and performers fill the stage of this Washington landmark on most weekdays from noon to 1 P.M. and 5 to 6 P.M. For information call (202) 289-4224.

• *Organization of American States.* Fall-spring concert series of musicians from 32 member countries. Sometimes the ambassador of the featured country hosts a reception following the concert. Concerts are given on alternate Wednesdays. Free. For information call (202) 458-3069.

• *Phillips Gallery.* Since the opening of the gallery in 1941, its Sunday 5 P.M. concerts have been a Washington tradition. A number of celebrated artists, among them Glenn Gould and Jessye Norman, had important early concerts in the paneled music room. Concerts run September through May. Free. For information (202) 387-2151.

• *Smithsonian Institution, Resident Associates Programs.* Concerts feature international performances held at various Smithsonian venues, including the Carmichael Auditorium, the Baird Auditorium, and the Palm Court, which is the site of jazz concerts. In the summer, jazz goes outdoors to the Smithsonian's bandstand at the corner of 14th Street and Constitution Avenue. Some concerts are free, but for others there is an admission fee. For information call (202) 357-0300.

• *World Bank.* Free noontime concerts cosponsored by one of the 152 embassies headquartered in Washington. The performances, which feature artists from the co-hosting country, are offered three times a month from September to June. In the past, offerings have included a Belgian jazz combo, a Malaysian pianist, flamenco dancers, German folksingers, and African musicians.

Chapter 7

Nature

C&O Canal, Georgetown

In no other capital can one so easily step from the bustle of the city into wooded country. That's because unlike other capitals, Washington, D.C., was created from scratch—superimposed on a wilderness. There's no need to bring the country to the city, because the city has been built around the country.

At least 250 native shrubs and trees line 300 miles of city streets, march in dense columns along Potomac River banks, and flourish in the woods of Rock Creek Park. Although many of the city's thousands of trees are native, more exotics grow here than in any other American city.

Over 1,800 varieties of flowers bloom, and 300 species of birds flutter across the sky. Within the boundaries of the nation's capital lives a scampering, squeaking, chirping, warbling, hooting population. Bald eagles nest. Immigrating Canadian geese and ducks stop to rest. Wild turkeys, bobcats, and white-tailed deer roam in bordering forests. Raccoons and squirrels forage along city streets.

This abundance of wildlife is due primarily to the fact that the edges of four different geological zones extend over the District and its environs. Thus, Washington is host to varieties and species that are native to both the North and the South. In addition, due to government expeditions and the gifts of foreign delegations, Washington boasts trees and flowers from around the world.

Discovering natural Washington is easy, even if you don't set out to hike or bike in Rock Creek Park or elsewhere. That's because flowers, trees, birds, and animals flourish in the heart of the city: the wisteria climbing the pink granite of the National Gallery of Art, the elm trees along Pennsylvania Avenue originally planted by Thomas Jefferson, the trees of the Capitol and the White House, the ducks at Constitution Gardens, the squirrels scampering in Lafayette Square.

You'll see many of Washington's most awesome natural sites as you follow the tourist trail to the monuments, museums, and historic homes. If you include time to explore the city's nearby parks and natural settings, you'll discover more. From the hundred or more parks in the greater Washington area, some stand out because they boast an unusual feature. The best are described here. All lie about 20 miles or less from the capital.

To see the best of natural Washington, follow the **Highlight Walk** and then venture to the **More Nature** sites in Maryland and Virginia.

Highlight Walk
Georgetown–Roosevelt Island

Three outstanding natural sites, which are within walking distance of one another, are also near Metro subway stations. This three-mile walk shows you the way on a route that takes you into one of America's most famous city parks, along a historic canal where barges are hauled by mules, and across the river to a pristine island preserved as a memorial to Theodore Roosevelt.

1. Rock Creek Park

Parts of Rock Creek Park today seem unchanged from the days Native American Indians hunted the bear, deer, and elk that roamed its wooded hillsides and verdant valleys. Perhaps nowhere east of the Mississippi does a more remote wilderness remain.

Theodore Roosevelt's efforts are credited with preserving this four-mile-long parcel of real estate bisecting the heart of the District of Columbia. In 1890, with pressure from this nature-loving future president, Congress authorized an appropriation of $10,000 for its purchase. Over 100 years later, the national park remains a natural woodland with a dense greenery of virgin forest and walls of shrubbery. Moss- and fern-covered rocks decorate the banks of Rock Creek and its tributary branches. In this wilderness live 40 varieties of mammal, 150 bird species, and 22 kinds of snakes.

Over 1,800 acres of parkland lie within District boundaries, with another 1,200 acres stretching into Maryland's Montgomery County. This portion is called Rock Creek Regional Park (see description below). Traversing the southern sections of the park is Rock Creek Parkway, one of the most scenic drives in the country.

To increase the diversity within the park, administrators initiated a program in 1977 to preserve 23 acres of meadowland. Rather than allowing the deep grass and wildflowers to be be overtaken by woods, once each spring mowers clear these areas. With management of the meadows, the flowers and grasses that attract birds and insects are nurtured and thus proliferate.

These preserved meadows occupy a dozen areas in the Rock Creek watershed. One meadow edges the woods at picnic site #17, east of Glover Road and north of its intersection with Ross Drive. Another is located about 200 feet east of Beach Drive at Pierce Mill. The National Park Service offers a free brochure entitled "Meadows," which lists 17 other meadow access points. The brochure also is a handy nature guide, since it lists the animal and plant life you can see each season.

Rock Creek Park offers 15 miles of hiking, biking and riding trails, and 70 groves with tables and fireplaces for picnics. Other attractions include the 1822 Pierce Mill, a 180-year-old gristmill where you can watch a miller grinding corn and wheat; the power of the tiny Rock Creek moves the great stone wheel inside. The National Zoo, within the bounds of the park, displays over 3,000 animals in natural settings. Also in the park are Thompson's Boat Center, Rock Creek Horse Center, and the Carter Barron Amphitheater.

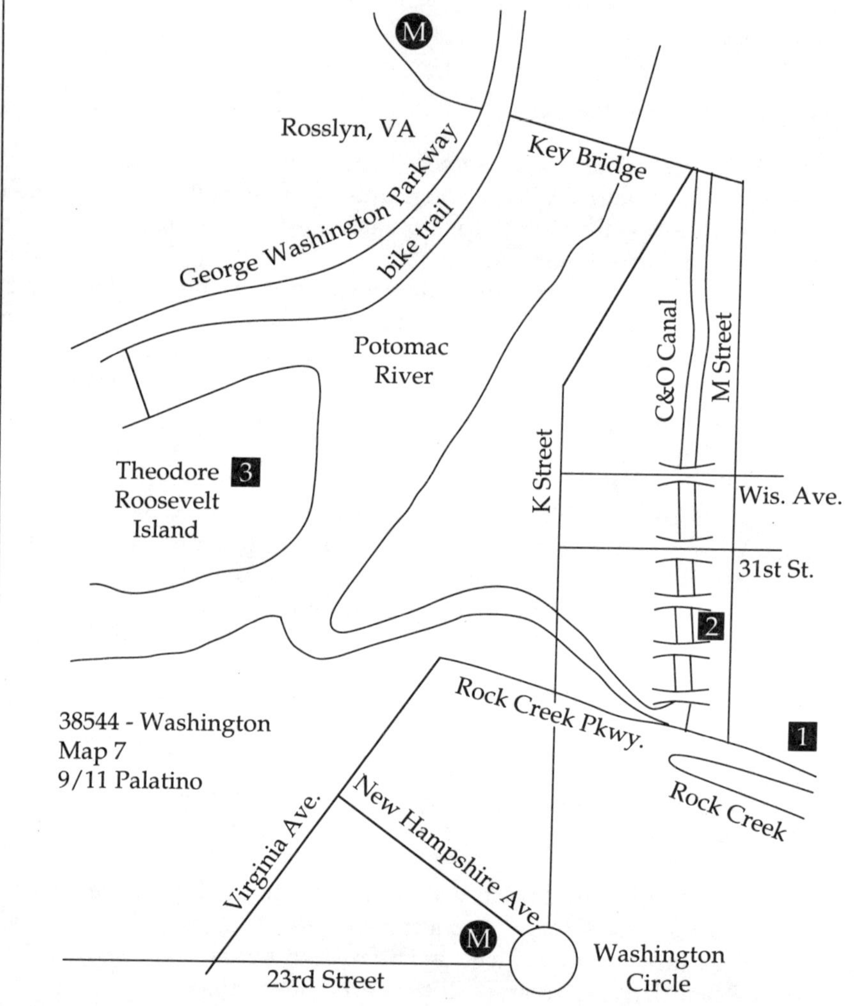

M Metro

1. Rock Creek Park, Rock Creek Parkway near K Street NW
2. C&O Canal National Historic Park, 31st Street above K Street NW
3. Theodore Roosevelt Island, George Washington Parkway near Key Bridge, Rosslyn, Virginia

Route

From the Foggy Bottom Metro subway station, walk south on New Hampshire Avenue to Virginia Avenue. Turn right, following Virginia Avenue to the bike trail that borders the river. Proceed north to the C&O Canal towpath that intersects the trail at the M Street ramp. Before you follow the towpath to the C&O Canal Historical Park, you may want to make a detour into Rock Creek Park. By walking about one mile from the M Street ramp you'll be able to savor one of the most idyllic sections of the park. The lure is the wooden bridge that overlooks the creek, which you reach after the trail turns off the busy Rock Creek Parkway into the woods. The walk along the parkway is particularly nice in the spring, when daffodils line the bordering hills.

When you return to the towpath, follow it three blocks to the C&O Canal's Georgetown headquarters, where canal trips begin. Continue along the C&O trail for the equivalent of four blocks, until you come to a bridge with a ramp that meets the trail. Follow the ramp up to M Street, turn left and continue across Key Bridge.

From the Virginia side of the bridge, walk to your left along the George Washington Parkway bike trail that leads to the causeway link to Roosevelt Island. From the island you can retrace your steps back to Key Bridge, and from there cross the traffic circles to Wilson Boulevard and the Rosslyn Metro subway station.

Since there are no concessions along the way or on Roosevelt Island, your best bet is to buy a picnic lunch in Georgetown on M Street near the C&O Canal Park.

A highlight for young nature lovers is the Rock Creek Nature Center, with its planetarium, elevated outdoor nature path, and exhibits of live animals and insects.

2. Chesapeake & Ohio Canal National Historical Park

Walking along a portion of the 185-mile C&O Canal towpath, your senses go on holiday. You see a dozen shades of green in the leaves of willow, beech, oak, poplar, and cottonwood trees. Wild flowers add color: blue delphinium, yellow buttercups, and violets. In the right season, you catch the scent of honeysuckle and roses. A symphony of sounds greet your ears: the hoot of a barred owl, the hammer of a woodpecker, the chirping of birds.

With a little luck, your tastebuds revel as you sample wild raspberries and persimmons.

The C&O Canal, paralleling the eastern shore of the Potomac River, climbs from the tidewaters of Georgetown to the mountains of Cumberland, Maryland. Along its banks live an extraordinary number of birds. Where elsewhere there are no more than five breeding birds per acre, along the canal up to 15 inhabit each acre. Wild animals also live along the canal: foxes, squirrels, opossums, raccoons, white-tailed deer, cottontail rabbits, otters, muskrats, and beavers.

The history of this unique canal goes back to George Washington. Although he never lived to see construction of a canal, he saw the need for harnessing the waters of the Potomac River and providing a transportation waterway. It was left to President John Quincy Adams to oversee construction of the C&O Canal, which began in 1828.

The canal's heyday was in the 1870s, when 500 barges carried almost a million tons of cargo a year: coal, wheat, lumber, corn. Traffic on the canal declined in the early 1900s as the new Baltimore & Ohio Railroad took most of the freight and passengers, thus reducing the canal's importance.

In the 1950s, a controversial proposal to pave the canal for a highway aroused concern. Supreme Court Justice William Douglas led a drive to defeat the highway and worked to turn the historic canal into a national park. A bust of Douglas at the locks in Georgetown reminds passersby of his role.

The towpath, along which boys once led the mules that pulled the canal boats, today survives as a popular recreation area. Bikers, hikers, and canoeists populate the best-preserved portion, which extends 14 miles from Georgetown to the Great Falls of the Potomac.

The park service offers hikes, campfire events, and other programs along the canal. One of the most challenging hikes is along the Billy Goat Trail, a two-mile circuit downstream from Great Falls, between locks #16 and #17. Scenic highlights include rocky pools bright with water lilies and prickly pear cacti.

Bikers enjoy ideal pedaling along the mostly flat towpath trail skirting the canal. Although canoeists can go the length of the canal (if they portage), the best waters stretch between Georgetown and lock #7 near Seneca. The most popular portion is in Great Falls vicinity.

Mule-drawn barge trips operate in the summer from both Great Falls Tavern and the Canal's Georgetown Visitor Center. During the 45-minute ride, you see how the locks lifted barges above the river level so they could negotiate the rising water level from tidewater to mountains. The canal ride also provides a sense of daily life in early canal days. Crew members dressed as nineteenth-century boatmen and women navigate the barge and entertain with period music on old-fashioned instruments.

In the summer the popular "Concerts on the Canal" series brings hundreds of spectators to the banks of the canal in Georgetown. The outdoor spectacular is staged every other Sunday from June to September. Musical offerings range from Dixieland, jazz, and bluegrass to reggae, gospel, and big band.

3. THEODORE ROOSEVELT ISLAND

"There are no words that can tell the hidden spirit of the wilderness, that can reveal its mystery, its melancholy, and its charm . . ." These simple words of Theodore Roosevelt, inscribed on granite tablets, sum up his delight in nature. They also capture the pleasure many feel upon discovering his island memorial, where words and trees immortalize this man who championed conservation.

When Roosevelt came into office in 1901, four-fifths of America's prime forests had been leveled. More than one-third of the wild population had been destroyed. With a belief in conservation that had grown from his boyhood enthusiasm for outdoor life, the new president set about rescuing the public domain. During his administration, more than 234 million acres were reserved for conservation. The U.S. Forest Service was created. Five national parks, fifty-one bird refuges, and four game refuges were established.

In the most appropriate way, the preservation of this wild refuge in the heart of a city pays tribute to Roosevelt the naturalist. The historic island, which has had many owners since it was granted by Charles I to Lord Baltimore, was purchased by the Theodore Roosevelt Memorial Association in 1931. The Olmsted brothers were hired to draw up a landscape plan. Sculptor Paul Manship was commissioned to create the 17-foot bronze statue of the nation's twenty-sixth president. Set on an oval terrace in front of a 30-foot shaft of granite, the statue is surrounded by a terrace, where a water-filled moat reflects the sky. Four granite tables inscribed with quotes from Roosevelt's philosophy of citizenship complete the memorial.

Beyond lies the 88-acre island sanctuary, where a rich variety of plants and animals flourish. Raccoons in search of crayfish inhabit the swamp where willow, ash, and maple trees root on mudflats. Marsh wrens, red-winged blackbirds, and kingfishers thrash amidst the cattails and pickerelweed. Woodpeckers, chickadees, wood thrushes, and squirrels share the treetops of elms, red maples, and oaks. You can hike along two and one half miles of foot trails that circle and bisect the island.

More Nature

Virginia

Bull Run Regional Park
Fairfax, Virginia

The largest stand of bluebells on the East Coast paints the woodland meadows for two weeks in mid-April in this, northern Virginia's most comprehensive park. The annual flooding and overflow of the Bull Run and Cub Run creeks nourishes the flower that proliferates over much of the 1,000-acre park.

By following the one-and-one-half-mile Bluebell Trail, you can enjoy the spectacle. The blooming bluebells are harbingers of spring. With their biological clocks triggered by the light and warming of longer spring days, they are a sign that the tender green leaves of trees and shrubs will soon appear. A glory of other wildflowers follows their lead, too, as adder's tongue, rue anemone, toothwort, Dutchman's breeches, and wild violets bloom.

Other attractions appeal to nature lovers in this spacious playground. Although the park's extensive facilities cater to the sports-minded, and it can accommodate thousands of picnickers and campers, it also preserves nature. Much of the land remains an untouched wilderness. A variety of ecosystems—deciduous forest, swamp, meadow, and two meandering creeks—attract wild animals and birds.

In addition to the Bluebell Trail, the park offers two others: the five-mile trail to Cub Run Bridge and the 14-mile Bull Run–Occoquan Trail. The second trail follows Bull Run Creek, passing a forest of 200-year-old trees, a hemlock grove, and banks of rhododendron.

Dyke Marsh
Alexandria, Virginia

Tennyson's poem "The Dying Swan" describes this strange and beautiful place, so near to the hustle of a major city and yet so far away from it in spirit.

> The plain was grassy, wild and bare,
> Wide, wild, and open to the air

The poet's "willow branches hoar and dank," "soughing reeds," and "silvery marish flowers" come together in the 240-acre wetland. The combination of marsh, flood plain, and swamp forest attracts over 200 species of meadow and shore birds. Terns, black fish crows, yellow warblers, sandpipers, wading birds, and Kadian flycatchers are just a few of the species that share this rich land with turtles, frogs, and reptiles.

On Sunday mornings when the bird-watchers arrive, the population in the marsh expands. Fortunately for the nature lover, an old road, once used to haul debris to be dumped in the marsh, bisects the marsh. This dry ground of the road provides the ideal means for entering the wilderness, which would otherwise be difficult to access.

That road came long after nature began creating the marsh thousands of years ago, as the current was slowed by the merging of Hunting Creek with the Potomac River. As the current slowed, the sediment carried by the water sank to the bottom. Gradually, as sediment and clay settled out of the slower-moving current, the environment began to support marsh flora and fauna.

Even before the modern days when the marsh was drained and filled to provide additional land for construction, the colonists altered the land. To create more land for grazing cattle, they constructed earthen walls to hold back the water. The colonial spelling of dike, "dyke," remained as the marsh's name long after the constructions were no longer maintained.

Aware that the marsh was the last of the once plentiful fresh-water wetlands that bordered the Potomac River, Congress enacted a law in 1956 that gave the National Park Service jurisdiction over the "irreplaceable wetlands." To assist the Park Service in preserving the marsh as a viable wetland wildlife habitat, a group called the Friends of Dyke Marsh formed in 1975. Members work with national and regional conservation groups to protect the marsh against development pressures, illegal uses, and contamination from pollution. They also sponsor cleanup days and conduct weekly guided bird walks on Sundays at 8 A.M. Information about the Friends is posted at the trail entrance off the parking lot.

Great Falls Park
Great Falls, Virginia

At Great Falls, the Potomac River drops 76 feet. The water dammed in an area of 11,460 square miles drains in a 50-foot waterfall. A torrent up to a half-mile wide rages. Freed of its bounds, it dashes down, over, and around boulders as it turns into an intricate system of channels, cataracts, rapids, and white-water pools.

At the full spring flood, park literature claims, the amount of water flowing over the falls surpasses the flow of Niagara Falls—480,000 cubic feet per second. The spectacle of unleashed power is unforgettable.

Divided by the Potomac River, Great Falls Park lies in both Virginia and Maryland. On the Maryland side, you can survey the falls from an overlook platform and visit park headquarters at the historic Great Falls Tavern. Inside this restored stone lock-house turned museum, you'll see a movie on the

Great Falls Park, Virginia

canal; historic photos and artifacts, including canal boat headlamps; and costumes worn by boat people. Also on display is a reproduction of a canal boat.

For a better view of the falls, head for Great Falls Park on the Virginia side of the river. There wooden platforms overlook the falls, as do picnic tables scattered beneath the pine trees. Several hiking trails lead through the woods, winding in and out of overlooks that you can enter much as you might a room. Each of these dozen or more vistas opens onto a different view of the gorge that the water flows through. The sight and sound of the gray-green water surging beside pale walls of stone is fascinating. Rock climbers make their way up and down small stone mountains as rappelers swing from boulders. On the river, kayakers congregate in peaceful pools or become part of the torrent as they propel their boats downstream.

Since Great Falls is a national park, there are facilities and programs to help you fully appreciate the primeval beauty of the site. Park rangers and naturalists conduct walks and occasionally present programs.

HUNTLEY MEADOWS PARK
ALEXANDRIA, VIRGINIA

Only in the last half-century has Huntley Meadows been a nature preserve. Before that, this rich combination of forest and wetland was farmed, timbered, and finally developed to accommodate several government agencies. When the last government tenant left in the 1940s, the only force shaping the land was the hand of nature.

Hand? Well, it's more like tooth. For natural forces at Huntley Meadows Park come primarily in the form of beavers. By gnawing and chewing with their sharp teeth, beavers have been reshaping the park ever since they reclaimed their habitat. They returned to Huntley Meadows shortly after the site became a preserve. Since the founding of the park, beavers have built the dams that have gradually turned forests into wetlands and meadows into marshes.

Gradually, too, the dams have raised the water level. In 1991, dammed water began flooding the boardwalk trail that crosses the beavers' domain. As a result some of the boardwalk washed out. Squarely facing the flooding caused by the beavers, which they refer to as their "hydraulic situation," park officials decided in that year to build a new boardwalk that would stand higher over the water.

With the new boardwalk, your feet will remain dry. But even without foot-in-the-water contact, you'll feel close to nature as you stroll the two-thirds-mile-long boardwalk. Although beavers aren't seen often in the daytime, with any luck you'll catch sight of a muskrat paddling by; observe herons, ducks, frogs, and butterflies; and hear songbirds. Whether or not you like snakes will determine whether you consider yourself lucky or unlucky should you spot one of the harmless creatures sunning itself on the boardwalk.

A number of other trails also take you into this 1,261-acre preserve. The variety of plant and animal life here is unrivaled. That's because over 120,000 years ago, this land, which lay at the bottom of a channel of the Potomac River, was surrounded by rich forests. The seeds of life nurtured in those prehistoric times produce the abundance of life that is apparent today. There are 275 plant, 60 bird, 36 mammal, 25 fish, 30 reptile, and 20 amphibian species.

Eagle's nest, Mason Neck National Wildlife Refuge

You can appreciate more of the abundance by following the boardwalk to Deer Trail. You can also climb a wooden observation tower for views of wildlife in the pond and meadow habitats. The Visitors Center offers nature exhibits, films, and lecture programs.

Mason Neck Peninsula
Lorton, Virginia

On this 14-square-mile finger of land where upland forest and rich marshlands meet, bald eagles soar. Half of the 6,000 acres that make up this unique ecosystem have been preserved as their refuge. With luck you'll see eagles and numerous other species where the Potomac meets Pohick and Belmont bays and feeds two freshwater marshes.

In the winter, you may catch sight of the eagles nesting high on bluffs overlooking bays and estuaries. In the spring, you're likely to glimpse the majestic birds flying between nest and marsh as they forage for food and nest-building materials.

Three parks offer a variety of attractions, including eagle-viewing sites and nature study exhibits:

Mason Neck National Wildlife Refuge

This facility was established in 1969 as the first federal refuge set aside specifically for the protection of the bald eagle. Administered by the U.S. Fish and Wildlife Service, the 2,277-acre refuge encompasses 2,000 acres of hardwood forest, the largest freshwater marsh in northern Virginia, and nearly 6 miles of shoreline. In this sanctuary, as many as 60 eagles come to rest, feed, and nest.

Other birds abound here as well. Of special interest are the blue-winged teal, the tree swallow, the Carolina wren, the wood thrush, the red-eyed vireo, the ovenbird, and the indigo bunting. Numerous other species visit the sanctuary, some only a few times a season and others as rarely as once every two to five years. A free brochure, "Birds of Mason Neck National Wildlife Refuge," lists 211 species plus 15 more "of accidental occurrence."

You hear the birds' sounds best, of course, as you distance yourself from the picnickers. Two trails offer the ideal escape: the Great Marsh Trail winds for three-quarters of a mile through forest to the marsh overlook. The three-mile Woodmarsh Trail loops through a century-old forest of oak, maple, hickory, and one of the southernmost stands of hemlock trees. Ferns, mosses, running pine, holly, mountain laurel, and wild cherry trees flourish in the forest. In the marsh, spatterdock grows in the shallow water, with wild rice commanding the slightly higher ground. On the driest parts, rose mallow and yellow iris abound.

Mason Neck State Park

This 1,804-acre park stretches along Belmont Bay adjacent to the Wildlife Refuge. It features extensive picnic, camping, and boating facilities. Two 1-mile trails wind through forest and marsh. One trail features an observation blind for viewing the wildlife, which, in addition to the 186 bird species seen on the site, includes red and gray fox, turkey, deer, and bobcat. At the beginning of one of the trails, the junior park rangers have constructed a huge eagle's nest. The visitors center offers exhibits on colonial life in the area, on the wildlife, and a wetlab. A slide show also does a good job of orienting visitors to Mason Neck and its conservation programs.

Pohick Bay Regional Park

This park, located at the top of the peninsula, sprawls along a spectacular bayside expanse. Because park naturalists lead excursions by canoe into the marsh, the park may be the best place for spotting the bald eagles. The half-day canoe trips conducted by park rangers offer the best chance for seeing the majestic birds.

This water-oriented park also offers one of the largest outdoor swimming pools on the East Coast, plus boat-launching facilities and sailboat and pedal-boat rentals. Naturalists lead hikes along the park's numerous trails.

Besides being noted for its natural beauty, the peninsula played an important part in the early history of our country. It was here that the father of our Bill of Rights, George Mason, established his Gunston Hall plantation. The colonial residence, now owned by the state of Virginia, can be visited. So can Pohick Church, where George Washington frequently attended services. Washington would journey by rowboat down the Potomac River to the church, and then have a midday dinner with his good friend at Gunston Hall.

W&O Railroad Regional Park
Northern Virginia

Probably nowhere else in the country will you find such a park. Where other parks ramble over field and meadow, this one follows the 100-foot-wide roadbed of a discontinued Washington & Ohio Dominion Railroad (W&O) line.

The narrow, 45-mile trail has become a national model for linear parks. Paved the entire distance, the trail is a haven for bikers and hikers, and it is the site of the annual National Wheelchair Race of Champions.

Between the beginning of the trail in Shirlington in Arlington and its terminus in Purcellville, the route passes a variety of urban and natural sites. Verdant terrain, lush woods, and rushing streams combine with old railroad bridges, former train stations, and even an antique caboose parked by a former whistle post. It also connects with numerous wayside parks and links with other bike trails.

Plans are being considered to extend the trail so that it will connect with the Appalachian Trail that runs through the Blue Ridge Mountains. The park is accessible from numerous cities along the route.

Other Virginia Parks

Some of the other major parks in Virginia include: Lake Fairfax Park, boasting a 30-acre lake and an Olympic-size pool; Laurel Ridge Conservation and Education Center, with displays on various wildlife management techniques and 12 miles of trails; Potomac Overlook Regional Park, with nature trails winding past old Indian springs and overlooking the Potomac River; and Riverbend Park, which offers hiking trails and a nature center.

Maryland

Rock Creek Regional Park
Derwood, Maryland

Where Rock Creek Park ends at the District border, this 3,000-acre park begins to the north in Maryland. In addition to the natural features you'll find in Rock Creek Park, the Maryland portion offers two artificial lakes. A good hiking trail skirts the 74-acre Needwood Lake. You can also rent a paddleboat, canoe, or fishing boat, or you can sightsee from aboard the Needwood Queen excursion boat.

The Meadowside Nature Center is one of the area's best. Here, students from the University of Maryland demonstrate wildlife management techniques for creating animal sanctuaries. Guided nature walks, films, and exhibits are also offered.

Woodend
Chevy Chase, Maryland

This 40-acre private estate was bequeathed by its last owners to the Audubon Naturalist Society in 1967. The property, part of a seventeenth-century colonial land grant, is dominated by magnificent old trees. The society has added new species to the original stands, including trees that are particularly attractive to wildlife. As a result, the estate has gradually become a sanctuary for the red fox, barred owl, opossum, raccoon, and cottontail rabbit, and even for wild turkey and deer.

Ponds burst with life, too, including crayfish, turtles, wood frogs, and salamanders. Tree branches are atwitter with Carolina wrens, American goldfinches, indigo buntings, white-throated sparrows, catbirds, and northern cardinals.

An enchanting nature trail takes you through a cross-section of nature preserves. As you walk through fields, thickets, and woods, along streams and beside a pond, you see a variety of habitats. Trees and plants are varied and lush. One moment you're in a conifer forest of spruce, hemlock, and cedar. In the next, you're passing beneath a copper beech into a wood of ferns and mosses. Ascending a hill, you come upon rows of tall, straight tulip trees. Trees march in tidy rows across fields of grasses and clover where small mammals make their homes.

Catering to its human visitors, the society opens the doors to the handsome Georgian-style mansion that is its headquarters. The mansion, which has stood here for 70 years, was designed by famed architect John Russell Pope. Visitors can step inside to see exhibits and visit the charming nature-lover's gift shop.

BEYOND

Also within a 50-mile drive of Washington are a number of other popular sites: 525-acre Cabin John Regional Park, with five miles of hiking trails; Eastern Neck National Wildlife Refuge, a Chesapeake Bay island of marshes and ponds populated each fall by migrating waterfowl; Patapsco Valley State Park with its 7,600 acres of dense forests, glades, and canyons, which boasts some of the area's most spectacular scenery.

Chapter 8

Science

The Museum of Natural History (*Courtesy of Smithsonian Institution*)

Washington, D.C., has been a major influence in the development of science in America. Government and private institutions have combined to stimulate scientific inquiry and to draw a remarkable parade of inventors, researchers, and explorers to the capital city. The history of our nation's emergence as a scientific power is recorded here in brick and stone. Several structures, including some that go back to pre–Civil War days, remind us of that story.

The story begins in 1790, when Congress established the U.S. Patent Office. Until 1935, this office was housed in the building that was renovated in 1968 to become the site of the National Portrait Gallery and the National Museum of American Art. Today the U.S. Patent Office continues its work in modern facilities in Virginia.

As our first federal agency, the U.S. Patent Office served a unique role. In addition to acting as the clearinghouse for inventions, the office also inadvertently fostered the growth of the Department of Agriculture.

The creation of that department is typical of the development of other federal agencies: It evolved out of a specific need. In 1802, the commissioner of the Patent Office asked Congress to appropriate $1,000 a year for the collection of information about agriculture and the purchase of seeds. With seeds and information to study, specialists had to be hired. More seeds . . . more information . . . more specialists—and before you knew it, a separate agency had to be created to handle the work. The Department of Agriculture, established in 1862, is today one of the largest government agencies.

Also in an indirect way, the U.S. Naval Observatory grew out of the old Naval Depot of Charts and Instruments. Congress originally had no intention of involving the government in scientific matters. From the start, when President John Quincy Adams proposed a naval observatory, congressional objections were voiced. Congress did, however, fund an agency to provide the U.S. Navy with navigational instruments and charts—the Depot of Charts and Instruments. Of course, in order to do that, the depot had to have an observatory. And one existed, unofficially. However, it wasn't until ten years after its construction that the presence of the observatory was officially recognized and it received the name it bears today.

The original observatory, capped with a 23-foot white dome, today looks much as it did upon completion in 1844. For a step back into the world of early-American science, you can visit the original Naval Observatory in Foggy Bottom. You can also see the famous facility to which it moved in 1893: the U.S. Naval Observatory on Massachusetts Avenue.

At the end of the Civil War, doors opened for the creation of a roster of new government science agencies. In the 1870s and 1880s, these new agencies began attracting top scientists. Among the new agencies were the Geological Survey, the Fishery Commission, the Department of Agriculture, the Weather Bureau, and the Army Medical Service.

During this period, some of the greatest names in science crossed the Washington stage: Joseph Henry, who built the first electromagnet, became the first secretary of the Smithsonian Institution; John Wesley Powell worked out procedures to expand the science of cultural anthropology; astronomer Simon Newcomb initiated a system of computing the positions of stars and for calculating the mass and path of planets; Matthew Fontaine Maury launched the science of oceanography; and Samuel Langley made a major contribution to astrophysics by measuring the radiant heat of the sun.

From the beginning, America's scientific orientation was applied rather than theoretical. The only fields that expanded in the nineteenth century were those that offered the hope of practical applications. "Most scientists were enlisted in the eminently practical task of describing the physical and natural characteristics of the nation, as well as other portions of the earth," Nathan Reingold writes in *Science in 19th Century America*. The work of describing the physical and natural character of the earth, of course, defines the science of geography, the queen of science in nineteenth-century America.

By appreciating the importance of geography in the minds of the early American scientists, one can see Washington's scientific institutions in a new light. One understands why the National Geographic Society achieved its prominence, as it served as a center for the collection and presentation of information about this, America's leading science. The Smithsonian Institution also reflects the importance of geography. The quasi-governmental facility was established with the bequest of an Englishman, James Smithson, who had never even visited America. Smithson asked that the $500,000 he gave to the U.S. government be used "for the increase and diffusion of knowledge among men."

From its beginning, the institution's focus has been on research into the physical and natural sciences—both subdivisions of geography. Toward that end, the institution established a national museum to serve as a repository for the specimens collected on expeditions to the West and overseas. Today its museum function dominates. The repository, begun almost 150 years ago, now boasts 100 million artifacts.

The Smithsonian Institution, the National Geographic Society, the Naval Observatory, the Patent Office, and other government agencies are among the highlights of a tour of American scientific roots. The trail into the past also takes you to the National Academy of Sciences, signed into existence by Abraham Lincoln in 1863 to advise the federal government on matters of science and technology. Progressing into the present, the trail links sci-

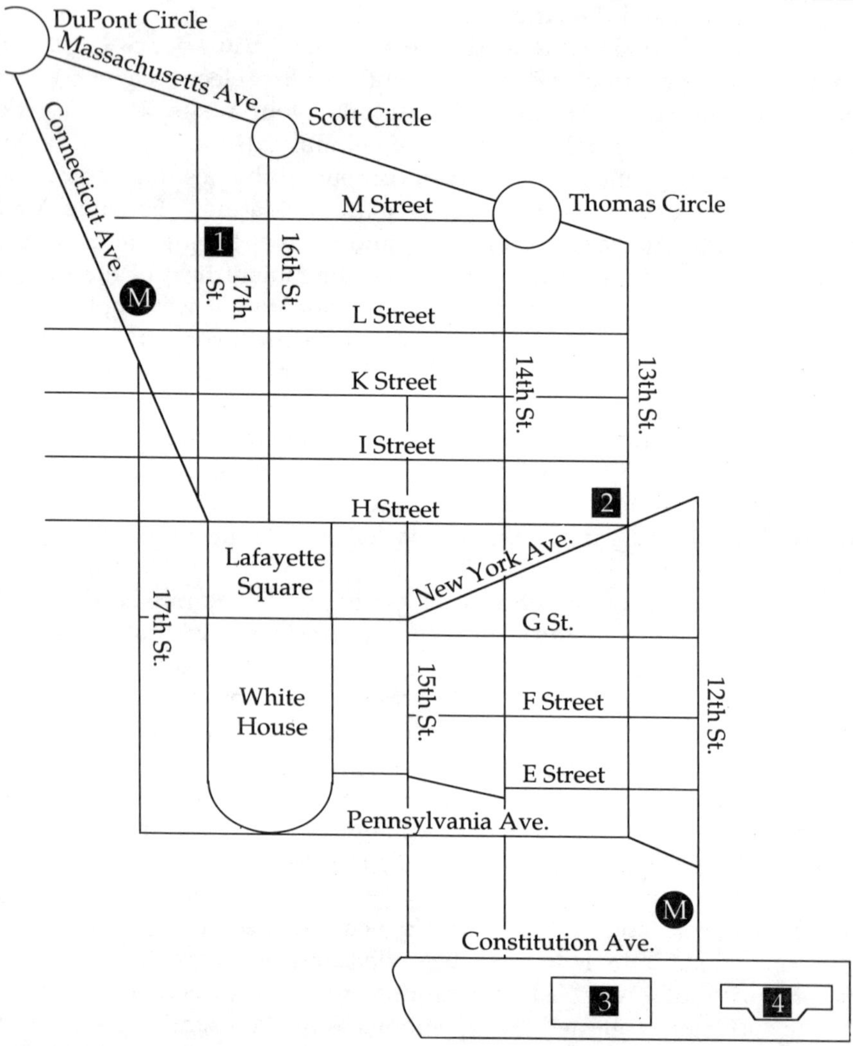

M Metro

1. National Geographic Society, 17th and M Streets NW
2. American Association for the Advancement of Science, 1333 H Street NW
3. National Museum of American History, 14th Street and Constitution Avenue NW
4. National Museum of Natural History, Constitution Avenue and 10th Street NW

Route

From the Farragut North Metro, walk east on L Street to 17th Street. Turn left and continue one block to the National Geographic Society. Next retrace your steps down 17th Street and continue, turning left on H Street. It's about five blocks to the American Association for the Advancement of Science. Next, walk down 12th Street to Constitution Avenue. The National Museum of American History is to your right, and the National Museum of Natural History is to your left. Retrace your steps north on 12th Street to the Federal Triangle Metro station (across from the Old Post Office).

entific Washington with the twentieth-century world of technological supremacy. See Chapter 9, "Technology."

You'll see the best of Washington's natural and physical sciences sites by following the **Highlight Walk** and by venturing on your own to the **More Science** sites on the Mall, along Embassy Row, in Foggy Bottom, and beyond.

Highlight Walk Downtown–The Mall

On this walk, which takes you from Mid Town to the Mall, you'll see two of the world's great natural history museums, fascinating new exhibits, plus an unusual gallery devoted to science art. You'll travel about a mile and a half, through the heart of downtown Washington, where you'll see some of the city's newest architectural marvels. You'll pass numerous cafés and restaurants along the way where you can stop for refreshment.

1. National Geographic Society

Geography 101 was never like this! Thanks to ground-breaking technology at the National Geographic Society's Explorers Hall, information about the physical features of Earth now comes with the push of a button.

A series of interactive exhibits in the society's newest installation, "Geographica," entertains and educates people about the many disciplines that geography encompasses.

Touch-screen modules, a live satellite feed, remote-controlled microscopes, and remote sensing imagery combine to produce some fascinating exhibits. In one, a simulated futuristic space station, you push a button beside your chair to ask a question, which is answered by a pilot computer and reflected on large screens. The weather module uses a live satellite feed to provide meteorological information, and also simulates a tornado graphically. The remote-controlled microscope you can manipulate zeros in on tiny land- and sea-dwelling creatures.

The centerpiece of "Geographica" hangs aloft on air bearings—a cushion of air only 1/200th of an inch thick. It's an 11-foot-diameter globe illustrating the earth's physical features. The fiberglass sphere is painted to show the world's rocky promontories and ocean trenches, areas of lush vegetation and desert stretches. There is no other globe in the world of its size that is so accurate and so detailed.

Explorers Hall exhibits dioramas that illustrate the lives of Southwest American cliff dwellers, one of the sleds used by Admiral Robert Peary to reach the North Pole, and a piece of moon rock. There's also a theater and a planetarium dome. Plans are afoot for a future exhibit in which you'll be able to carry on a simulated talk with some of the great explorers who have been supported by the society.

Explorers Hall, the Society's permanent exhibit space, went high tech in 1989. Now you can learn by interacting with state-of-the-art video monitors that respond to your touch with pictures, data, and even sound effects. Of these, the interactive kiosk that most enchants children of all ages is "Mam-

Globe at the National Geographic Society.

mals: A Multi-Media Encyclopedia." You can get a picture and information about any of hundreds of animals, and remarkable renderings of the sounds they make. With a little imagination you'll orchestrate a raucous zoo of sounds: roaring lions, trumpeting elephants, crying sea lions, and howling wolves.

As fascinating in a different way is the exhibit that features a bio-scanner. By manipulating this microscope, you can study the chameleon and the tarantula that live—separately—behind glass. With a zoom lens you see more than you could with your naked eye even if you had the chance—and nerve—to get eyeball-to-eyeball with either creature.

2. American Association for the Advancement of Science

This organization, which seeks to advance education in science, offers something special to visitors. A large atrium in the heart of the association's headquarters displays work that reflects the centuries-old interaction of art and science.

Contemporary subjects and historical materials are brought together in new ways. The eclectic mix in the past has included computer-based murals, fossil-like clay prints, geometric sculptures, textiles woven with ancient techniques, and photographs taken in the restricted areas of important research laboratories. The artists whose works are shown either create by using scientific processes or principles, or they use scientific subjects as their inspiration. Sometimes the scientific association is obvious, as in computer art. Other times the connection is more esoteric, as in the textile woven by the St. Louis chemist who uses a mathematical base for her design.

The art gallery is part of the association's Art of Science and Technology Program, established in 1985. The exhibits are often shown in the New York Academy of Sciences in New York City as well.

Should you show a particular interest in science-related art, you may be lucky enough to inspire one of the staff to show you more works, hung in offices throughout the building.

3. National Museum of American History

When you have 100 million objects in your attic and have space downstairs for only one percent of the total, making selections can be tough. One of the ways the Smithsonian Institution handles the problem is by coming up with a particular aspect of American life to interpret. Then curators go into "the nation's attic" and bring down the specimens and artifacts that best illustrate that theme. That's the trend these days at the world's largest museum complex: to show objects of interest in a context that helps people understand their world.

Understanding trends and targeting themes that most interest people is an important aspect of the Smithsonian's work. Nowhere are the results of this orientation more in evidence than in the National Museum of American History. Old exhibits are constantly being dismantled and new ones created. Often artifacts from the old are used in the new in fresh ways.

One example of this process can be seen in the restructuring of the former "Hall of Physical Sciences" into the "Science in American Life" exhibit, which focuses on chemistry and other physical sciences. The $5-million exhibit, devoted to the history of modern science and science-based technologies, aims at expanding scientific literacy.

By involving visitors in scientific investigation, the exhibit, with the help of full-time staff members, encourages visitors to take on the role of scientist to discover the scientist in themselves. One section of the science center will focus on the complexity of science by depicting the interconnections between science and world issues. Ethical, technological, and political issues, such as alternative solutions for waste management, will be explored.

But of all the exhibits devoted to the physical sciences, one dominates all others: the Foucault Pendulum that greets visitors entering on the Mall side of the museum. The pendulum, invented by French physicist Jean Foucault in 1851, was the first laboratory apparatus to demonstrate the Earth's rotation. For 20 years the pendulum swung across the compass rose on the first floor of the museum; then it was raised to the second floor. Now, from both above and below, you see the swinging ball knock over pins as the Earth spins on its axis.

Among the museum's newest exhibits is "Health in America," which opened in 1991. It displays objects from the 100,000-piece collection encompassing the fields of medicine, pharmacy, dentistry, and public health, and interprets the history of medicine from the eighteenth century to the present day.

For more information on the National Museum of American History, see **Literature, Military,** and **Technology.**

4. Museum of Natural History

If you don't have a lifetime to roam the world, spend a day or more at the Museum of Natural History. Under one roof, you'll discover exhibits that tell the story of our planet and all the beings and creatures on it.

Only a fraction of the 80 million objects gathered in nineteenth-century expeditions are on display. Those artifacts and specimens that are exhibited show human evolution, culture, and civilizations, along with the history of life on land and sea, with a special emphasis on the splendors of nature.

Millions of objects are arranged in 34 exhibits on two floors. Most people tackle the museum sights in one of two ways: by attempting to see everything and come away with a mind-boggling overview of the natural world, or by concentrating on a few favorites, picking and choosing from the huge smorgasbord of offerings.

Among the exhibits focusing on human life are "Native People of the Americas," "Cultures of the Pacific," "Cultures of Asia and Africa," "Western Civilization," and "Human Origins and Variations." Other exhibits highlight various aspects of the natural environment. These include "Birds of the World," "Life in the Sea," "The World of Mammals," "Ice Age Mammals, Fossils, Reptiles," "Earth, Moon, Meteorites," "Jade, Gems, Minerals, and Fossils."

The new "Life in the Ancient Seas" exhibition, which opened in 1990, tells a story that has never been treated before in a major museum: the evolution of life in the sea, beginning with the Paleozoic era, 570 million years ago. The $4-million exhibit hall, under construction for four years, combines the talents of 100 scientists, designers, artists, and carpenters. The new exhibit completes the museum's paleontology project, which also includes the Dinosaur Hall.

Lighting effects that simulate sunlight filtering through water give you the sensation of being submersed in the sea in the company of strange creatures. Models of fish, squid, and other ancient sea creatures, suspended overhead, move through imaginary waters. On the walls, two huge murals depict life-size prehistoric animals swimming underwater. To create the murals, the artist painstakingly studied the fossil skeletons of the creatures and made models of each before beginning to paint. Her largest mural features a 20-foot-long marine lizard and an ancient whale, along with 30 other marine animals characteristic of the time.

Other highlights of the "Life in the Ancient Seas" include:

- *A reef diorama.* Composed of more than 100,000 models of bryozoans, sponges, brachiopods, and other marine animals from the 250-million-year-old Paleozoic era.

- *Trilobite's eye simulation.* A specially constructed lens fitted with a camera that allows you to see yourself on a monitor as you would have been seen by this Paleozoic sea creature.

- *Clay-animated short film.* Shows marine creatures of the food web at the end of the Mesozoic era. (Made by the creators of the popular "California Raisins" commercial.)

Other favorites:

• *Eight-ton mounted African bush elephant.* The first thing you see upon entering the main rotunda.

• *Life-size tableau of a Neanderthal burial.* This would have taken place 70,000 years ago.

• *Living coral reef.* Created and maintained in a 300,000-gallon aquarium. Electronic, mechanical, and biological devices simulate natural conditions on the reef, providing a natural environment in living color for such creatures as parrot fish, crabs, and algae.

• *Dinosaur skeletons.* Including the 80-foot-long diplodocus, the largest land-living animal ever to have appeared on earth.

• *Meteorites.* The largest collection on exhibit in the world, including fragments of extraterrestrial matter that formed a 4,000-foot-wide crater in Arizona.

• *"Insect Zoo."* Thousands of live insects fly, swim, and climb about in their Plexiglas-walled cages. You can watch volunteer keepers feed tarantulas three times a day, peer into a beehive, and touch a giant grasshopper.

• *"Discovery Room."* Hundreds of specimens to touch, including elephant tusks, petrified wood, woolly mammoth teeth, and a crocodile head. You can also taste and smell herb seeds and try on costumes from around the world.

Of all the exhibits, one particularly appeals to almost everyone: the 1,000 exotic and rare cut, polished gemstones on display in the "Geology, Gems, and Minerals Hall." Most people come to see the legendary 45.5-carat Hope diamond and, once there, linger awestruck by the dozens of other outstanding jewels.

To better show off what some call "the world's greatest collection of gems and minerals," a new, larger area is in the works. Portions of the new facility will probably be ready by 1994. During construction, portions of the exhibit may be closed.

The new $6-million facility will be worth the wait. Instead of simply displaying items, exhibits will tell stories: how atoms form crystals; how historic jewels were cut; why minerals have brilliant colors; how minerals occur in nature.

Note: If time allows, you may want to include a stop at the National Aquarium, which is along the route, in the Department of Commerce building. This, the oldest aquarium in the United States, displays tropical and freshwater fish. Crabs and oysters in an open tank that's low enough for children to reach invite pats and taps. Sharks and piranhas are fed on alternate days at 2 P.M. (except Fridays).

MORE SCIENCE

THE MALL

NATIONAL AIR AND SPACE MUSEUM

Amidst the technological wonders of this famous museum, scientific displays also clamor for attention. Information on astronomy, cosmology, and the science of flight beckon the science buff. Sometimes the scientifically oriented displays can't be missed, while at other times they're less obvious parts of large galleries.

One gallery you'll want to seek out is the "Stars Gallery," which tours the known universe from ancient to the present time. Artifacts include a Lear jet infrared telescope, the prototype of the ATM x-ray mirror, and an IVE Scientific Control Console.

Seeing scientific instruments educates, but if you're the type who learns by doing, you'll want to be on hand for the three live demonstrations. New science demonstrations are now available at two different times each day. Check with the information desk as to time and place.

After introducing the scientific principle that is the focus of the demonstration, the leader gives you the chance to experiment for yourself. The demonstration programs, which last about 20 minutes, include "Forces of Flight" and "The Space Show."

"Forces of Flight" demonstrates the four forces of flight: lift, weight, thrust, and drag. To make the principles come alive, you are invited to help launch a hot-air balloon model and to manipulate the controls that keep an airplane in the air.

"The Space Show" demonstrates the instruments used to explore our galaxies—primarily the telescope, camera, and spectrometer. You'll hold a diffraction grading, which is a glass with minuscule lines that improves on the properties of a prism. Using it, you see more sharply how white light, when diffracted, separates into a spectrum of individual colors.

You also experiment with the ways the various atmospheres of other planets affect matter. You see how the nitrogen atmosphere of Neptune's satellite Triton (which is 320 degrees below zero) affects matter; when a flower is dipped in liquid nitrogen, it becomes brittle and crumbles like glass.

A third demonstration, available only to groups and by reservation, is connected with the gallery called "Beyond the Limits: Flight Enters the Computer Age." The demonstration shows the computer's impact on flight.

For those with a yen for astronomy, the museum's world-class Albert Einstein planetarium will need no introduction. From 10 to 13 times a day, the facility presents 28-minute shows that send skywatchers into orbit. The planetarium is one of the world's best. Banks of slide projectors cast the images of 8,910 stars onto its 70-foot dome. The audiovisual system is of the first magnitude, with four video projectors and a new state-of-the-art sound system. In addition, a magician's bag of special effects simulate mind-boggling space events, including the pyrotechnics of the aurora borealis, rotation of the galaxies, meteor showers, and exploding stars. Program designers also choose from almost 400,000 still images of planets, space missions, stars, and nebulas. Often they run the images in sequences to create motion pictures.

For more information on the National Air and Space Museum, see **Military** and **Technology**.

Foggy Bottom

National Academy of Sciences

The ornate bronze doors opening into this "temple of science" hint at the treasures to be found within. Once you're inside, however, the small foyer fails to prepare you for the grandeur of the Great Hall. Sixty-four feet square, the Great Hall shines with a gold-embellished vaulted ceiling capped by a dome that simulates the sun. Brilliantly painted tiles and paintings adorn the ceiling. Symbolism speaks volumes. Sculpture, paintings, and tiles highlight the mythological roots of science. Medallions filled with insignia and symbols represent the world's oldest academies of science. A painting portrays Prometheus, aided by Athena, stealing the divine fire from the chariot of the sun god. Bas-relief figures represent darkness and light.

Opening off the Great Hall is a walnut-paneled gallery where science-related artworks are exhibited as part of the "Arts in the Academy" program. Some of the artists shown apply scientific technology to their work: holography, high-speed photography, photomicrography, medical photography. Others use unconventional materials like epoxy resin or light or even flowing oil to form sculptures. Some artists are exhibited whose work, although not about scientific subjects, is strongly influenced by scientific imagery and concepts.

When its founders established the "Arts in the Academy" program in 1970, they undoubtedly took to heart the words of Albert Einstein, which they quote today in their literature: "All religions, arts, and sciences are branches of the same tree. All these aspirations are directed toward ennobling man's life, lifting it from the sphere of mere physical existence and leading the individual toward freedom. . . ." Recalling the connection Einstein made between art and science, the monument that the academy erected to his memory in 1979 is very appropriate.

Situated in a grove of elm and holly trees on the corner of Constitution Avenue and 22nd Street, the monument features a statue of the seated Einstein. Sculptor Robert Berks depicted the scientist holding a paper inscribed with the mathematical equations that summarize three of his most important scientific contributions. On the back of the bench, three quotations reflect the scientist's integrity, endless sense of wonder at the world, and concern for social justice. The kindly face of the great scientist, based on a portrait bust sculpted from life, looks down with a mixture of compassion and humor. Most visitors respond with a smile. Some give in to another urge; they climb up into his welcoming lap for a photo.

Note: The academy has a cafeteria, which is usually open to the public.

Old Naval Observatory

In 1873, with the acquisition of the largest telescope in the world, the U.S. Naval Observatory ascended to star status. Prior to that time, the observatory had used small telescopes to establish standards for the almanacs and star catalogs it prepared to aid navigation. With the 26-inch refractor, however, the observatory's role expanded to include astronomical research. Today the observatory ranks as a world-class research institution.

Visitors can chart this growth and also discover the evolution of the science of astronomy in America by joining tours offered at both the original Naval Observatory and the U.S. Naval Observatory that replaced it.

The white dome of the nineteenth-century Naval Observatory gleams on a hilltop in Foggy Bottom. Although the site is now home of the Bureau of Medicine and Surgery, the original structures look much as they did in 1844, when the observatory was known as the Depot of Charts and Instruments. In those days, the facility repaired and rated ship chronometers and maintained charts.

Gradually, the depot turned to astronomy to establish time standards that would enhance its navigational guidance operation. As an outgrowth of this service, the depot became the nation's official timekeeper.

Today, you can still climb the worn wooden stairway that leads to the central rotunda where the first telescope rested on a two-story stone pier. You can stand where the dome once opened to the sky, on the same spot where Abraham Lincoln stood long and silent one night during the Civil War. In the south-wing rotunda, which once housed the 26-inch great equatorial telescope, you can stand where astronomer Asaph Hall discovered the faint objects that turned out to be the moons of Mars.

You can also see the observation shutters through which astronomers charted the stars. And continuing to the east-wing residence of the first superintendent, Matthew Fontaine Maury, you can climb red sandstone stairs to the parlor where Maury launched the science of oceanography.

EMBASSY ROW

U.S. NAVAL OBSERVATORY

The observatory was moved to its current Massachusetts Avenue site in 1893, when smog (the combination of river haze and the smoke of nineteenth-century industrial pollution) affected the quality of observations.

At the second observatory site, you can peer through the old 26-inch telescope moved from the first observatory. Also, you can look through the eyepiece of the century-old 12-inch refractor that the astronomers usually focus on Jupiter or Mars. In contrast to the old telescopes, with their brass fittings that are as beautiful as they are functional, a modern 24-inch steel telescope made in 1960 is strictly utilitarian.

In addition to giving you the chance to observe the night sky through the telescopes, the tour also shows you the facility that is the source for the nation's official timekeeping. Walking through a separate building, you see the latest in clock technology, including the so-called atomic clock. This clock, accurate to within one-billionth of a second, operates on the frequency of a cesium beam shifting between orbits.

BEYOND

NATIONAL INSTITUTES OF HEALTH
BETHESDA, MARYLAND

For budding research scientists and medical buffs, the center of the universe has to be the National Institutes of Health. Over 14,000 employees work in the 21 institutes housed in 50 buildings on the 310-acre campus. By offering tours and exhibits, the Visitors Center gives the curious a chance to see what goes on behind the scenes.

Depending on the weather, the one-hour tour either takes you around the grounds or inside the buildings. On the inside tours you get a look at a couple of labs: one devoted to basic research, another to clinical pathology. At the Visitors Center, you can interact with a half-dozen touch-screen and computer exhibits, including one that gives you a sense of what it's like to do scientific research.

NATIONAL MUSEUM OF HEALTH AND MEDICINE
NORTHWEST WASHINGTON

Tucked away well off the tourist trail at Walter Reed Army Medical Center lies a little-known site that will fascinate medical buffs. Begun in 1862 as the Armed Forces Medical Museum, the National Museum of Health and Medicine today documents the birth of modern medicine.

When the U.S. government began collecting medically related documents, photos, historical artifacts, and anatomical specimens in 1862, the modern science of medicine had just been born. Since those days over 100 years ago, the techniques and practices identified with modern medicine have developed. By viewing the artifacts, you combine the study of history and the study of medical technology. The two fields are brought together in exhibits that illustrate the state of Civil War medicine, the military contribution to medicine, and landmarks in the conquest of disease.

Only a portion of the huge collection can be exhibited in the small museum. Most of the 2.2 million documents and photos, the 12,000 anatomical specimens, and the 325,000 historic artifacts must be stored elsewhere. But you do see a representation of the largest microscope collection in the United States, the bullet—with skull fragments still attached—that killed Abraham Lincoln, a model of a horse-drawn ambulance, and an autopsy kit circa 1871. The artifacts are grouped into four exhibit areas: "Viewing the Body," "Perspectives from the Past," "Exploring Inner Space," and "The Culture of Medicine."

When the medical museum was located on the Mall in the 1960s, it attracted over one million visitors a year. Moved to the Walter Reed Army Medical Center in 1968, it now attracts only 35,000 a year. However, all that may change. Sometime within the decade, the museum hopes to move to a more accessible downtown site. Plans call for a facility with six halls of exhibits that go beyond the present focus on American medical history. The new museum could include exhibits on how the body works, the causes and treatments of common diseases, and how diet and life-style affect health.

Chapter 9

Technology

A Soviet SS-20 missile and a U.S. Pershing II missile. National Air and Space Museum (*Courtesy of the National Air and Space Museum*)

Although technologies may be created and manufactured elsewhere, Washington, like a parent, both nurtures and shows off the new baby. The nurturing, of course, comes from the U.S. government. Funding for research and development originates with such giants as the Department of Defense, NASA, the Federal Aviation Administration, the Environmental Protection Agency, the Federal Communications Commission, and the Department of Commerce.

Because government makes Washington a national stage, new technologies often make their debuts here. Samuel Morse in 1844 tapped out his historic telegraph message, "What hath God wrought," from beneath the dome of the U.S. Capitol. Over 100 years later, in 1965, President Johnson participated in the first commercial communication satellite transmission between the White House and Europe.

Between these two events and since, information technology has been Washington's lifeblood. Communication—the creation of information and its transmission—continues to be the city's number-one activity. Whether a military command, a medical report, or a legislative bill, information technology moves the message from one brain to another. Public broadcasting (PBS and NPR), MCI, COMSAT, and the country's greatest concentration of telecommunication companies are brought together here.

This focus on information technology is reflected in the wealth of exhibits featured in the city's museums and galleries. For the "techie" visitor or resident, this means abounding opportunities to interact with leading-edge computers and media.

The sightseer also discovers a wealth of sites that are technological feats. In few other cities can more structures be described with superlatives: the biggest, the tallest, the first. Some also boast the first use of a state-of-the-art material:

- Washington Monument, the tallest masonry structure in the world, is topped by the country's first aluminum roof.
- The U.S. Capitol dome, made of nine million pounds of cast iron, is one of the world's largest.
- The Pentagon, the largest office building in the world, covers 29 acres with 17 miles of corridors.
- Supreme Court building, probably the the largest marble building in the world.
- U.S. Marine Corps Memorial (Iwo Jima) the largest cast bronze figure in the world.
- The Metro subway system is the largest urban public works project ever undertaken as a single unified design. Built at a cost of $7.1 billion, its 90 miles of track threads through Virginia, Maryland, and the District.

- Washington National Cathedral, begun in 1907 and completed in 1990, triumphs as one of the tallest such structures in the world.

Technological feats, leading-edge information technology—riches await discovery in Washington. In few other cities can one indulge in so many pleasures: touring the headquarters of the world's leading satellite operation, surveying 100 years of industrial and aviation history, seeing state-of-the-art computers and multimedia technology. You'll see the best of Washington's technological sites by following the **Highlight Walk** and by venturing on your own to **More Technology Sites** in the downtown area and beyond.

Highlight Walk
Capitol Hill–The Mall

Even though this walk takes you to familiar landmarks and museums, by focusing on technology, you'll experience them in new ways. On the two-mile walk you'll sample the finest delicacies on Washington's table of technological wonders. At three world-class museums, you'll see the machines that have changed our world. As you focus on the inventors and the technology depicted in the artwork that ornaments the U.S. Capitol, you may come away with a deeper appreciation of America's technological roots.

1. U.S. Capitol

America's reverence for technology reaches new heights—literally and figuratively—in the dome of the U.S. Capitol. Among the frescoes painted 180 feet above the rotunda floor, Aphrodite holds the Atlantic cable and Ceres rides a reaper. The glorified George Washington in the company of gods smiles down on Minerva, who speaks with three inventors: Benjamin Franklin, Samuel Morse, and Robert Fulton.

The tribute to American technology continues in the frieze in the collar of the dome, which presents scenes from American history. Of the eight panels that sum up our nation's greatest moments, the last to be executed, *The Birth of Aviation*, shows the Wright brothers' flight of 1903.

Other references to technology can be seen as you walk the halls of the Capitol. On one ground-floor corridor, panels painted by Constantine Brumidi show Benjamin Franklin in his laboratory, and inventors Robert Fulton and John Fitch with early steamboat models. Most popular is the mural executed by Allyn Cox, which shows the American astronauts who landed on the moon in 1969.

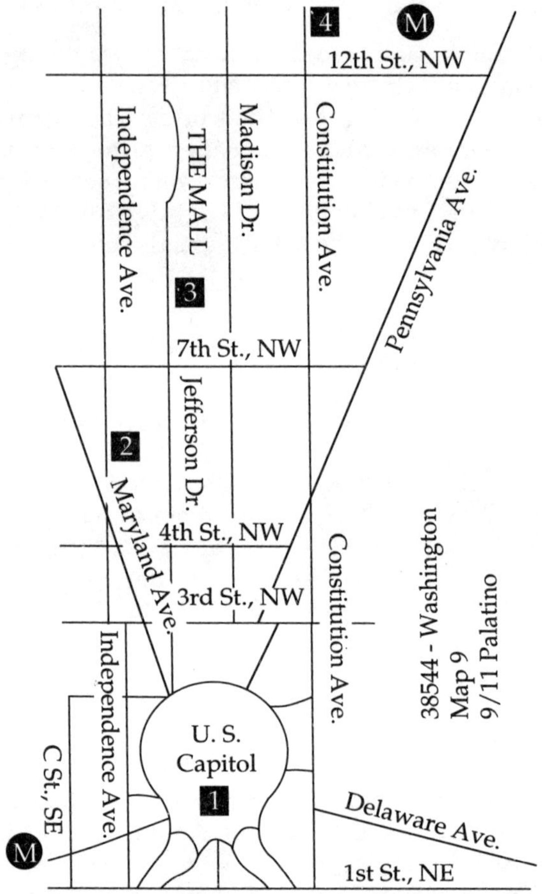

M Metro

1. U.S. Capitol, Capitol Hill
2. National Air and Space Museum, Independence Avenue between 4th and 7th Streets SW
3. Arts and Industries Building, 9th Street at Independence Avenue SW
4. National Museum of American History, 14th Street and Constitution Avenue NW

Route

Begin at the Capitol South Metro subway station and walk to the U.S. Capitol. After your visit, walk around to the West front of the Capitol and head down the stairs. Turn left to Independence Avenue and walk three blocks to the National Air and Space Museum. Continue to the Arts and Industries Building and then cross the Mall to the National Museum of American History. Conclude your tour by walking to the Federal Triangle Metro station at 12th Street between Pennsylvania and Constitution avenues NW.

But of all the tributes to technology, none surpasses the dome itself. Considered a technological tour de force, the Capitol dome marks an innovation in dome engineering. A new technology made that innovation possible: cast iron. With this strong yet lightweight material, designers were freed of the restraints of the coffered masonry domes that had been built since Roman times.

Cast-iron technology came along at the right time. It provided a solution to the problem of how to add a massive dome to the rotunda, which had been built 50 years before. The old foundation and walls were tested and found strong enough to carry the additional weight of the new cast-iron dome. Today, the nine million pounds of cast iron that went into the two trussed shells that make up the dome lie hidden behind a dazzling white veneer. As a result, most who see the dome rarely guess that it is made of cast iron and not the marble that it is painted to resemble.

Neither do most know that beneath the U.S. Capitol, modern technology of another kind made its debut in 1909. In that year, battery-powered coaches made their first runs in the subterranean tunnel that links the Capitol with the Russel Senate Office Building. Today electric subway cars, added in 1939, whisk members and the public between the Capitol and the Rayburn Office Building on the House side, and the Dirksen and Russel Senate Office Buildings. One of the original 1909 coaches, purchased from the Studebaker Company, is on exhibit in the rotunda of the Russel Office Building.

Note: Dining rooms in the Dirksen Senate Office Building and in the Rayburn and Longworth House Office Buildings are open to the public before 11:30 A.M. and after 1:15 P.M. There is also a rooftop restaurant in the Madison wing of the Library of Congress, which offers a spectacular view.

For more information on the U.S. Capitol, see **Gardens** and **Literature**.

Underground Senate Transport

2. National Air and Space Museum

Technology soars in more ways than one in this shrine to the air age. First, in 23 galleries under one 200,000-square-foot roof, you see the evolution of America's technological know-how. Second, because of the technological wizardry used in the design of the building and its exhibit areas, you get the feeling some of the most historic aircraft and spacecraft are flying indoors.

That's because aerospace design strategies were used in the design of the building and its exhibits. On the team, working with the architect, was the museum director—a former aviator-astronaut—and the exhibit designer—an aeronautical engineer; both brought to the project their unique expertise.

They created an extraordinary museum. The three-block-long structure features tinted glass bays and skylights that bring the outdoors in. Suspended from tubular steel trusses that span the ceiling are a half-dozen aircraft, including a DC-3 that weighs eight tons. The trusswork is so unobtrusive that the airplanes seem magically to fly through the air.

In the main exhibition hall, the DC-3 and other of the "Milestones of Flight" take wing. Stars include the Wright brother's *Flyer*, the *Spirit of St.*

Louis, the Bell X-1 that broke the sound barrier in 1947, the Apollo 11 command module that took three astronauts from the moon in 1969, and the Jupiter explorer *Pioneer 10*.

In halls filled with thousands of other aircraft, space vehicles, and flight artifacts, you see aviation history exhibits from "Early Flight" to "World War II Aviation" and "Exploring the Planets." Some of the specimen aircraft and spacecraft were chosen for their historic importance, others for their fame, still others because of the technological triumphs they manifest.

Of the many objects that fall into the category of technological triumph, these are most outstanding:

• *Tracking and Data Relay Satellite replica.* The largest and most sophisticated communications satellite in space. The 57-foot-long, full-scale replica, plus information about an exhibit of photos of the satellite and its terminal, are displayed in the Space Hall.

• *Hubble Space Telescope Test Vehicle.* The largest astronomical space telescope ever built. The full-size structural and dynamic test vehicle, nearly

Lockheed U-2, National Air and Space Museum (*Courtesy of the National Air and Space Museum*)

43 feet high, is displayed in the Space Hall together with photos of the vehicle being built and tested.

• *Voyager 1 Planetary Probe.* The most sophisticated spacecraft sent to explore other worlds. Among the most dramatic discoveries made by its robots were the rings around Jupiter and the active volcanoes on one of its moons. Located in "Exploring the Planets."

• *Viking Lander test capsule.* Refurbished to resemble as closely as possible the landers on the Martian surface. In addition to measuring such natural phenomena as wind velocity and atmospheric pressure, the spacecraft explored the physical properties of surface materials and searched for living organisms. Located in the "Milestones of Flight" gallery.

• *Lockheed U-2C.* The first high-altitude photo-reconnaissance plane to fly over the Soviet Union. The craft's 80-foot wingspan aids in achieving maximum altitude. Soviet jets and antiaircraft missiles were unable to match its performance until 1960, when the U-2 piloted by Francis Gary Powers was brought down in the Soviet Union. The aircraft has played a vital role in reconnaissance in Cuba, China, Vietnam, and the Middle East, and has done civil disaster assessment and environmental monitoring as well. Located in the "Looking at Earth" gallery.

• *Geostationary Operational Environmental Satellite.* The model of the craft first launched in 1976 to provide intensive coverage of a region's daily weather developments, as well as severe storm warnings. Full-scale model located in the "Looking at Earth" gallery.

• *Multi-Spectral Scanner.* Engineering model of the sensor carried on all Landsat satellites. The mechanics, which acquire data in both visible and infrared wavelengths, produce images of Earth that cover an area of about 13,000 square miles. Located in the "Looking at Earth" gallery.

Technology of another sort reaches new heights in the Samuel P. Langley Theater, where motion pictures are projected on the five-story-high IMAX screen. Movies include *On the Wing,* a thrilling film that simulates the wonders of flight; *Flyers,* about American pilots; *To Fly,* an aerial tour of America; and *Living Planet,* an armchair tour of the great monuments of the past. The newest film, *Blue Planet,* features scenes shot on several space shuttle flights by astronauts trained to use the IMAX camera.

Like the Garber Facility, the Air and Space Museum's technological triumphs are often also military high points. Thus, if you're interested in technology, be sure to read the entries on the Garber Facility and the Air and Space Museum in **Military**.

For computer buffs, the highlight of the National Air and Space Museum is the recently opened "Beyond the Limits: Flight Enters the Computer Age." The gallery, organized in seven exhibit areas, illustrates the primary applications of the computer in aerospace design, aerodynamics, computer-aided manufacture, flight testing, air operations, flight simulation, and space operations.

In this gallery reigns the revolutionary CRAY-1. This supercomputer is the first with enough speed (more than 200 million operations per second) to predict complex aerodynamic behavior. With its ability to generate graphics that can model aerodynamic forces as accurately as the most sophisticated wind tunnel, the CRAY-1 changed aerodynamic research.

The result of the first use of computer-aided design to develop an entire airframe is also on exhibit in this galley: the Grumman X-29 Research Aircraft. It is the first plane to combine the canard wing design with ultralight composite materials and fully computerized controls. Completely dependent on three on-board computers, the fighter aircraft is highly maneuverable.

Note: A cafeteria and restaurant are located at the east end of the museum.

For more information on the National Air and Space Museum, see **Military** and **Science**.

3. Arts and Industries Building

Stepping back 100 years into early industrial America, you hear the clank, bang, whir, and squeak of a dozen machines. That's because the Smithsonian Institution, in its bicentennial exhibit, displays many of the actual machines that drew throngs to the Philadelphia Centennial Exposition of 1876. On regularly scheduled tours, sound effects are added as volunteer docents monitor the gauges that crank, turn, and pull a fantasy of levers, ropes, and wheels.

When the bicentennial exhibit, officially entitled the "1876 Centennial Exhibition," opened in 1976, it rambled through four halls in the vintage Arts and Industries Building. In addition to machinery, the original exhibit included displays from individual states and a hall of manufactured goods, including French lace, clocks, steel forgings, telescopes, perfume, and pistols. One hall featured objects from U.S. government agencies, including the Alaskan totem pole that's now in the Museum of Natural History.

Although the space devoted to centennial displays will dwindle, some objects most likely will remain—for good reason. Finding alternative space for such giants as a 19-ton steam engine, and then actually moving them, isn't easy, even for the Smithsonian. So, if you're a technology buff, you're pretty sure of discovering some fascinating machinery when you stop by.

The wonders of nineteenth-century America await your inspection. Here are steam-powered machines of every description—pumps, printing presses, machine tools, dynamos, plus a 19-ton refrigeration compressor.

These are must-see stars:

• *Corliss steam engine.* A 1/12th model of a machine similar to the one that 1876 exposition-goers hailed as "the ultimate manifestation of American technological prowess." The largest steam engine in the world, the 700-ton Corliss drove all the machinery in Machinery Hall and was the focal point of the entire exposition. The Corliss Centennial Engine became a monument to be matched by only the Statue of Liberty herself. But it wasn't only the size of the original machine that awed visitors. As remarkable were the innovative features that it boasted. One of the most outstanding is the pinion gear under the floor that transfers power by engaging teeth on the face of the flywheel; the 30-foot flatbelt around the flywheel was the largest gear-wheel ever made.

Railroad man George Pullman appreciated both the monumental character of the Corliss engine and its efficiency. He bought the engine after the exposition closed and used it to power the machinery in his car works outside Chicago. Robert Post, writing in the exhibition catalog, notes that Pullman had an impressively appointed engine house erected for the Corliss engine "and there it worked in awesome grandeur for nearly thirty years."

• *Military steam engine.* Constructed in 1864 to power machine-shop equipment. It's one of the few such all-purpose machines still in existence. Also, it's of historical importance, as it kept railroad equipment running during the Civil War and thus added greatly to the success of the Union forces.

• *Linde-Wolf ammonia compressor.* The first means of mechanical refrigeration. In the early 1870s a group of brewers commissioned inventor Carl P. G. Linde to come up with an alternative to ice as a means of keeping their product cold. Linde applied the vapor-compression principle, using ammonia as a refrigerant. The machine here was once installed at the John F. Wiessner Brewery in Baltimore. Built in 1884, it may be the earliest surviving refrigeration compressor in America.

• *Otis steam elevator machine and freight platform.* This is the two-cylinder machine installed in 1873 in the Grand Union Hotel in Saratoga Springs. The engine drives the primary shaft through a leather flatbelt; this shaft, in turn, drives the winding drum and the double gears. Note the service brake on the primary shaft, the endless rope passing beneath the platform floor that controls the mechanism, and the "wagon spring" safety stop mounted under the overhead hoist beam. If the cable breaks, the spring (normally held in stress by normal tension) relaxes. The relaxation movement causes pawls on the side columns to move out and engage racks on the shaftway guides, thus stopping the platform.

• *"The Jupiter."* An American-type locomotive, the 4-4-0 was built in 1876 by the Baldwin Locomotive Works for the Santa Cruz Railroad. This mainstay of American railroads has a 3-foot gauge engine with 12 x 18-inch cylinders and 42-inch wheels. Similar engines were used in the golden spike ceremony that celebrated the completion of the transcontinental railroad in 1869. Relatively few have survived.

Also worth special attention is the Rogers woodworking machine and, in the Connecticut state exhibit in the manufacturing hall, the Pratt-Whitney Company display of two varieties of machine tools.

4. National Museum of American History

Once called the Museum of History and Technology, the famous collection here retains much of its original focus. Most of the first floor bursts with the tools and machines that dramatize our technological evolution.

You get an overview of America's transformation from an agricultural economy to an industrial power in the centerpiece exhibit "Engines of Change: The American Industrial Revolution, 1790–1860." The exhibit tells the story of the people and machines that contributed to the revolution that focused international attention on the superiority of American technology. Most important for the technology buff, it spotlights the nineteenth-century innovations in machinery, interchangeable parts, and the factory system. Over 250 objects are featured in the exhibit.

Highlights of "Engines of Change":

- *McCormick reaper.*
- *Spinning machine.* From the first successful spinning mill in the United States.
- *John Bull locomotive.* The oldest operable, self-propelled vehicle in the world.
- *John Howe's 1840 pin machine.* One of the oldest surviving pieces of automated machinery.
- *Models of some of the best-known inventions.* The Whitney cotton gin, the Howe sewing machine, and the Morse telegraph can all be seen.

In addition to the machines and models spotlighted here, you'll discover milestones of American technology in eight other exhibit areas.

Hall of Agriculture:

- *Old Red.* The International Harvester cotton harvester of 1942, symbol of the transformation of the labor-intensive old cotton culture to a new one dominated by machines.
- *J. I. Case Company's first portable steam engine.* Built in 1869.
- *Benjamin Holt's combination harvester and thresher.* An early version of a modern combine.

Hall of Road Transportation:

- *Duryea (1893) steam-powered carriage.*
- *Haynes (1894) experimental automobile.* America's earliest.
- *1903 Oldsmobile Curved Dash Runabout.*
- *1913 Model-T Ford.* One of 15 million sold between 1909 and 1927.
- *1902 Winton Bullet racing car.*

Railroad Hall:

- *Promontory, Utah, ceremony spike.* Used to mark the 1869 opening of the transcontinental railroad and the unification of the country by rail.
- *Stourbridge Lion of 1829.* The first steam locomotive to operate in the Western hemisphere.
- *Southern Railway's "1401."* Built in 1926, the 92-foot engine and tender hauled passengers over two million miles from 1926 to 1951.
- *Pioneer.* The 12½-ton engine of 1851 served for 40 years on the Cumberland Valley Railroad.

Hall of Power Machinery:

- *1880 Francis reaction turbine.* Typifies the most efficient later water turbines.
- *1901 Riedler pumping engine.* Driven by a Pelton impulse turbine.
- *1819 Holloway ten-horsepower engine.* The oldest surviving relic of American-built stationary steam engines.
- *1905 turbogenerator of Charles Parsons.* Parsons was a pioneer designer of the commercially successful steam turbine.
- *1927 Curtis-General Electric steam turbine.*
- *Steam-driven Frick ammonia compressor from 1898.* A standard of the refrigeration industry from 1880 to 1920.

Hall of American Maritime Enterprise:

- *Oldest commercial marine propeller known.* Survived from the *Indiana,* which sunk in Lake Superior in 1858.
- *Oldest surviving steam plant built in the United States.*
- *Engine and boiler of John Steven's* Little Julilana.
- *Whaleboat from the SS* Charles W. Morgan.

Hall of Bridges and Tunnels:

- *The world's only major railroad suspension bridge.* Section of the original cable, and model of the bridge built over the Niagara River in 1855. Brooklyn Bridge designer John August Roebling proved the strength and practicality of iron-wire suspension bridges with his 821-foot span.

The 1990 debut of the "Information Age: People, Information and Technology" exhibit at the National Museum of American History changed forever the possibilities of a museum visit. Now, for the first time, you not only see and hear the artifact of the information revolution, you also interact with state-of-the art technology. Remote concepts become real as you become personally involved.

The real genius stroke of the exhibit is the bar-coded brochure that you receive when you enter. As you walk through the exhibit area, you'll undoubtedly stop at some of the 14 video stations or 24 computer-driven workstations. If you place the bar-coded brochure against the scanner at a workstation, your activities will be logged and stored on the exhibition's computer network. When you leave, you'll receive a printout souvenir of what you did at the exhibit. Making all this possible is a complete computer network that ties together the interactive workstations, videos, films, and radio recordings in the exhibit hall.

In addition to viewing the exhibit as a state-of-the-art interactive experience, you can also tour the world of communication technology from the micro to the macro. If you concentrate on the individual objects, you'll have 700 gems to discover. You'll get an overview that encompasses 150 years of history within the confines of the 14,000-square-foot exhibit hall.

The exhibit breaks down the history of information technology chronologically into three sections: 1835 to 1939, World War II, and 1946 to the present. Other areas are devoted to a multimedia film presentation that uses the latest video technology, and to an interactive gallery where visitors try their hand at computer-aided design, on-line data bases, and experiments with computer voice recognition.

Highlights among the artifacts on display include Samuel Morse's original telegraph, Alexander Graham Bell's original telephone, the Hollerith tabulating system, and the R2D2 and C-3PO robotic heroes of *Star Wars*. Hands-on displays include a re-creation of a Combat Information Center, where visitors will be able to encipher their own names using the ENIGMA code, and the "Finder," where they can have their thumbprints read.

Note: Both a cafeteria and the Palm Court restaurant are available to visitors.

For more information on the National Museum of American History, see **Literature**, **Military**, **Music**, and **Science**.

More Technology

The Mall

National Gallery of Art

State-of-the-art technology and the works of the world's greatest artists come together as never before at the new high-definition video theater opened here in the winter of 1991. The electronic imaging system that makes sharp, brilliant pictures possible has been installed in cooperation with the Sony Corporation of America. Now, seated in a comfortable theater, you see the ultimate in visual projection as works from the collection are presented in special shows. As one of the country's only high-definition video facilities open to the public, it's an exciting example of the wedding of technology and art.

Downtown

Union Station

One of the great monuments to the heyday of railroad passenger travel stands on the edge of Capitol Hill. Union Station, built in 1908, has recently undergone a $160-million restoration.

Tributes in stone celebrate the technology that made the emergence of the railroad possible. Foremost are the statues of heroic figures that top the columns at the entrance and look down from balconies inside. These 18-foot figures, inspired by the Golden Age of Greece, symbolize the forces that made the railroads possible: fire, electricity, and mechanics. The inscriptions over the arches also pay eloquent tributes to technology:

> Electricity: carrier of light and power, devourer of time and space, bearer of human speech over land and sea, greatest servant of man, itself unknown. Thou hast put all things under his feet.

Group tours that highlight the history and architecture of the station can be arranged.

Note: Union Station offers an array of restaurants and a fast-food court.

Tech 2000 Gallery

If you've ever envied Mr. Spock of "Star Trek" as he manipulates those futuristic control panels, this is the place for you. With a visit to this new gallery of interactive multimedia technology, you'll be masterminding the universe in no time.

Developed by the Interactive Multi-Media Association, Tech 2000 features a hands-on exhibit of more than 85 video, computing, and telecommunication technologies. The showcases exhibit $1.5 million worth of emerging technologies, with the emphasis on interactive systems and media.

Even without a high-tech orientation, you can operate the user-friendly machines; instructions posted beside each exhibit help. The lifelike manikins that populate the gallery add to the user-friendly atmosphere.

With the help of the gallery staff or by reading the instructions beside each exhibit, you easily become a participant in this electronic festival. You can choose from a large menu of intellectual and sensory experiences. Among the exhibits are those that simulate riding a bobsled, flying a plane, driving a car, and playing golf on a private course. Other interactive programs offer instructions on operating such things as forklifts and cash registers. Interactive educational programs include one called G.T.V., produced for National Geographic by Lucas Films and Apple Computer. This computer-controlled TV allows the user to pick and choose what he or she wants to see. You can click on a certain period of a time line and pick a subject area.

By using the "Interactive Landscape and Design" program, you can plan a garden. At last—planting a tree without picking up a shovel! This new technology also allows you to decorate an interior, changing the color of the drapes and moving furniture around without any lifting.

But of all the exhibits, nothing beats—in more ways than one—the Mandala System. This "virtual reality machine" allows you actually to beat a drum as you interact with an imaginary rock band or other musical group. The revolutionary technology is the first of its kind. The mechanism (reminiscent of that in the movie *Tron*) uses a video camera and software to insert your image into the computer animation. When specific graphics functions are touched, they trigger animation and sound. You see yourself beating the drum or cymbal and you hear the sounds the instruments make as you do.

Much more awaits discovery in the 10,000-square-foot gallery that is divided into nine subject areas. In organizing the gallery, curators have grouped the exhibited pieces into categories that relate to their application: Areas are designated for the home, work, art and culture, town square, and learning.

National Building Museum

The restored Pension Building, completed in 1887, boasts a central Great Hall that is large enough to contain a 15-story building placed sideways. This astonishing interior space (the site of 12 inaugural balls), together with the galleries that surround it, now houses the National Building Museum.

Mandated by Congress in 1980, the museum focuses on various aspects of the building industry. Craftspeople, engineers, architects, developers, and preservationists are represented in the exhibitions that fill its galleries. Previous exhibits have spotlighted the use of materials in building, current issues, architectural styles, and tools. The museum's annual "Festival of the Building Arts" brings together craftspeople who demonstrate their skills and invite participation.

Foggy Bottom

Lincoln Memorial

From a technological viewpoint, the Lincoln Memorial is a marvel of engineering. To appreciate it, you'll want to see the display beneath the monument that chronicles the construction of the memorial. A window overlooks the foundation, where stalactites and stalagmites have formed. Despite rumors to the contrary, the tours that once took place beneath the monument have been discontinued permanently.

Beyond

Intelsat
Northwest Washington

If you've ever imagined how the world will look a 100 years from now, you've probably pictured a building like the INTELSAT World Center. Communications satellites from the International Telecommunications Satellite

Intelsat (*Courtesy of Intelsat*)

Organization (INTELSAT) provide 180 countries with their internal and international communications links.

The future seems to have materialized here under a huge atrium that arches 80 feet into the sky. Set on 18 acres of grounds, the square atrium, flanked by steel and glass-block towers and pods, shines like a highly polished spaceship. Dwarfed by the sheer cliff of soaring glass and steel, the satellites positioned at the base of the building tilt their antennae toward the sky. Contrasting shapes, the mammoth scale of the structure, and its gleaming skin of glass add up to a unique visual experience.

Inside in the lobby, the fantastic journey continues. Suspended from the stainless steel ceiling are models of seven different satellites INTELSAT has launched into space in the last 25 years. The models, one-half or three-quarters their actual size, give you a rare overview of the evolving technology.

You see the world's first commercial communications satellite, the *Early Bird,* launched in 1965. In contrast, a model of the newest generation of satellites, INTELSAT VI, features digital circuit multi-impactation equipment that multiplies the capacity of the *Early Bird* 500 times.

Before pointing out the various models, the tour guide leads the way into the theater, where visitors see a ten-minute multi-screen film. The presentation includes information on the role of the international organization and its satellite network.

Highlights for "techies" are views of two work areas, which are seen from glassed-in balconies. One balcony overlooks the Satellite Control Center, where technicians jockey the spacecraft into geosynchronous orbit. They also reposition and maneuver space station satellites to keep them in orbit.

The second balcony overlooks the Operations Center, or Earth station, which handles the traffic over the system. You see the staff and mechanisms that control access to the Earth station links in the INTELSAT network. Video monitors flicker with the images that coordinate various verification tests and demonstrations. A huge world map that reaches almost two stories high from floor to ceiling shows the locations of satellites in space and the Earth stations. Although you don't hear the beeps, bells, and hum of the operations room, the guide's commentary helps you understand what's going on.

As the guide tells the story of the 1990 mislaunch of the $150-million IS-VI F3, you can almost feel the tension. During that launch from this control center, a mechanical failure in the rocket caused the F3 to spin into space. Just in time, the experts at control headquarters located the spacecraft, opened communication lines, and issued commands that boosted it into a low Earth orbit, where it would be safe until it could be rescued. The drama continued in 1992 when, in the same control room, the rescue mission attempted to reboost the recalcitrant spacecraft.

The 45-minute tour is available by reservation for both individuals and groups. The regular tour is slanted toward the layperson, but a more technologically sophisticated tour can be arranged.

Alexandria Waterfront Museum
Alexandria, Virginia

A pre–Civil War lift lock that was once a link in the seven-mile extension of the C&O Canal into Alexandria is the centerpiece of the Alexandria Waterfront Museum. Excavated in 1978, the lock is listed on the National Register of Historic Places. In addition to seeing the lock and the pool, you can see changing exhibitions that relate to the development of Alexandria's waterfront.

Garber Facility
Suitland, Maryland

Anyone who's had an overflowing closet knows the problem. With more possessions than space, some things simply must go into storage. When the National Air and Space Museum runs out of room to display the aircraft it owns, the overflow goes to the 14 warehouses at the Paul E. Garber Preservation, Restoration, and Storage Facility.

Since the mid-1950s, when the Smithsonian Institution began using the facility, 160 historically significant aircraft and spacecraft have been sent to the facility. On behind-the-scenes tours, visitors see the collection that also includes thousands of air and space artifacts.

As part of the museum's increasing emphasis on conservation, work includes not only restoration but also preservation. Increasingly, technicians at the facility save the history of air- and spacecraft technology by preserving original paint, fabric, and parts.

Sometimes conservation only involves cleaning the vehicle. In other cases the craft must undergo a total restoration down to the last nut and bolt. Every effort is made to restore the craft to a condition as close to original as possible.

The Paul E. Garber Facility was named in honor of the man who played a key role in establishing the facility. Garber, who joined the Smithsonian Institution staff in 1920, was instrumental in acquiring such aircraft as Charles Lindbergh's *Spirit of St. Louis;* Wiley Post's *Winnie Mae;* and the Curtiss NC-4, the first airplane to cross the Atlantic.

During the two-hour tours, trained guides tell the stories of the most famous aircraft. Some are notable for the historical role they played, or for a particular accomplishment. Others represent a technological milestone or stage of aeronautical development. Still others are the sole surviving examples of their type.

Although it might be argued that almost all of the 150 aircraft being preserved at the Garber Facility are technologically noteworthy, some shine like suns among mere stars. In the selection here, those aircraft with primarily military associations have been excluded. You'll find a separate highlight list in **Military**.

Here, then, are some of the advanced prototypes, important firsts, and crafts considered innovative and technological breakthroughs.

HIGHLIGHTS:

• *Bellanca C.F.* The 1922 airplane that was the most efficient of its day. With a string of 13 first-place wins at major air meets, the elegant airplane accommodated four passengers luxuriously in its fully enclosed cabin. Advanced as it was, however, the *Bellanca C.F.* was the only one of its type ever built; the days of cost-effective passenger service had not yet arrived.

• *Benoist Type XII.* A prime example of pre–World War I American aeronautical technology. The 1912 two-place biplane featured the first closed-fuselage, tractor-type (engine up front) aircraft built in the United States. Rather than copying the Wright and Curtiss machines or popular European models, the designer created a completely original design.

• *Stinson SR-10F Reliant.* The first craft to perform an aerial pickup of a human.

• *Northrop N-1M Flying Wing.* The first true flying wing produced in the United States. The attempt at creating an aerodynamically clean craft, unveiled in 1940, removed as unnecessary drag the engine nacelles, fuselage, and tail surfaces. Two engines within the fuselages drove two pusher propellers; elvons on the wing's trailing edge served as both elevators and ailerons; a split-flap device on each wing tip replaced the conventional rudder. Although the craft performed poorly on test flights, the flying wing design of the B-2 Stealth bomber is a direct descendant.

For more information on the Garber Facility, see **Military**.

TOURIST RESOURCES

Washington D.C. Convention and Visitors Association, 1212 New York Avenue NW, Washington, D.C. 20005, (202) 789-7000. Request information by phone or letter and you'll receive a variety of brochures on sites, tours, and transportation, including a good map.

Washington Visitor Information Center, 1455 Pennsylvania Avenue NW, Washington, D.C. 20004, (202) 789-7038. A walk-in center for brochures and information on special events. Open 9 am to 5 pm Monday through Saturday.

Washington Metropolitan Area Transit Authority, 600 5th Street NW, Washington, D.C. 20001, (202) 637-7000. The authority offers bus and subway service in the District and to suburban Maryland and Virginia. The Metro subway serves many of the major tourist sites. Write or call for the brochure "All About the Metro System," or pick it up at the Metro Center station office.

National Park Service, U.S. Department of the Interior, 1100 Ohio Drive SW, Washington, D.C. 20242, (202) 485-9666. Write for brochures on the memorials.

Smithsonian Institution Visitors Information and Associate Reception Center, 1000 Jefferson Drive SW, Washington D.C. 20560. (202) 357-2700. Staff at the center answers questions and hands out information on the museums and special programs. Also, the Smithsonian's Resident Associate office runs numerous half- and full-day tours in and around Washington. For a membership fee, you can join and get a newsletter of scheduled tours.

Special Interest Tours Inc., P.O. Box 33033, Washington, D.C. 20033, (202) 467-4402. Offers VIP and group tours with special interest itineraries and commentary; arranges special VIP on-site tours, walking tours or transportation, guide service, imaginative meals, refreshments, and special events.

REFERENCES

Adams, Henry. *Democracy*. New York: Farrar Straus & Young, 1879.

Ames, Mary Clemer. *Ten Years in Washington City*. Hartford: A.D. Worthington, 1874.

Cable, Mary. *Avenue of the Presidents*. Boston: Houghton Mifflin, 1969.

Choukas, Bradley and Melanie Choukas. *City of Trees*. Baltimore: Johns Hopkins University Press, 1987.

Cooling, Benjamin Franklin. *Symbol, Sword and Shield*, Hamden, Conn.: Archon Books, 1975.

Corcoran Gallery of Art. *Handbook of American Painting in the Collection of The Corcoran Gallery of Art*. Washington: Corcoran Gallery of Art, 1947.

Cutler, David. *Literary Washington*. Lanham, Md.: Madison Books, 1989.

Dickens, Charles. *American Notes and Pictures from Italy*. New York: Pollard and Moss, 1885.

(Dolkart, Andrew). *The Old Executive Office Building: A Victorian Masterpiece*. Washington: U.S. Government Printing Office, 1984.

Getlein, Frank. *The Washington D.C. Art Review*. New York: Vanguard, 1980.

Green, Constance McLaughlin. *Washington: Capital City 1879–1950*. Princeton, N.J.: Princeton University Press, 1963.

Green, Eleanor. *Master Paintings from The Phillips Collection*. Sandy Hook, Conn.: Pennhurst Books, 1988.

Halle, Louis. *Springtime in Washington*. New York: Atheneum, 1963.

Hawthorne, Nathaniel. *The American Notebook*. New Haven: Yale University, 1933.

James, Henry. *The American Scene*. Bloomington: Indiana University Press, 1968.

Lee, Douglas Bennet, Roger L. Meersman, and Donn L. Murphy. *Stage for a Nation: The National Theatre 150 Years*. Lanham, Md.: University Press of America, 1985.

Lee, Richard M. *Mr. Lincoln's City: An Illustrated Guide to the Civil War Sites of Washington*. McLean, Va.: EPM Publications, 1981.

Peters, James Edward. *Arlington National Cemetery: Shrine to America's Heroes*. Rockville, Md.: Woodbine House, 1986.

Post, Robert. *1886: A Centennial Exhibition*. Washington, D.C.: Smithsonian Press, 1976.

Reingold, Nathan. *Science in 19th Century America*. Chicago: University of Chicago Press, 1985.

Riley, Laura and William Riley. *Guide to the National Wildlife Refuges*. Garden City, N.Y.: Anchor Press, 1979.

Rosenberger, Francis Coleman. *Washington and the Poet*. Charlottesville: University Press of Virginia, 1977.

Small, Herbert. *The Library of Congress: Its Architecture and Decoration*. New York: W. W. Norton & Co., 1982.

Southwick, Louise Hardin. *Avenue of the Presidents*. Boston: Houghton Miffin Co., 1969.

Thomas, Bill and Phyllis Thomas. *Natural Washington*. New York: Holt, Rinehart and Winston, 1980.

Whitman, Walt. *Specimen Days in America*. London: G. Routledge, 1887.

Wilmerding, John. *American Masterpieces from the National Gallery of Art*. New York: Hudson Hills Press, 1980.

WHERE AND WHEN

African Museum of Art. See National Museum of African Art.

Air and Space Museum. See National Air and Space Museum.

Alexandria Waterfront Museum, 44 Canal Center Plaza, Alexandria. (703) 838-4288. Exhibits, canal lock remnant. Open 11 A.M. to 4 P.M. Tuesday through Friday; 1 to 4 P.M. weekends. Free. **Technology** (pg. 204).

American Association for the Advancement of Science, 1333 H Street NW. (202) 326-6672. Art exhibits in atrium. Open 9 A.M. to 5 P.M. Monday through Friday. Free. **Science** (pg. 177).

American History Museum. See National Museum of American History.

American Red Cross National Headquarters, 17th and D streets NW. 737-8300. Tiffany windows. Open 9 A.M. to 5 P.M. weekdays. Free. **Art** (pg. 36).

Anderson House, 2118 Massachusetts Avenue NW. (202) 785-2040. Historic residence, garden, library. Open 1 P.M. to 4 P.M. Tuesday thru Saturday. Tours. Free. **Antiques** (pg. 14), **Gardens** (pg. 65), **Literature** (pg. 106), **Military** (pg. 120), **Music and Theater** (pg. 152).

Aquarium. See National Aquarium.

Arboretum. See National Arboretum.

Arlington National Cemetery, Arlington, Virginia. (703) 692-0931. Military gravesites, memorials, Tomb of Unknown Soldier, Custis-Lee House, tours, services. Open 8 A.M. to 7 P.M. in summer; 8 A.M. to 5 P.M. in winter. The changing-of-the-guard ceremony is held on the hour and the half-hour during the summer, and on the hour during the winter. Tourmobile tours. Free. **Military** (pg. 125).

Army Ordnance Museum, Army Proving Ground, Aberdeen, Maryland, reached via U.S. 40 or I-95. (301) 278-3602. A laboratory in which students from the Army Ordnance School study the evolution of the tools of war. Features hundreds of exhibits, including scores of tank designs. Open noon to 4:45 P.M. Tuesday through Friday, 10 A.M. to 4:45 P.M. weekends. Free. **Military** (pg. 136).

Art Museum of the Americas (formerly Museum of Modern Art of Latin America), 201 18th Street NW. (202) 458-6016. Art gallery, gardens, tours, programs. Open 10 A.M. to 5 P.M. Tuesday through Saturday. Free. **Art** (pg. 36).

Arthur Sackler Gallery. See Sackler Gallery.

Arts and Industries Building, 9th Street at Independence Avenue SW. (202) 357-2700. Exhibits, demonstrations, shop. Open 10 A.M. to 5:30 P.M. daily. Free. **Technology** (pg. 195).

Australian Embassy, 1601 Massachusetts Avenue NW. (202) 797-3000. Open 9 A.M. to 4:30 P.M. weekdays. Art gallery.

Austrian Embassy, 3524 International Court NW. (202) 895-6700. Periodic art exhibits. Gallery open 9 A.M. to 5 P.M. weekdays. **Art** (pg. 30).

Barney Studio House, 2306 Massachusetts Avenue NW. (202) 357-3111. Historic residence, tours. Open by reservation only, 11 A.M. and 1 P.M. Wednesday and Thursday; 1 P.M. on the second and fourth Sunday, October through June. Free. **Music and Theater** (pg. 147).

Botanic Garden, U.S., First Street and Maryland Avenue SW. (202) 226-4082. Greenhouse gardens. Open 9 A.M. to 5 P.M. daily, until 9 P.M. in June, July, and August. Free. **Gardens** (pg. 73).

Brazilian-American Cultural Institute, 4100 Connecticut Avenue NW. (202) 362-8334. Open 9 A.M. to 9 P.M. weekdays. Art gallery, films, language classes.

Brookside Gardens, 1500 Glenallan Avenue, Wheaton, Maryland. (301) 949-8230. Gardens, conservatory. Open 9 A.M. to 5 P.M. daily. Free. **Gardens** (pg. 89).

Bull Run Regional Park, Fairfax, Virginia. (703) 631-0550. Trails, programs, annual Blue Belle Walk. Open dawn to dusk from March through November. Free to local residents. Directions: From the Beltway take I-66 west, exit at Centreville, turn right on Route 29 and continue three miles to park sign. Free. **Nature** (pg. 162).

Cabin John Regional Park, 7400 Tuckerman Lane, Rockville, Maryland. (301) 299-4555. Open year-round. Free. **Nature** (pg. 170).

Canadian Embassy, 501 Pennsylvania Avenue NW. (202) 682-1740. Art gallery, exhibits, theater, tours. Open 10 A.M. to 5 P.M. weekdays. Free. **Art** (pg. 30).

Capitol, U.S. Capitol Hill. Monument, exhibits, tours, shop. Open 9 A.M. to 4:30 P.M. daily (until 8 P.M. in summer). Historic site, tours. Tour office (202) 225-6827. Free. **Gardens** (Pg. 72), **Technology** (pg. 189).

Chesapeake & Ohio Canal National Historical Park. Visitor center at Great Falls Tavern, 11710 MacArthur Boulevard, Potomac, Maryland. (202) 472-4376. Canal trail, boat trips, programs. There is a second visitor center at 1057 Thomas Jefferson Street (between K and M streets) in Georgetown. (202) 653-5844. Both offer mule-drawn barge trips along the canal. Fee. **Nature** (pg. 159).

Christian Heurich Mansion. See Heurich Mansion.

Columbian Consulate, 1825 Connecticut Avenue NW, Suite 218. (202) 387-8338. Open 9 P.M. to 1 P.M. weekdays, and afternoons by appointment. Art gallery.

Confederate Memorial Hall, 1322 Vermont Avenue NW. (202) 483-5700. Exhibits, library, special events. Open by appointment. Free. **Military** (pg. 137).

Constitution Gardens, between 17th and 23rd streets NW. Memorial, gardens. Open dawn to dusk. Free. **Gardens** (pg. 77).

Corcoran Gallery of Art, 17th Street and New York Avenue NW. (202) 638-3211. Art museum, shop, cafe. Open 10 A.M. to 5 P.M. Tuesday through Sunday; 10 A.M. to 9 P.M. Thursday. Donation. **Antiques** (pg. 9), **Art** (pg. 35), **Music** (pg. 152).

DAR Museum, 1776 D Street NW. (202) 628-1776. Period rooms, antique exhibits, library, tours. Open 8:30 A.M. to 4 P.M. Monday through Friday; Sunday, 1 to 5 P.M. Tours. Free. **Antiques** (pg. 10).

Decatur House, H Street and Jackson Place NW. (202) 842-0920. Historic residence, shop, tours, programs. Open 10 A.M. to 2 P.M. Tuesday through Friday; noon to 4 P.M. weekends. Admission. **Antiques** (pg. 21).

Diplomatic Reception Rooms. See State Department.

Dirksen Senate Office Building, 1st Street and Constitution Avenue NE. Public cafeteria open weekdays before 11:30 A.M., after 1:15 P.M. **Technology** (pg. 191).

Dumbarton House, 2715 Q Street NW. (202) 337-2288. Historic residence, gardens, tours, programs. Open 9 A.M. to 12:30 P.M. Monday through Saturday. Tours. Free. **Antiques** (pg. 15), **Gardens** (pg. 68).

Dumbarton Oaks, 31st and R streets NW. (202) 342-3200. Historic residence, gardens, tours, programs. Collection open daily except Mondays, 2 to 5 P.M. Garden open 2 to 6 P.M. April through October; 2 to 5 P.M. November through March. Tours, concerts. Admission to garden only. **Antiques** (pg. 18), **Art** (pg. 38), **Gardens** (pg. 69), **Music and Theater** (pg. 148).

Dumbarton Oaks Park, behind Dumbarton Oaks off unmarked road on the north side of R Street, near 31st Street NW. Trails. Open daylight hours but closes during the winter. (202) 426-6832. Free. **Gardens** (pg. 71).

Dyke Marsh, George Washington Memorial Parkway at Belle Haven picnic area. (703) 285-2225. Trails, bird-watching tours. Entrance is about one mile south, beyond the intersection of I-95. Open dawn to dusk. Free. **Nature** (pg. 162).

Eastern Neck National Wildlife Refuge, Rockhall, Maryland. (301) 639-7056. Trails, bird-watching, boating facilities. From Rockhall via Maryland 445, south across the bridge. Open daily dawn to dusk. Free. **Nature** (pg. 170).

Einstein Planetarium. See National Air and Space Museum.

Federal Reserve Board, C Street between 20th and 21st streets, NW. (202) 452-3686. Art gallery, garden. Open 11:30 A.M. to 2 P.M. Tuesday through Friday. Free. **Art** (pg. 37), **Gardens** (pg. 73).

Folger Shakespeare Library, 201 East Capital Street SE. (202) 544-7077. Theater, library exhibits, concerts, garden, tours. Open 10 A.M. to 4 P.M. daily, except Sundays. Free. **Gardens** (pg. 71), **Literature** (pg. 102), **Music and Theater** (pg. 144).

Ford's Theater, 511 10th Street NW. (202) 426-6924. Theater, museum exhibits, tours. Open 9 A.M. to 5 P.M. daily, except during matinees and afternoon rehearsals, when the theater is closed. Free. **Music and Theater** (pg. 144).

Fort Ward Museum and Historic Site, 4301 West Braddock Road, Alexandria, Virginia. (703) 838-4848. Museum, grounds, tours, special events. Open 9 A.M. to 5 P.M. Tuesday through Saturday; noon to 5 P.M. Sunday. Free. **Military** (pg. 133).

Fort Washington Park, Prince Georges County, Maryland. (301) 763-4600. Historic fort, trails, tours, programs. Open 7:30 A.M. to 8 P.M. daily in summer; closes at 5 P.M. in the winter. Admission. To reach the fort, take Beltway exit 3 (Indian Head Highway, Route 210) south. Drive 4½ miles south. **Military** (pg. 137).

Franciscan Monastery, 1400 Quincy Street NE. (202) 526-6800. Shrines, gardens. Open 9 A.M. to 5 P.M. daily. Donations. **Gardens** (pg. 82).

Freer Gallery of Art, 12th Street and Independence Avenue SW. (202) 357-2700. Exhibits, tours, programs. Open 10 A.M. to 5:30 P.M. daily. Free. **Art** (pg. 46).

Garber Facility, Saint Barnabas Road at Silver Hill Road, Suitland, Maryland. (202) 357-1400. Exhibits, tours. Open 9 A.M. to 5 P.M. Monday through Friday; 10 A.M. to 1 P.M., Saturday and Sunday. Tours by reservations. Free. **Military** (pg. 129), **Technology** (pg. 204).

Great Falls Park, 9200 Old Dominion Drive, Great Falls, Virginia. (703) 759-2915. Trails, tours, programs. Accessible both from the Virginia side of the Potomac River and from the Maryland side. Admission on Virginia side. **Nature** (pg. 163).

Haupt Victorian Garden, behind the Smithsonian Castle, accessible from both Jefferson Drive and Independence Avenue NW. Gardens. Open daily from dawn to dusk. Free. **Gardens** (pg. 74).

Heurich Mansion, Historical Society of Washington, 1307 New Hampshire Avenue NW. (202) 785-2068. Historic residence, gardens, library, tours. Open noon to 4 P.M. Wednesday, Friday, Saturday. Admission. **Gardens** (pg. 65), **Literature** (pg. 107).

Hillwood Museum, 4155 Linnean Avenue NW. (202) 686-5807. Mansion residence, decorative art collection, gardens, cafe, tours. Open daily except Tuesdays and Sundays. Tours by reservations at 9 A.M., 10:30 A.M., noon, and 1:30 P.M. Self-guided garden tours, concerts, lecture program. Admission. **Antiques** (pg. 25), **Gardens** (pg. 80), **Music** (pg. 152).

Hirshhorn Museum and Sculpture Garden, 8th Street and Independence Avenue SW. (202) 357-2700. Art exhibits, shop, tours, programs. Open 10 A.M. to 5:30 P.M. daily. Free. **Art** (pg. 48).

Historical Society of Washington. See Heurich Mansion.

Huntley Meadows Park, 3701 Lockheed Boulevard, Alexandria, Virginia. (703) 768-2525. Boardwalk, trails, Visitor Center displays, tours, programs. Open dawn to dusk, Visitor Center, 9 A.M. to 5 P.M. except Tuesdays. Free. Directions: Take Beltway exit 1 (Richmond Highway Route 1) south 3.5 miles to Lockheed Boulevard. Turn right and continue .5 mile to the park entrance on the left at Harrison Lane. Note: There is another entrance to the park that accesses a picnic area. **Nature** (pg. 165).

International Monetary Fund, Visitors Center 700 19th Street NW. (202) 623-6869. Exhibits. Open 10 A.M. to 5 P.M. weekdays. Free.

INTELSAT Visitors Center, 3400 International Drive NW. (202) 944-7841. Exhibits, tours. Tours by reservation on Tuesday at 10 A.M. and Thursday at 3 P.M. Free. **Technology** (pg. 202).

Japan Information and Culture Center, 1155 21st Street NW, basement of Lafayette Center Galleria. Exhibits. Open 9 A.M. to 5 P.M. weekdays. Free. **Art** (pg. 30).

Jewish War Veterans National Memorial Museum, Archives, and Library, 1811 R Street NW. (202) 265-6280. Exhibits. Open 10 A.M. to 4:30 P.M. Monday through Friday, Sunday by appointment. **Military** (pg. 136).

Joaquin Miller Cabin, Rock Creek Park at Beach and Military Drives. Poet's cabin, poetry readings. Free. **Literature** (pg. 110).

Kahlil Gibran Garden, Massachusetts Avenue near 30th Street NW. Park, wooded path. Free. **Gardens** (pg. 71).

Kenilworth Aquatic Gardens, Kenilworth Avenue and Douglas Street NE. (202) 426-6905. Gardens, tours. Open 7:30 A.M. to 6 P.M. (until 8 P.M. in summer) daily. Free. **Gardens** (pg. 83).

Kennedy Center for the Performing Arts, New Hampshire Avenue and Rock Creek Parkway. (202) 785-4600. Theater, library, tours. Open 10 A.M. to midnight. Tours 10 A.M. to 1 P.M. Monday through Saturday. Library, terrace level, (202) 707-6245. Open 11 A.M. to 8:30 P.M. Tuesday through Friday; 10 A.M. to 6 P.M. Saturday. Free. **Music and Theater** (pg. 147), **Literature** (pg. 109).

Lake Fairfax Park, 1400 Lake Fairfax, Drive, Reston, Virginia. (703) 471-5415. Open daylight hours. Noncounty resident admission. **Nature** (pg. 168).

Lafayette Square, Pennsylvania Avenue NW. Jackson Place, H Street, Madison Drive. Park. Free. **Literature** (pg. 93), **Military** (pg. 115).

Laurel Ridge Conservation and Education Center, 8925 Leesburg Pike, Vienna, Virginia. (703) 790-4000. Center open 8 A.M. to 4:30 P.M. Monday through Friday. Grounds open daily. Free. **Nature** (pg. 168).

Library of Congress, Jefferson Building, 1st Street between East Capitol Street and Independence Avenue SE. Madison Building, Independence Avenue and 1st Street SE. (202) 707-5000. Exhibits, concerts, tours. Open weekdays 8:30 A.M. to 9:30 P.M.; Saturday 8:30 A.M. to 5 P.M.; Sunday 1 to 5 P.M. Oval Gallery, 6th floor Madison Building, open 8:30 A.M. to 5 P.M. Monday through Friday. Free. **Gardens** (pg. 73), **Literature** (pg. 102), **Music and Theater** (pg. 145).

Lincoln Memorial, 23rd Street and Constitution Avenue NW. (202) 426-6895. Memorial, tours. Although tours have been suspended indefinitely, the exhibit area at the base of the monument has windows overlooking the fountain. **Technology** (pg. 202).

Longworth House Office Building, Independence Avenue and South Capitol Street SW. Public cafeteria open weekdays before 11:30 A.M., after 1:15 P.M. **Technology** (pg. 191).

Madison Hotel, 15th and M Streets NW. (202) 862-1600. Lobby exhibits. **Antiques** (pg. 21).

Marine Corps Air Ground Museum, Quantico Marine Base, Quantico, Virginia. (703) 640-2606. An impressive collection of planes, tanks, machine guns, and more. Open Tuesday through Saturday, April through November 28, 10 A.M. to 5 P.M. Sunday noon to 5 P.M. Tours. Free. The Quantico National Cemetery, adjacent to Quantico Marine Base, Quantico, Virginia. (703) 221-2183. Open Monday through Friday 9 A.M. to 4:30 P.M. Veteran's Day Services. Free. **Military** (pg. 136).

Marine Corps Museum. See Washington Navy Yard.

Marine Corps War Memorial, (Iwo Jima Statue), Virginia side of Memorial Bridge between the main entrance to Arlington Cemetery and Arlington Boulevard. (202) 433-6060. Memorial, parades. Open always, but be wary after nightfall. Free shuttle bus service from Arlington Cemetery parking lot during the day and on parade evenings. Marine Corps sunset parade on grounds at 7 P.M. from late May to late August. Free. **Military** (pg. 134).

Mason Neck National Wildlife Refuge, Lorton, Virginia. (703) 690-1297. Trails, tours. Open daily, April through November. Free. Directions: From Washington (I-495), take U.S. 1 south, turning left (east) at VA 242 (Gunston Hall Road). Turn right on High Point Road for a half mile, then left into Woodmarsh parking lot. **Nature** (pg. 167).

Mason Neck State Park, Lorton, Virginia. (703) 339-7265. Trails, tours, camping facilities. Open first weekend in April through last weekend in October. Free. **Nature** (pg. 167).

Meadowlark Gardens Regional Park, 1624 Beulah Road, Vienna, Virginia. (703) 255-3631. Gardens. Open 10 A.M. to dusk daily. Programs, walking tours. Donation. **Gardens** (pg. 89).

Meridian House, 1630 Crescent Place NW. (202) 939-5558. Historic residence, gardens. Open 2 P.M. to 5 P.M. Tuesday through Friday, and Sunday. Free. **Gardens** (pg. 80).

Mexican Cultural Institute, 2829 16th Street NW. (202) 728-1628. Exhibits, historic residence. Open 10 A.M. to 6 P.M. Tuesday through Sunday. Free. **Antiques** (pg. 21) **Art** (pg. 30).

Middle East Institute, 1761 N Street NW. (202) 785-1141. Library. Open 10 A.M. to 5 P.M. Mondays, Wednesdays, and Fridays (Fridays 10 A.M. to noon in summer); 10 A.M. to 8 P.M. Tuesdays and Thursdays. Closed in August. Free. **Literature** (pg. 108).

Mount Vernon, George Washington Parkway south of Alexandria, Virginia. (703) 780-2000. Historic residence, Washington tomb, outbuildings, gardens, museums, shops. Open weekdays 9 A.M. to 5 P.M. March through October; 9 A.M. to 4 P.M. November through February. Admission. **Antiques** (pg. 22), **Gardens** (pg. 87).

Museum of the National Guard, One Massachusetts Avenue NW. (202) 543-5148. Exhibits, store. Open 8 A.M. to 4:30 P.M. Monday through Friday. Free. **Military** (pg. 120).

National Academy of Sciences, 2101 Constitution Avenue NW. (202) 334-2000. Rotunda, art gallery, concerts. Open 9 A.M. to 5 P.M. weekdays, but sometimes closed without notice for private event. Einstein Statue at corner of Constitution Avenue and 22nd Street NW. Free. **Music and Theater** (pg. 153), **Science** (pg. 182).

National Air and Space Museum, Independence Avenue between 4th and 7th streets SW. (202) 357-2700. Exhibits, films, planetarium, shop, restaurants. Open 10 A.M. to 5:30 P.M. daily. Tours, special events. Free. Einstein Planetarium, ten shows each day. Admission. Langley Theatre films *To Fly*, *Blue Planet*, etc. Admission. **Literature** (pg. 105), **Military** (pg. 121), **Science** (pg. 181), **Technology** (pg. 192).

National Aquarium, Commerce Department Building, 14th Street between Pennsylvania and Constitution avenues NW. (202) 377-2825. Exhibits. Open 9 A.M. to 5 P.M. daily. Admission. **Science** (pg. 180).

National Arboretum, 3501 New York Avenue NE. (202) 475-4815. Gardens, exhibits, shop, tours. Open 8 A.M. to 5 P.M. weekdays; 10 A.M. to 5 P.M. weekends. Bonsai Pavilion open 10 A.M. to 2:30 P.M. daily. Free. **Gardens** (pg. 83).

National Archives Exhibition Hall, 7th Street and Constitution Avenue NW. (202) 501-5000 recorded schedule. Exhibits, shop. Open 10 A.M. to 9

P.M. April 1 through Labor Day; 10 a.m. to 5:30 p.m. September through March 31. Tours, lecture programs. Free. **Literature** (pg. 100).

National Building Museum, F Street between 4th and 5th streets NW. (202) 272-2448. Exhibits, shop. Open 10 A.M. to 4 P.M. Monday through Saturday; noon to 4 P.M. Sunday. Special events, tours. Free. **Technology** (pg. 201).

National Gallery of Art–East Building, Pennsylvania Avenue between 3rd and 4th streets NW. (202) 737-4215. Exhibits, tours, shops, cafe. Open 10 A.M. to 5 P.M. Monday through Saturday; 11 A.M. to 6 P.M. Sunday. Special programs, tours. Free. **Art** (pg. 53).

National Gallery of Art–West Building, Pennsylvania Avenue between 4th and 7th streets NW. (202) 737-4215. Exhibits, concerts, tours, cafe, shops. Open 10 A.M. to 5 P.M. Monday through Saturday; 11 A.M. to 6 P.M. Sunday. Free. **Art** (pg. 50).

National Geographic Society, Explorers Hall. 17th and M streets NW. (202) 857-7589. Exhibits, shop, tour. Open 9 A.M. to 5 P.M. Monday through Saturday; 10 A.M. to 5 P.M. Sunday. Free. Library, 16th and M streets NW. (202) 857-7883. Open 8:30 A.M. to 5 P.M. Monday through Friday. **Science** (pg. 173).

National Guard Museum. See Museum of the National Guard.

National Institutes of Health, 9000 Rockville Pike, Bethesda, Maryland. Visitors Center (301) 496-1776. Exhibits, tours on Monday, Wednesday, and Friday, 11 A.M. Free. **Science** (pg. 184).

National Library of Medicine, 8600 Rockville Pike, Bethesda, Maryland. (301) 496-6308. Exhibits, tours. Open 8:30 A.M. to 9 P.M. Monday through Thursday; closes at 5 P.M. on Friday and Saturday during the summer. Tours at 1 P.M. from adjacent Lister Hill Building. Free.

National Museum of African Art, 960 Independence Avenue SW. (202) 357-2000. Art gallery, shop, tours, programs. Open 1 A.M. to 5:30 P.M. daily. Free. **Art** (pg. 45).

National Museum of American Art, 8th and G streets NW. (202) 357-2700. Exhibits, tours, shop, cafe. Open 10 A.M. to 5:30 P.M. daily. Exhibits, shop, special programs, tours. Free. **Art** (pg. 57).

National Museum of American History, Smithsonian Institution, 14th Street and Constitution Avenue NW. (202) 357-2700. Exhibits, cafe, shop, tours. Open 10 A.M. to 5:30 P.M. daily. Free.

National Museum of Health and Medicine, Walter Reed Medical Center, 16th and Georgia Avenue NW. (202) 576-2348. Open 9:30 A.M. to 4:30 P.M. weekdays; 11:30 A.M. to 4:30 P.M. weekends. Exhibits. **Science**. (pg. 178).

National Museum of Natural History, Constitution Avenue at 10th Street NW. (202) 357-2700. Open daily 10 A.M. to 5:30 P.M. Exhibits, shops, tours. Free. **Science**. (pg. 184).

National Museum of Women in the Arts, 801 13th Street NW. (202) 783-5000. Exhibits, cafe, shop, tours, special programs. Open 10 A.M. to 5 P.M. Tuesday through Saturday; noon to 5 P.M. Sunday. Donation. **Art** (pg. 60).

National Portrait Gallery, 8th and F streets NW. (202) 357-2700. Exhibits, tours, special programs, cafe. Open 10 A.M. to 5:30 P.M. daily. Free.

National Theater, 1325 E Street NW. (202) 783-3370. Theater tours 11 A.M. most Mondays, and by special arrangement. Free. **Music and Theater** (pg. 143).

Natural History Museum. See National Museum of Natural History.

Naval Observatory, 34th Street and Massachusetts Avenue NW. (202) 653-1507. Tours of exhibits and telescope-viewing by reservation: 653-1543. Free. **Science** (pg. 184).

Navy Memorial, Pennsylvania Avenue between 7th and 9th streets NW. (202) 737-2300. Visitor Center open 10 A.M. to 5 P.M. daily except Sunday, noon to 5 P.M. Exhibits, concerts, free. Film *At Sea,* admission. **Military** (pg. 119).

Naval Memorial Museum. See Washington Navy Yard.

Octagon House, 1799 New York Avenue NW. (202) 638-3105. Historic residence, garden, tours. Open 10 A.M. to 4 P.M. Tuesday thru Friday, 1 P.M. to 4 P.M. Saturday. Admission. **Gardens** (pg. 76).

Old Executive Office Building, 17th Street and Pennsylvania Avenue NW. (202) 395-5895. Historic office building tours on Saturdays by reservation. Free. **Military** (pg. 116).

Old Post Office, Pennsylvania Avenue and 12th Street NW. (202) 289-4224. Shops, restaurants, observation tower. Tower open 8 A.M. to 11 P.M. daily, mid-April through mid-September; other periods from 10 A.M. to 5:45 P.M. Free. **Music and Theater** (pg. 153).

Old Naval Observatory, 23rd and D streets NW. (202) 653-1297. Tours offered on weekdays at 10 A.M. and 2 P.M. Reservations necessary. Free. **Science** (pg. 183).

Old Stone House, 3051 M Street NW. (202) 426-6851. Historic residence, gardens, musical evenings. Open 9:30 A.M. to 5 P.M. Wednesday through Sunday. Free. **Gardens** (pg. 68).

Organization of American States (OAS) Patio and Aztec Garden, 17th Street and Constitution Avenue NW. (202) 458-3000. Tropical courtyard, art gallery, gardens, concerts, tours. Open 9 A.M. to 4:30 P.M. weekdays. Free. **Art** (pg. 36), **Gardens** (pg. 76), **Music and Theater** (pg. 153).

Patapsco Valley State Park, Baltimore, Maryland. (410) 461-5005. Trails, camping. Open dawn to dusk. Admission. **Nature** (pg. 170).

Patuxent River Park, Upper Marlboro, Maryland. (301) 627-6074. Trails, nature study area, boating. Park entrance off Croom Airport Road via Croom Road. Open dawn to dusk. Admission fee.

Pentagon, Arlington, Virginia, at Pentagon Metro. (703) 695-1776. Tours weekdays every half hour from 9:30 A.M. to 3:30 P.M. Free. **Military** (pg. 131).

Philips Collection, 21st and Q streets NW. (202) 387-2151. Exhibits, concerts, shop, cafe, tours. Open 10 A.M. to 5 P.M. Monday through Saturday; noon to 7 p.m. Sunday. Fee. **Art** (pg. 40).

Pohick Bay Regional Park, Lorton, Virginia. Visitor Center (703) 339-6104. Trails, boat facilities, Visitor Center displays. Open year around. Free. Directions: Take I-95 south, exit at Lorton, follow Gunston Hall signs to park. **Nature** (pg. 167).

Potomac Overlook Regional Park, Military Road at Marcy Road, Arlington, Virginia. (703) 528-4506. Park open year round. Visitor Center open 10 A.M. to 5 p.m. Tuesday through Saturday; 1 to 5 P.M. Sunday. Free. **Nature** (pg. 168).

Rayburn House Office Building, Independence Avenue at South Capitol Street SW. Cafeteria open before 11:30 A.M., after 1:15 weekdays. **Technology** (pg. 191).

Renwick Gallery, Pennsylvania Avenue at 17th Street NW. (202) 357-2700. Exhibits, special programs, concerts, shop, tours. Free. **Art** (pg. 31).

River Farm, American Horticultural Society Headquarters, 7931 East Boulevard, Alexandria, Virginia. (703) 768-5700. Gardens, special programs, tours. Open 9 A.M. to 5 P.M. weekdays; open some Saturdays during summer. Free. **Gardens** (pg. 90).

Rock Creek Park, extends from East-West Highway in Maryland to Memorial Bridge in the District. (202) 426-6832. Hiking, biking, horse riding trails, and other facilities. Numerous roads access park attractions, including Rock Creek Parkway, Military Road, Tilden Street, Park Road. The Rock Creek Nature Center and Planetarium is in the northern portion of the park at 5200 Glover Road; (202) 426-6829. The Nature Center is open year round from 9 A.M. to 5 P.M. except Mondays. Free. **Nature** (pg. 157).

Rock Creek Regional Park, Visitor Center, 6700 Needwood Road, Derwood, Maryland. (303) 762-7494. Directions: Take exit 21 off the Capital Beltway (Georgia Avenue, MD 97) north to Norbeck Road. Turn left, then right on Muncaster Mill Road to Needwood Road. Turn left and follow signs to Visitor Center. Free. **Nature** (pg. 169).

Russell Senate Office Building, 1st Street and Constitution Avenue NE. Subway car exhibit. Open 9 A.M. to 5 P.M. weekdays. Free. **Technology** (pg. 191).

Sackler Gallery of Art, 1051 Independence Avenue SW. (202) 357-2700. Exhibits, shop, tours. Open 10 A.M. to 5:30 P.M. daily. Free. **Art** (pg. 54).

Saint Sophia Greek Orthodox Cathedral, 36th Street and Massachusetts Avenue NW. (202) 333-4730. Mosaics. Call first. **Art** (pg. 42).

Scottish Rite Temple, 1733 16th Street NW. (202) 232-3579. Exhibits, library, tour. Open 8 A.M. to 4 P.M. weekdays. Free. **Literature** (pg. 110).

Sherman Monument, E Street, 15th Street, Treasury Place, South Executive Place. Memorial. Free. **Military** (pg. 118).

State Department Diplomatic Reception Rooms, C and 22nd streets NW. Tour office (202) 647-3241. Tours of decorated rooms by reservation, Monday through Friday at 9:30 A.M., 10:30 A.M., and 2:45 P.M. Free. **Antiques** (pg. 12).

Sumner School Museum and Archives, 1201 17th Street NW. (202) 727-3419. Historic school, art gallery, exhibits, concerts. Open 10 A.M. to 5 P.M. Monday through Friday. Free. **Music and Theater** (pg. 146).

Tech 2000, Techworld Plaza, 8th and K streets NW. (202) 842-0500. Exhibits, hands-on media, tours. Open 11 A.M. to 5 P.M. Tuesday through Sunday. Admission. **Technology** (pg. 200).

Textile Museum, 2320 S Street NW. (202) 667-0441. Exhibits, gardens, tours. Open 10 A.M. to 5 P.M. Monday through Saturday; 1 to 5 P.M. Sunday. Donation. **Art** (pg. 42), **Gardens** (pg. 67).

Theodore Roosevelt Island, George Washington Memorial Parkway, Virginia. (703) 285-2598. Trails, tours. Open dawn to dusk. Free. Naturalist-led hikes on weekends. **Nature** (pg. 161).

Tudor Place, 1644 31st Street NW. (202) 965-0400. Historic residence, gardens, house tour. Open 10 A.M. to 4 P.M. Tuesday through Saturday by reservation. Admission. **Antiques** (pg. 16), **Gardens** (pg. 68).

Union Station, Massachusetts Avenue between North Capital Street and Second Street NW. (202) 347-9491. Restored train station, tours, shops, restaurants. **Technology** (pg. 200).

Venezuelan Embassy, 1099 30th Street NW. (202) 342-2214. Art and cultural exhibits. Open 9 A.M. to 1 P.M. and 2 P.M. to 5 P.M. weekdays. Free. **Art** (pg. 30).

Vietnam Veterans War Memorial, Constitution Avenue and Henry Bacon Drive NW. (202) 485-9666. Memorial. Open 24 hours daily, park ranger on site 8 A.M. to midnight. **Military** (pg. 123).

Washington Navy Yard, 9th and M streets SE. Naval Memorial Museum (202) 433-2651. Exhibits, tours. Open 9 A.M. to 4 P.M. weekdays; 10 A.M. to 5 P.M. weekends. Free. Marine Corps Museum, (202) 433-3534. Exhibits. Open 10 A.M. to 4 P.M. Monday through Saturday; noon to 5 P.M. Sunday. Free. **Military** (pg. 134).

Washington National Cathedral, Massachusetts and Wisconsin avenues. (202) 537-6200. Cathedral artistry, observation gallery, garden, special programs, concerts, tours. Open 10 A.M. to 4:30 P.M. Monday to Saturday; 7:30 A.M. to 4:30 P.M. Sunday. Donation. Fee for observation gallery. **Art** (pg. 43), **Gardens** (pg. 79), **Literature** (pg. 107), **Music and Theater** (pg. 149).

W & O Railroad Regional Park, Northern Virginia. (703) 689-1437. Bike and jogging trail. Directions: Accessible from numerous cities along its route, including Arlington, Falls Church, Vienna, Herndon, Reston, Sterling, Leesburg, Purcellville. **Nature** (pg. 168).

White House, 1600 Pennsylvania Avenue NW. Tour information (202) 456-7041. Historic residence tours 10 A.M. to noon, Tuesday through Saturday. **Antiques** (pg. 18), **Gardens** (pg. 75).

Wilderness Society, 900 17th Street NW. (202) 833-2300. Photo exhibit. Open 10 A.M. to 5 P.M. Monday through Friday. Free. **Art** (pg. 31).

Woodend, 8940 Jones Mill Road, Chevy Chase, Maryland. (301) 652-9188. Audubon Nature Center with trails, historic residence, shop. Grounds open dawn to dusk, shop open 10 A.M. to 5 P.M. weekdays (until 8 P.M. Thursdays) and 9 A.M. to 5 P.M. Saturdays. Free. Directions: Take exit 20 of the Capital Beltway, following Connecticut Avenue south to Jones Bridge Road. Turn left and watch for signs. **Nature** (pg. 169).

Woodrow Wilson House, 2340 S Street NW. (202) 387-4062. Historic house, garden, tours. Open daily except Monday 10 A.M. to 4 P.M. Admission. **Gardens** (pg. 67).

World Bank, 701 19th Street NW. (202) 458-2649. Art gallery by appointment only. Free. **Music and Theater** (pg. 153).